WRITERS IN THEIR TIME
General Editor: Norman Page

Published titles

GEOFFREY CHAUCER	*Janette Dillon*
JOSEPH CONRAD	*Brian Spittles*
GEORGE ELIOT	*Brian Spittles*
THOMAS HARDY	*Timothy Hands*

Forthcoming titles

CHARLES DICKENS	*Angus Easson*
GEORGE ORWELL	*Norman Page*
WILLIAM SHAKESPEARE	*John Drakakis*
VIRGINIA WOOLF	*Edward Bishop*

The 86-year-old Thomas Hardy surrounded by characters from *The Mayor of Casterbridge* before the performance of the Barnes Theatre Company in Weymouth, 1926 (*Trustees of the Thomas Hardy Memorial Collection in the Dorset County Museum, Dorchester*)

Thomas Hardy

Timothy Hands

First published 1995 by
MACMILLAN PRESS LTD
Houndmills, Basingstoke, Hampshire RG21 2XS
and London
Companies and representatives
throughout the world

ISBN 0–333–54998–8 hardcover
ISBN 0–333–54999–6 paperback

A catalogue record for this book is available
from the British Library.

10 9 8 7 6 5 4 3 2 1
04 03 02 01 00 99 98 97 96 95

Printed in Malaysia

Series Standing Order
If you would like to receive future titles in this series as they are
published, you can make use of our standing order facility. To place a
standing order please contact your bookseller or, in case of difficulty,
write to us at the address below with your name and address and the
name of the series. Please state with which title you wish to begin your
standing order. (If you live outside the United Kingdom we may not have
the rights for your area, in which case we will forward your order
to the publisher concerned.)

Customer Services Department, Macmillan Distribution Ltd
Houndmills, Basingstoke, Hampshire, RG21 2XS, England.

For my teachers,
and especially David, Charles, Richard, John and Glenn

Contents

Acknowledgements

The first debt is to Norman Page, for commissioning this volume in the series and for his characteristically helpful general editorship.

Expert assistance on a number of matters has been given by Jennie Barbour, Julian Budden, James Gibson, Peter Henderson, Charles Osborne and Georgina Salmon. Catherine Hands compiled the index, and Peter Henderson gave much help with the proofs. June Dixon Millar kindly loaned a number of rare editions from the specialist library of the architectural historian Roger Dixon. Much assistance has of course been given by library staff, especially those of the British Library, Dorset County Library and the library of the University of Kent at Canterbury.

The genesis of the book is in a number of courses given over the past fifteen years, and the stimulating co-operation of many pupils and students in them is gratefully acknowledged. A special word is reserved on another page for my many teachers. Much of Chapter 4 was given to the Thomas Hardy Society Summer School in Dorchester in 1992, and published in *New Perspectives on Thomas Hardy*, edited by Charles P. C. Pettit. The material is here reproduced by kind permission of Macmillan Press.

Though helping little with the text proper, many people have assisted in its completion. These especially include my parents, my wife, Sheila Bennett, Peter Brodie, Alan Bullock, Reggie Burton, Anthony Phillips, Ian and Ann Smart, and the beautifully behaved young men of Galpin's.

General Editor's Preface

In recent years many critics and teachers have become convinced of the importance of recognizing that works of literature are grounded in the conditions of their production in the widest possible sense of that phrase – in the history, society, ideas and ideologies of their time, the lives and careers of their authors, and the prevailing circumstances of the literary market-place and the reading public. To some extent this development reflects both a disenchantment with the 'practical criticism' approach that held sway for so long in school, college and university teaching of literature and a scepticism towards the ahistorical biases encouraged by some more recent schools of critical theory.

It is true that lip-service has long been paid to 'background': the English Tripos at Cambridge, for instance, embodied the 'life, literature and thought' formula from its early years. Such an approach, however, tended to treat 'background' as distinct and detachable from literary works and as constituting a relatively minor, marginal and even optional element in the study of a text. What is now perceived to be in question is something more vital and more central: not a loosely defined relationship between certain novels, plays and poems on the one hand and 'history' or 'ideas' on the other, but an intimate informing and shaping of the one by the other. Colonialism in Conrad or Kipling, Christian theology in Milton or Bunyan, scientific discovery in Tennyson or Hardy, politics in Yeats or Eliot: these are not background issues against which the texts can be foregrounded but crucial determinants of the very nature of the texts themselves without which they would be radically different and which profoundly affect the way we understand and value them.

At the same time, as most teachers are ready to attest, even a basic knowledge of the historical and cultural conditions of past, including recently past, generations cannot be taken for granted. To many students, periods as recent as the 1930s or the Great War are largely a closed book, while key concepts of earlier generations such as Darwinism or Puritanism, and major movements such as the spread of literacy and the growth and decline of imperialism, are known in the sketchiest outline if at all.

This series is intended to provide in an accessible form materials that will make possible a fuller and deeper understanding of the work of the major authors by demonstrating in detail its relationship to the world, including the intellectual world, in which it was produced. Its starting-point is not a notion of 'background' but a conviction that many, perhaps most, great writers are in an integral sense *in* and *of* their time. Each volume will look afresh at the primary texts (or a selection of them) in relation to the ways in which they have been informed and shaped by both the external and the ideological conditions of their worlds. Historical, political, scientific, theological, philosophical and other dimensions will be explored as appropriate. By understanding more fully the contexts which have made particular works what they are and not otherwise, students and others will be able to bring new understanding to their reading of the texts.

NORMAN PAGE

Introduction

Sometime in the late 1880s, Thomas Hardy copied in to his *Literary Notebooks* a passage from an article entitled 'The Decline of Art' in the magazine *Nineteenth Century*. The article was by Tennyson's friend F. T. Palgrave, then professor of poetry at Oxford, and quoted one of his predecessors in that post:

> Mr M. Arnold has a fine remark, that 'for the creation of a master-work in literature two powers must concur – the power of the man, and the power of the moment.'[1]

Despite Hardy's interest in this view, writing a volume on Thomas Hardy for a series on writers in their time is not easy. For Hardy, the series needs retitling. As writer he was novelist and poet; in period he was Victorian, Edwardian and, in the view of some critics, Modernist. Hardy had the power of several men, and lived through not a few significant moments.

Nor do the problems end here. Or rather, their ending is with Hardy's beginnings, with a biography full of false starts, concealed or mistaken feelings and misleading statements. Born in 1840 and mistaken for dead, Hardy died in 1928, ending a life he had written as well as lived. *The Life of Thomas Hardy*, nominally by Hardy's second wife Florence, was in fact almost exclusively planned and written by himself, Florence being left to manage those passages (such as that describing Hardy's death) which even the Grand Old Man of English Letters could not pen. Hardy's body was interred in Poet's Corner at Westminster Abbey, but his excised heart was placed in the grave of his first wife Emma, in Hardy's native parish of Stinsford. The dislocation is representative. Disabled (or in some cases liberated) by the lack of records which Hardy and his assistants so assiduously gathered together and destroyed, Hardy's biographers have searched for the true character and life of Thomas Hardy ever since. Hardy the man, like Hardy the author and Hardy the creature of his time, is a difficult person to locate.

Selectivity is therefore unavoidable, not least with regard to works discussed. Accessibility to the general reader has been the guiding principle. Subsequent writers and readers have consistently disagreed with the verdict of 106 young writers, marshalled by St John Ervine, who in a tribute to Hardy on his eightieth birthday wrote: 'We thank you, Sir, for all that you have written ... but most of all, perhaps, for *The Dynasts*' (*Life*, p. 446). Hardy created – and finished – a whole idiosyncratic epic-dramatic genre with this extraordinary piece, but the present volume can have no mission for reclaiming the work from the widespread neglect posterity has accorded it. There has recently been a welcome critical trend to discuss all of Hardy's novels (fourteen, published 1871–95), and (less enthusiastically) to pay increased attention to his short stories. The former trend is reflected in this study; though, again for practical reasons, greater reference has had to be made to the moiety better known by the general reader: *Under the Greenwood Tree* (1872), *Far from the Madding Crowd* (1874), *The Return of the Native* (1878), *The Mayor of Casterbridge* (1886), *The Woodlanders* (1887), *Tess of the d'Urbervilles* (1891) and *Jude the Obscure* (1895). These provide a representative glimpse of Hardy's experimentation with the novel form in, respectively, two early novels of pastoral exposition, one transitional novel of over-reaching expansion, two late novels of organic (if sometimes flawed) achievement, and two final novels of considered but provocative social exploration. A wide variety of poems is mentioned, though obviously it has only been possible for close attention to be paid to fewer than thirty. For the convenience of readers as bewildered by the choice of anthologies as the anthology selectors are bewildered by decisions over which of Hardy's 900-plus poems to include, these poems are when possible quoted in full.

Chapter 1 gives a general guide to Hardy's life and literary products. Chapters 2 and 6 form a frame for the remaining chapters and provide, respectively, a retrospect to the Romantic period and Hardy's interest in it, and a guide to Hardy's critical reputation, chiefly through a study of criticism published from Hardy's lifetime to the present day. The remaining chapters cover Hardy's views on society, contemporary ideas and the arts. Each chapter is prefaced by a quotation from a Hardy poem. A Select Bibliography and a Chronological Table are provided at the end of the volume.

Quotations are taken from the Macmillan hardback New Wessex edition (1975–8). Chapter references (common to all editions of the novels) and references to Hardy's *Collected Letters* (Oxford, 1978–88) and *Life* (ed. Michael Millgate, London, 1984) are given in the text when appropriate.

1

'I lived in quiet, screened, unknown':* The Lives of Thomas Hardy

Thomas Hardy was born in Upper Bockhampton, in the parish of Stinsford, near Dorchester, Dorset, on 2 June 1840, at 8 a.m. At first put aside as dead, he was rescued, by the observation and slap of the midwife, in an episode which somehow seems symbolically appropriate. Initial perception of death preceded a life of exceptional longevity; yet that longevity, and the prolific creativity that accompanied it, were themselves frequently to be accompanied by longings for obscurity and oblivion, an exit from what 'A Necessitarian's Epitaph' calls 'A world I did not wish to enter'. 'Ere nescience shall be reaffirmed', questions 'Before Life and After', 'How long, how long?'

The world of 1840 was distinctive. Queen Victoria had been on the throne three years, and the country over which she ruled was becoming conscious of its position at the fore-front of world affairs and development. 'The history of England is emphatically the history of progress', wrote the pre-eminent Victorian historian, Lord Macaulay,[1] yet with that progress there was developing a tendency towards doubt and even self-destruction that in Hardy's lifetime was to become intense. Already in 1838 Thomas Arnold, who as Headmaster of Rugby was closer to the young than most, could note 'A sort of new atmosphere of unrest and paradox hanging around many of our ablest young men'.[2]

The Dorset dweller of 1840, however, was far removed from the centre of this intellectual and material storm – to put the matter more precisely, he found himself approximately fourteen and a half hours from London by stage-coach. Life

* From 'A Private Man on Public Men'.

in Upper Bockhampton represented something of a still point at the centre of the ever more rapidly turning wheel of national progress and change, and Hardy chose to present his roots as extending very deep. 'On the maternal side', the *Life* (p. 10) stolidly informs us, 'he was Anglo-Saxon.' Various family trees, of differing degrees of reliability and provenance, accompany this dubiously supportable claim; but, as so often in Hardy's biography, students of the author have to come to appreciate that the created fiction contains as much significance as the distorted and often unestablishable fact. Hardy was, in short, determined to view himself as age-old even before he was one.

Thomas Hardy – as though to increase this tendency – found himself the third of that name, following his grandfather and father before him. Thomas Hardy the First (perhaps represented as old William Dewy in *Under the Greenwood Tree* and various poems commemorating the Stinsford parish choir) was provided by his father John Hardy with a cottage at Bockhampton (now preserved by the National Trust as Hardy's Birthplace) and set up in John's own occupation as a master mason-cum-builder. Thomas, by turns Napoleonic volunteer, enthusiastic church and dance musician and storer of illicit contraband, died in 1837, and thus never lived to meet his grandson; but that grandson's memory of his grandmother, Mary, and his early years in the family home, are recalled in 'Domicilium', Hardy's earliest known poem.

Thomas Hardy the Third would recall his father with evident attraction: handsome, with teeth regular into old age, and blue eyes that never faded to grey, musician, dancer, walker and, most of all, ladies' man. But with Thomas the First's inherited charm went also that grandfather's casualness about business ways, for Thomas also recalled his father as unpossessed of 'the tradesman's soul' (*Life*, p. 501). To these charms fell victim Jemima Hardy, née Hand, cook to the aristocratic vicar of Stinsford, Edward Murray. The daughter of an occasionally employed Dorset labourer, George Hand, renowned for drunkenness, violence and opposition to religion, Jemima found herself thrust early into the world to survive upon her not inconsiderable wits. Purposeful, intolerant and sprightly, Jemima had intelligence and ambitions; her son recalled her as a woman of 'unusual ability and judgement, and an energy that might have carried her to incalculable issues' (*Life*, p. 12). In the poem 'A Church Romance' Hardy gives an ecclesiastical view of his parents' early encounter, Jemima admiring the energy of the violinist in the choir in the church gallery:

> One strenuous viol's inspirer seemed to throw
> A message from his string to her below,
> Which said: 'I claim thee as my own forthright!'

Hardy family tradition tells an earthier story: that Thomas, on catching sight of the young servant-woman while working on a nearby building, promptly seduced her under the bushes by the neighbouring River Frome. Whichever is true, it is certain that sacred and sexual combined beside the banks of the same river on 22 December 1839, the solemnisation of Hardy's parents' marriage having been precipitated by Hardy's conception some weeks previously. Less than two months later, on 10 February 1840, Queen Victoria married Albert of Saxe-Coburg.

It is possible that Hardy was born prematurely: certainly he suffered much physical weakness in early years and was not expected to survive. Jemima too had a grip on life which was precarious: some time between 1843 and 1846 she became dangerously ill following a miscarriage. The illness probably affected Hardy emotionally and certainly altered Jemima temperamentally: her determination that her son should make a mark in the world (as also perhaps her feeling that her husband was failing to do so) increased substantially. It was she who proved the driving force in her son's education, and especially in the gratification of his desire for books, for both he and Jemima claimed that he was able to read at the age of three. Hardy read with enthusiasm, but not with the catholicity which greater family wealth would have rendered possible. In 1847 he was presented by his godfather with a copy of *The Rites and Worship of the Jews*; other owned childhood favourites which he particularly recalled include Dryden's translation of the *Aeneid*, Johnson's *Rasselas* and a translation of Bernardin de Saint-Pierre's *Paul et Virginie*.

In 1848 Hardy became the first pupil to enter the newly built National School in Upper Bockhampton, an event which

is recalled in 'He Revisits His First School'. The school was
the product of the twin enthusiasms of the new vicar of
Stinsford, Arthur Shirley, and Julia Augusta Martin, wife of
the local landlord. Hardy's talents and his mother's ambition
for them, however, ensured that his stay at the school was a
limited one, for in 1850 Jemima decided to send Hardy to the
British and Foreign Bible Society School in Dorchester, run by
Isaac Last. The quality of Last's tuition was undoubtedly
superior to that offered in Stinsford, but there was an acute
social snag. Last's school was Nonconformist, and Jemima's
decision thus endeared the Hardy family to neither their
vicar nor, more particularly, Julia Augusta Martin, who had
grown inordinately fond of the young child, whilst Hardy for
his part had grown 'more attached than he cared to own . . .
his feeling for her was almost that of a lover' (*Life*, p. 24).
Hardy's father lost the estate business as a consequence,
whilst Hardy himself had to endure an encounter with Mrs
Martin at a Harvest Supper whose emotional intensity he
was long to recall.

For Hardy himself, however, the consequences of the move
to Last were certainly beneficial. In 1852 he began Latin
under Last's tuition, continuing his studies with some
success; and in the three years following Last's setting up of a
new independent academy in 1851 Hardy, as well as building
up physical strength, made rapid intellectual strides.

Nor were the consequences of the move merely academic:
by 1850 a fuller experience of the manifold everyday workings of the county town had begun to become an important
by-product of the change in schooling, and readers of the
fiction will recognise in Hardy's early journeyings to school a
pattern of progression from isolated country to bustling town
familiar to them. School also helped to remove Hardy from
the influential company of an almost exclusively adult and
largely feminine world, allowing him to form at school the
first of an extensive series of attractions to members – especially the more unattainable – of the opposite sex. Hardy's
dislike of being touched by his schoolfellows went, so to
speak, hand in hand with an interest in female relationships,
which began early and strong. A fellow pupil at the
Bockhampton National School, Fanny Hurden, was probably
Hardy's first experience of the wounded and wounding

heart: Hardy never forgot one incident in their relationship, when, in play or anger, he burnt her hand badly by pushing her against the classroom stove.

Admirers of Hardy's style and achievement must be grateful that his education was not so advanced or so demanding that it prevented the cultivation of the more individual interests and enthusiasms which his environment rendered at hand. As early as 1844 or 1845 Hardy was given a toy concertina, and soon afterwards was introduced to the violin. This instrument allowed him to contribute to the secular activities of the Stinsford string band, and by 1852 the young boy was already winning local approval as a violinist of enthusiasm and sensitivity. Most of all life at home kept Hardy in contact with an oral tradition far removed from the principles and subjects of his formal education, a home background based on a culture steeped in folk-lore and the more vital and primary aspects of story-telling, all imbibed within a family atmosphere of love and unease rendered more memorable by its musical accompaniments. All this is recorded vividly in the poem 'The Self-Unseeing', with its characteristically heart-felt yet un-indulgent lament for an intimacy savoured yet unappreciated, passed and yet constantly remembered:

> Here is the ancient floor,
> Footworn and hollowed and thin,
> Here was the former door
> Where the dead feet walked in.
>
> She sat here in her chair,
> Smiling into the fire;
> He who played stood there,
> Bowing it higher and higher.
>
> Childlike, I danced in a dream;
> Blessings emblazoned that day;
> Everything glowed with a gleam;
> Yet we were looking away!

Hardy's biographer Michael Millgate remarks that 'Hardy was – to an extraordinary degree – a child of the oral tradition, and perhaps, in England, that tradition's last and greatest product.'[3] But the duality goes deeper than this. Hardy's childhood was characterised by contrasts: country and town, educated and illiterate, rural and 'respectable', loved and anxious, petted and alone. Hardy's early life has an acutely bipartite feel to it.

A period of particular transition followed Hardy's departure from Last's academy in 1856. The *Life* speaks of Hardy as 'a child till he was sixteen, a youth till he was five-and-twenty, and a young man till he was nearly fifty' (p. 37): probably a hint at considerable adolescent emotional development this year. Certainly his range of feeling increased substantially through unrequited love for a local farmer's daughter, Louisa Harding, recalled in the poems 'Louie' and 'To Louisa in the Lane'. Hardy was in addition finding himself drawn, as he later recalled, into three separate existences, 'the professional life, the scholar's life, and the rustic life' (*Life*, p. 36).

The professional life consisted of apprenticeship, on 11 July, to the Dorchester architect John Hicks at his premises at 39 South Street, Dorchester. Hardy's interests, like those of the practice, seem to have been largely ecclesiastical: several designs and sketches from the period survive. In Hicks's office Hardy became closely involved with a fellow apprentice, the earnest Henry Robert Bastow: a heated debate on the merits of infant baptism, and Hardy's purchase of a Greek New Testament, resulted.

The scholar's life was furthered by the proximity of Hicks's office to the school kept by the poet and scholar William Barnes, and by the friendship which Hardy soon developed with Horace Moule, son of the vicar of the Dorchester suburb of Fordington, and Hardy's subsequent partial acceptance into the Moule family circle. Henry Moule, famous for a diversity of achievements, ranging from courage in ministering to his flock in cholera epidemics to invention of the patent earth closet, fathered seven sons of remarkable ability, energy and religiosity. In such a family there almost had to be a black sheep, and Horace was it. Handsome but dissipated, talented but rootless and alterable, scholarly but incapable of completing a degree despite attendance at both Oxford and Cambridge, Horace Moule was as charming as he was unstable: Hardy was to be deeply grieved by his suicide on 21 September 1873. For now, however, Hardy could only wonder at and admire Moule's wide knowledge and questioning unconventional intellect, read up the modern authors (such as Bagehot, Mill, Darwin and the contributors to *Essays and Reviews*) to which Moule either directly or by example introduced him – and feel acutely the social and intellectual gap (lessening, but never much) that divided them.

Hardy was also commencing his own literary endeavours. As early as 1856 he was beginning to contribute to the *Dorset County Chronicle*. A local skit (probably 'The Town Clocks' in the issue for 17 January) was followed by a series of articles on Hicks's church restorations. Such endeavours soon became less public but more self-consciously literary. Productions in 1858 and 1859 include lost essays on Lamb and Tennyson as well as several poems, but uncertainty prevails on the subject because of Hardy's secrecy: they were possibly shown to no one even at the time of writing.

These manifold Dorchester activities culminated not in elation but depression. By early 1862 Hardy, though retained in employment by Hicks at the end of articles, had lost his sense of direction and was suffering from listlessness of spirits. 'Why then cast down, my soul? and why / So much oppress'd with anxious care', he marked in his Prayer Book on 8 February. Hardy's emotional life was not proceeding well: there is some evidence that a proposal of marriage to a Dorchester shop assistant, Mary Waight, was turned down this year. Nor were his academic studies capable of proceeding, for social and financial reasons, as far as Hardy would have liked to take them: Horace Moule was advising him against considering a university education. On the other hand Hardy's ambition and sense of potential were crescent, as the verse he marked in Habbakuk on 23 March suggests: 'For the vision is yet for an appointed time, but at the end it shall speak, and not lie: though it tarry, wait for it; because it will surely come, it will not tarry' (Habbakuk 2:3).

What came to Hardy was a move away from Dorchester – his first. Purchasing with characteristic caution a return ticket, he set out on 17 April 1862 for London. 'It may be hardly necessary to record', the *Life* remarks, '. . . that the metropolis into which he . . . plunged at this date differed greatly from the London of even a short time after. It was the London of Dickens and Thackeray' (p. 43). Here was amusement and contrast a-plenty: extremes of rich and poor on crowded streets, entertainments from public executions to music halls, aggressive prostitution and persuasive phrenologists, and all the trappings of an all-judging, all-praying, all-governing state and empire – the metropolitical city of the world, in short, at a young man's feet.

Hardy took advantage. He heard Palmerston speak, Dickens read, Shakespeare and many other dramatists performed, and by 1866 was so far into his ambivalent relationship with the theatre as to be taking a walk-on part, for one night only, in Gilbert à Beckett's pantomime *Ali Baba and the Forty Thieves*. Self-education proceeded. There was wide reading: Newman, Comte and Fourier, for example, as well as Marcus Aurelius, whose *Thoughts*, given him by Horace Moule, always remained by his bedside. An early passion was for trips to the International Exhibition at South Kensington, which was intended, like its more famous Crystal Palace predecessor of 1851, as a showcase of the nation's wealth, power and expertise. Lunchtimes were often spent at the National Gallery. Hardy started to read Ruskin, and in May 1863 began to summarise details of painters since the Renaissance in a notebook entitled 'Schools of Painting'. Architectural employment was congenial in the offices of Arthur (later Sir Arthur) Blomfield, a keen amateur musician with a practice at once happy, harmonious and too busy for the good of its principal's long-term reputation.

However, with so many recreational activities, and notwithstanding some success in prize competitions, it soon became plain that architecture was unlikely to prove a satisfactory form of long-term employment. The *Life* recounts consideration of the life of an art critic or London correspondent for a provincial newspaper, but in fact all the literary and journalistic schemes of this time seem to have been directed towards a university education leading to a career in the church. Ecclesiastical aspirations, however, were also to prove short-lived. Although Hardy was continuing, with noteworthy individuality, to attend in London both evangelical and high churches concurrently, religious doubts were soon to set in. By 1865 Hardy's once copious annotations of his church attendance had declined completely; and, before long, any thought of university entrance would also be abandoned.

Writing, more and more essential for Hardy as a means of self-expression and recreation, began to attract him as a possible career. The *Life* reports that 'by 1865 he had begun to write verses, and by 1866 to send his productions to magazines' (p. 49). Hardy, with characteristically earnest painstakingness, was clearly attempting to set himself up as an author, and especially as a poet. Purchases included Nuttall's *Standard Pronouncing Dictionary*, Walker's *Rhyming Dictionary*, Henry Read's *Introduction to English Literature* and several volumes of verse. Attempts at verse publication were none the less not successful, and much early work was destroyed. In March 1865, however, *Chambers's Journal* published an article Hardy had submitted the previous December, 'How I Built Myself a House', and, as Hardy later remarked, the acceptance of the piece determined his career. Architecture provided a livelihood but, as the many poems dated 1866 suggest, writing had become the main interest.

Hardy's relationships with the opposite sex, however, continued to be problematic. In 1863 he appears to have become more or less formally engaged to a lady's maid, Eliza Bright Nicholls, a relationship which was to provide the basis for the 'She, to Him' sequence of poems. But by 1865 the relationship was floundering, as a note for 2 June, Hardy's twenty-fifth birthday, suggests: 'Not very cheerful. Wondered what woman, if any, I should be thinking about in five years' time' (*Life*, p. 52). The end of the Eliza affair, in 1867, is almost certainly the occasion of one of Hardy's most anthologised poems, 'Neutral Tones':

> We stood by a pond that winter day,
> And the sun was white, as though chidden of God,
> And a few leaves lay on the starving sod;
>   – They had fallen from an ash, and were gray.
>
> Your eyes on me were as eyes that rove
> Over tedious riddles of years ago;
> And some words played between us to and fro
>   On which lost the more by our love.

The smile on your mouth was the deadest thing
Alive enough to have strength to die;
And a grin of bitterness swept thereby
Like an ominous bird a-wing . . . .

Since then, keen lessons that love deceives,
And wrings with wrong, have shaped to me
Your face, and the God-curst sun, and a tree,
And a pond edged with grayish leaves.

As this poem suggests, Hardy's five years in London were
not entirely happy ones, characterised on the one hand by
great intellectual development, but on the other by personal
loneliness and emotional disturbance, in the end giving rise
to depression. Affected also by ill health, Hardy quit London
in July 1867, returning to Dorset and the employment of John
Hicks with, as the *Life* expresses it, 'very different ideas of
things' (p. 57).

Hardy now began an affair with his cousin, Tryphena
Sparks, which lasted perhaps until 1870, and certainly led to
the exchange of rings. He also started work on a novel, *The
Poor Man and the Lady*, whose conception partly resulted from
the contrasts now experienced between cosmopolitan and
provincial existence. Each of these activities, and especially
Hardy's first novel, was to entail disappointment or disruption. 'Lord, how long wilt thou look upon this: O deliver my
soul from the calamities which they bring on me', Hardy
underlined in his Prayer Book on 7 November 1869. Various
publishers, including Macmillan, to whom the book had been
submitted in July 1868, took their time before rejecting the
manuscript; though Hardy did gain from Chapman & Hall's
reader, George Meredith, the advice that it would be better
for the author to postpone publication of *The Poor Man* while
he attempted a novel with more plot. In February 1870 Hardy
returned from Weymouth where, following the death of John
Hicks, he had been employed by the architect G. R. Crickmay,
to live with his parents. He settled to work in the quieter surroundings on his new project, a novel partly plundered from
the manuscript of *The Poor Man and the Lady*, and entitled
Desperate Remedies.

At Crickmay's request, Hardy set off from Bockhampton at 4 a.m. on 7 June on an architectural mission to St Juliot in Cornwall. On arrival he met the rector's sister-in-law Emma Lavinia Gifford, by turns attractive, impulsive, vivacious, eccentric and alluring. Four years later Hardy was to marry her. On her death, 42 years later, Hardy was to turn his desk calendar to this date, and leave it unaltered. To be in love with Emma, as 'When I Set Out for Lyonnesse' and other poems which recount this professional visit (such as 'A Man Was Drawing Near to Me' and 'At the Word "Farewell"') make clear, was a blindingly momentous experience, and especially so in such surroundings.

> When I set out for Lyonnesse,
>   A hundred miles away,
>   The rime was on the spray,
> And starlight lit my lonesomeness
> When I set out for Lyonnesse
> A hundred miles away.
>
> What would bechance at Lyonnesse
>   While I should sojourn there
>   No prophet durst declare,
> Nor did the wisest wizard guess
> What would bechance at Lyonnesse
> While I should sojourn there.
>
> When I came back from Lyonnesse
>   With magic in my eyes,
>   All marked with mute surmise
> My radiance rare and fathomless,
> When I came back from Lyonnesse
> With magic in my eyes!

Whatever the defects in her character which subsequent events and biographers have revealed, it cannot be doubted that Emma's belief in Hardy's creative ability substantially increased the effectiveness with which he was to set about his change of career. In May 1870, with *Desperate Remedies* finished, Hardy abandoned his employment with Crickmay and moved to London, keeping in touch with Emma, to whom he now considered himself betrothed. He continued to work as an architect, but in a piecemeal and comparatively unrooted style, for practices in both London and Dorset. On 25 March 1871 Hardy's first accepted novel was published by Tinsley's, much of the manuscript having been recopied in Emma's hand. Less than a year and a half later, in June 1872, a second novel, *Under the Greenwood Tree*, was published. The following September *A Pair of Blue Eyes*, supplied at Tinsley's own suggestion, began serial appearance in *Tinsley's Magazine*. In November, Hardy was invited by no less eminent a figure than Leslie Stephen to contribute a serial to the prestigious *Cornhill*. This commission was to be called *Far from the Madding Crowd*. Hardy could now afford to be confident. When in September he was offered employment on preferential terms by the architect T. Roger Smith he declined. His career as a novelist had begun.

Of Hardy's first four published novels – the first three heavily reliant upon *The Poor Man and the Lady* – *Desperate Remedies* and *A Pair of Blue Eyes* represent a lower plane of achievement. The former, a pot-boiler which is Wilkie Collins-like in its accumulation of connected data and incident, has an uneven consistency but at times a certain vigorous rawness of appeal. In it, as in the highly autobiographically suggested *A Pair of Blue Eyes*, much of which is set in Cornwall, many prefigurations of the later fiction can be observed, though expressed in ways which as yet lack much refinement. 'That's convenient, not to say odd', Stephen Smith remarks in *A Pair of Blue Eyes*, on discovering that he is staying in the same hotel as his rival Knight (xxxvii). The phrase might serve as a motto for the novel as a whole. Coincidences abound, at times garishly. At the end of the book, Knight and Smith find themselves on the same train, neither realising that the body of their beloved Elfride is contained in a funeral carriage at the front. Some of the rustic writing is mechanical, some of the characterisation and dialogue stagey, and the plotting overall has a vigour yet bizarreness of conception that Hardy has not yet learnt to accommodate.

The same criticism can hardly be levelled at the exquisite but brief *Under the Greenwood Tree*, the deftly expressed account of the romance between Dick Dewy and the local schoolteacher Fancy Day, or Hardy's first mature masterpiece, *Far from the Madding Crowd*. 'To myself, on the rare occasions on which I look into it', Hardy wrote of *Far from the Madding Crowd* to Frederic Harrison, 'it has a growing tendency to appear as the work of a youngish hand, though perhaps there is something in it which I could not have put there if I had been older' (*Letters*, II, 294). 'It may easily be maintained', an early critic remarked, 'that his later fiction has done no more than equal this exquisite early thing.'[4] The novel has a sweep and a homogeneity that make it unique in the Hardy corpus.

With the completion of *Far from the Madding Crowd* in July 1874 Hardy's last extended period of residence in his birthplace came to an end. The transference of lifestyle was palpable: from rural to urban, and from instinctive to intellectual. The suicide of Horace Moule in September had deprived Hardy of an indispensable mentor, but he was beginning to gain acceptance into the sort of intellectual circles that Moule himself had enjoyed, especially that of Leslie Stephen. In a letter of the period Hardy speaks of himself as 'denied by circumstances until very lately the society of educated womankind', whilst confessing to a 'bearishness' characteristic of those who live much alone (*Letters*, I, 26). It was, however, at the Stephen's that Hardy first met the illustrator of *Far from the Madding Crowd*, Helen Paterson, to whom he felt strongly attracted and whom he subsequently wished he had married.

Hardy in fact married Emma Gifford at St Peter's, Elgin Avenue, Paddington, on 17 September 1874. Neither family attended on what Emma described as a perfect September day.

Hardy's writing now, ironically, took a wrong direction. Invited by Stephen to provide another story for the *Cornhill*, Hardy found himself urged into 'the unfortunate course of hurrying forward a further production before he was aware of what there had been of value in his previous one: before learning, that is, not only what had attracted the public, but what was of true and genuine substance on which to build a career as a writer with a real literary message'. This confession in the *Life* (p. 105) cannot be disputed: *The Hand of Ethelberta* is Hardy's sally, strikingly unsuccessful, into a novel of high society: 'I do not wish to attempt any more original writing of any length for a few months, until I can learn the best line to take for the future' (*Letters*, I, 34), Hardy correctly told a correspondent after completing the novel.

What now followed was a substantial period of taking stock. Hardy confirmed his change of home away from London by moving into the couple's first house, Riverside Villa, Sturminster Newton, which, though small, was 'probably that in which they spent their happiest days' (*Life*, p. 115). This happiness derived not only from marriage, but also from an intimacy with the plenitude and hardships of nature and rural life (reflected in a number of Sturminster poems), and a growing confidence and ambition as an author (as evidenced in the *Literary Notebooks*, probably started in the first half of this year and kept with autodidactic zeal), and in the ambitious style of *The Return of the Native*, largely written at Sturminster. Such happiness had, however, to be set against a developing frustration at remaining childless: 'We hear that Jane, our late servant is soon to have a baby', Hardy noted. 'Yet never a sign of one is there for us' (*Life*, p. 119). The ambivalences of the time are beautifully caught in the final stanza of 'A Two-Years' Idyll', Hardy's poetic reflection on the Sturminster years:

> What seems it now?
> Lost: such beginning was all;
> Nothing came after: romance straight forsook
> Quickly somehow
> Life when we sped from our nook,
> Primed for new scenes with designs smart and tall. . . .
> – A preface without any book,
> A trumpet unlipped, but no call;
> That seems it now.

The novel of the Sturminster years, *The Return of the Native* (published 1878), sets from the outset a new tone. 'The new Vale of Tempe may be a gaunt waste in Thule', the sixth paragraph speculates. 'And, ultimately, to the commonest tourist, spots like Iceland may become what the vineyards and myrtle-gardens of South Europe are to him now; and Heidelberg and Baden be passed unheeded as he hastens from the Alps to the sand-dunes of Scheveningen' (I, i). Hardy sets himself up as an extensive tourist of Europe and literature, well travelled amongst the rarer folios. A chapter such as the ninth of Book I, in which the early relationship between Venn and Thomasin is described, clearly reveals that the old blueprints remain underneath: this is the kind of relationship that the reader of *Far from the Madding Crowd* can compare with that of Bathsheba and Oak. But, as the opening makes clear, the novel tries to set things out in an altogether more grand literary manner. Allusions, many of them taken from the *Literary Notebooks*, abound – and sometimes rather overshadow Hardy's own material. Wildeve is 'the Rousseau of Egdon' (III, vi), Clym is 'a John the Baptist' (III, ii), and Eustacia a Mozartean 'Queen of Night' who looks 'like the Sphinx' (I, vii), with superadded 'side shadows from the features of Sappho and Mrs Siddons' (I, vi). She is 'restless as Ahasuerus the Jew' (II, vii) but may finally 'take her place between the Héloïses and the Cleopatras' (I, vii). The allusions which dog the characters positively supercharge the heath, which has accordingly been seen by some as the novel's protagonist. *The Return* shows Hardy attempting, with new ambition, to reach remote heights, but the impression is of someone who, having doggedly scaled the Victorian Parnassus with ropes and mountain-pick, finds himself breathless and not a little heady, unaccustomed both to the view and the shortage of oxygen. Leslie Stephen, no mean mountain climber himself, rejected the book for the *Cornhill*, doubtless realising that though Hardy had found a new voice, he was not yet used to it.

In 1878, the Hardys moved into 1 Arundel Terrace, Wandsworth. Hardy applied for a British Museum reader's ticket, and there carried out much research on the Napoleonic period to be used in his next novel, *The Trumpet-Major*. By degrees, the *Life* claimed, he 'fell into line as a London man again' (p. 125). Hardy was elected a member of the Savile Club and the Rabelais Club, and his circle of social acquaintance grew considerably: meetings with Browning, Matthew Arnold and Tennyson, for example, were all to take place in the coming two years. Relationships between the Hardy and Gifford families, however, were no easier, and it was at 1 Arundel Terrace that the Hardys began to feel, echoing Wordsworth, that 'there had past away a glory from the earth'. 'It was in this house', the *Life* with uncharacteristic bluntness acknowledges, 'that their troubles began' (p. 128). Little of this is shown in the texture of Hardy's romance of the Napoleonic period, *The Trumpet-Major*: 'a cheerful, lively story' as Hardy described it (*Letters*, I, 65), which began serialisation in January 1880. However, Hardy's next novel, *A Laodicean*, clearly shows the detrimental effect of the severe internal bleeding which kept him in bed for long periods of time later in the year and had him confined to the house from October until the following April: much of the novel had to be dictated to Emma from Hardy's sick-bed. The story of the marriage choice facing Paula Power, daughter of a railway magnate, *A Laodicean* possesses an interesting and carefully conceived Arnoldian ideological ground plan, but the lack of cohesion and proportion is unfortunate.

Two on a Tower, a romance set in the perhaps over-ambitious if highly romantic context of the stellar universe, began serialisation in the *Atlantic Monthly* in May 1882, after the Hardys had moved to Wimborne in Dorset. 'The execution is hurried, and far from what I intended', Hardy told Edmund Gosse, '– but it could not be avoided' (*Letters*, I, 110). The relationship between an astronomer, Swithin St Cleeve, and his aristocratic lover, Viviette (Hardy's latest variation on the poor man and lady motif), is an attempt at making science 'not the mere padding of a romance, but the actual vehicle of romance' (*Letters*, I, 110). Unfortunately, like *A Laodicean*, its infrastructure of self-consciously modernistic ideas fails to find adequate concealment in creations of character and plot.

A return to Dorchester in June 1883 brought better health and better writing. Hardy had decided to build himself a house, Max Gate, just at the outskirts of the town, on the Wareham Road; the Romano-British remains found there partially explain the Roman background to his next novel, *The Mayor of Casterbridge*, which began publication on 2 January 1886. *The Mayor* is a novel of considerable emotional power, over-filled with incident (a fault attributed by Hardy to the pressures of serialisation) but none the less governed by a disciplined and carefully worked scheme.

If *Far from the Madding Crowd* and *The Return of the Native* can be seen as novels of experiment in which Hardy tried out his subject matter and how he could adapt it, with under- and over-reaching consequences, *The Mayor* and its successor

The Woodlanders (which Hardy often felt in some respects his best novel; *Life*, p. 520) may be seen as organic novels, with an artistically worked wholeness and professionalism about their conception and execution. In both, there is a carefully devised harmony of character and environment with dominant image and motif. 'The home corn trade, on which so much of the action turns, had an importance that can hardly be realized', the Preface to *The Mayor* makes plain. Grain is central not only to the Casterbridge economy, but also to the novel's language and imagery – as also to the patterns of germination, growth and fruit-bearing which affect the characters' lives. 'My great creditor is Grower' (xxix), the debt-ridden Henchard perhaps a little too over-symbolically remarks; just as a small incident represents 'the seed that was to lift the foundation' of the Henchard–Farfrae friendship (xv).

Though unassuming in character and incident, the opening pages of *The Woodlanders* represent an intricately prepared scheme offering several versions of invasion. Mrs Dollery's passengers approach Hintock, Percomb approaches Marty, and one party then informs the other of Fitzpiers, who has designs of invasion on many. In the next chapter, economic repression is examined through the twin symbols of the injuries to Marty's hand and the designs which Mrs Charmond has on Marty's hair, a rape of the lock and a disfiguring of the body that confirm the novel's dominant pattern of invasion, both metaphorical and physical.

With the creation of these two major works in his *oeuvre* behind him, Hardy attained a lifelong ambition by leaving in March 1887 for a tour of Italy. For Hardy, deprived of the financial resources for early travel, this was a liberating and fascinating experience, and the 'Poems of Pilgrimage' in *Poems of the Past and the Present* derive from it. Hardy at last saw those sights of which he had so long read: 'I am so overpowered by the presence of *decay* in Ancient Rome that I feel it like a nightmare in my sleep', he reported (*Letters*, I, 163). The year, also characterized by an increasing absorption in London society, was one on which Hardy could look back with satisfaction and a sense of achievement: 'The year has been a fairly friendly one to me. It showed me ... the south of Europe – Italy, above all Rome, – and it brought us back unharmed and much illuminated. It has given me some new acquaintances, too, and enabled me to hold my own in fiction' (*Life*, p. 212).

With a volume of short stories, *Wessex Tales*, completed and another, *A Group of Noble Dames*, in progress, Hardy was now able to turn his attention to what is generally seen as his *magnum opus*, *Tess of the d'Urbervilles*. The subject matter of the novel was for some tastes too sordid, and Hardy had trouble in securing serial publication: for example, Mowbray Morris, the editor of *Macmillan's Magazine*, commented on 'rather too much succulence'.[5] Several cuts had to be made in the serial version; they were then restored in the printed book, for which Hardy supplied a controversial subtitle ('A Pure Woman / Faithfully Presented by Thomas Hardy') and epigraph ('. . . Poor wounded name! My bosom as a bed / Shall lodge thee'). 'Much of my work hitherto has been of a tentative kind, and it is but latterly that I have felt any sureness of method' (*Letters*, I, 239), Hardy told John Lane a few days before *Tess* began serialisation. Here, indeed, Hardy the late developer had at last found his method: though controversial in effect, the novel is in achievement undoubtedly splendid, with a formidable emotional sweep, a tightly worked intellectual background and a coherence of vision and technique.

The *Life* remarks that *Tess*, 'notwithstanding its exceptional popularity, was the beginning of the end of his career as a novelist' (p. 252). More immediately, however, its notoriety brought financial stability, with increased fame and social encounters. With the latter, though, went increasing difficulties in Hardy's marriage. Female distractions – such as Rosamund Tomson – were beginning to abound. At the Gosses' on 2 July Hardy sat next to Agatha Thornycroft, wife of a famous sculptor and appraised by Hardy as the most beautiful woman in England. Perhaps she forms a physical model for Tess; certainly she gave cause for Hardy still to be reflecting on the perfection of her mouth three weeks later.

Emma Hardy was now beginning to keep private and critical diaries recording her husband's behaviour. Her interest in women's rights was also beginning to grow: 'He understands only the women he *invents* – the others not at all', she told her friend Mary Haweis.[6] The death of Hardy's father on 20 July 1892 did little to help the Hardys' marital difficulties, removing a source of good humour that had helped keep the troubled relationship between the Bockhampton and Max Gate households from excessive deterioration.

The greatest test of the marriage came with Hardy's liaison with Florence Henniker, the daughter of the first Lord Houghton and wife of an army officer, whom he met for the first time in Dublin on 13 May 1893, and with whom an intimacy quickly developed. Hardy introduced her to the proper study of architecture, collaborated with her on a short story, 'The Spectre of the Real', and by August 1893 was probably to be found clasping her hand behind the high altar of Winchester Cathedral.

Little of this showed either in Hardy's unusual novel *The Well-Beloved* (which started as a serial in October 1892 and appeared in revised book form five years later) or, more surprisingly, in his new volume of short stories *Life's Little Ironies*. The same can hardly be said, however, of Hardy's last major novel *Jude the Obscure*, which Hardy claimed to have begun writing in detail in August 1893. The novel addresses the marriage issue with aggressive gusto – and was to fall prey to problems of censorship as a result. Nor is this entirely surprising, for *Jude* is not the product of a man with a quiet or balanced mind: the strain shows in the quality of the writing and threatens the artistic achievement.

This was, in a way, a novel about which Hardy cared too much and with which he was too closely involved emotionally. From the beginning of its conception, the temptation to polemic loomed: 'Never retract. Never explain. Get it done and let them howl', Hardy quoted in the *Life*, recording the publication of the novel (p. 286). Hardy's sense of humour, no less than his sense of balance, here appear to have deserted him. As one critic has remarked, Sue's departure from Jude's Melchester lodging, disguised in men's clothing, belongs obviously to comedy; only a writer with too great a sense of mission could fail to notice that actually this is the world of *Figaro*, unperceived as such by its author.

The parts of *Jude*, it is generally agreed, are greater than its whole. This may suggest that the author was already thinking in shorter poetic episodes than in the longer sweeps of the novel: it should not, however, be misunderstood as suggesting that the novel lacks an overall plan. In its hour-glass structure, its dramatic contrasts of male and female, believers and unbelievers, flesh and spirit, ethics and law, self-indulgence and self-denial, the novel is if anything overwrought. *Jude* reads not as the novel of an incompetent, but as the novel of a competence overstrained, and with it Hardy bade farewell to novel-writing.

The reasons for this farewell have been much discussed, and few subsequent commentators have felt able to equal the clear-mindedness of Max Beerbohm: 'Mr Hardy writes no more novels because he has no more novels to write.'[7] In the first place, Hardy's move to poetry was not a sudden or a clear-cut one. The year 1889, for example, had been one of considerable poetic activity, whilst experimentation with the short story rendered the farewell to prose prolonged. Certainly, Hardy now felt that he had the financial stability to follow his inclinations with less circumspection. The labour – considerable and frequently tedious – involved in revising versions of novels for publishers wary of prudish readers was demanding. Indeed, the intensity of concentration required for any kind of lengthy prose fiction was cause for reflection for a man in his fifties who was beginning to feel – particularly after a back injury sustained in the summer of 1894 – signs of impending old age. Critical outcry at the novels did not encourage. Hence Hardy's reaction to the review of *Tess* in the *Quarterly*: 'Well, if this sort of thing continues no more novel-writing for me. A man must be a fool to deliberately stand up to be shot at' (*Life*, p. 259). Poetry offered hopes of less controversy and a new beginning. 'While thinking of resuming "the viewless wings of poesy" before dawn this morning, new horizons seemed to open and worrying pettinesses to disappear', Hardy had recorded on Christmas Day 1890 (*Life*, p. 241).

For Emma's sake, perhaps, the gradual transition was just as well. She made no secret of the fact that she disapproved of her husband's growing reputation as a novelist of a new morality. For his part, Hardy was beginning to tire exceptionally of his wife's idiosyncratic character, even if references to this were kept general: 'I feel that a bad marriage is one of the direst things on earth, and one of the cruellest things, but beyond that my opinions on the subject are vague enough',

Hardy told his friend Sir George Douglas, with an unconvincing disclaimer.

Matters cannot have been helped by Hardy's growing attraction for the married daughter of General Augustus Pitt-Rivers, Agnes Grove, who increasingly succeeded Florence Henniker in his affections as a literary pupil, or by the critical reception of the book version of *The Well-Beloved* in 1897. 'Of all forms of sex mania in fiction we have no hesitation in pronouncing the most unpleasant to be the Wessex-mania of Mr. Thomas Hardy', proclaimed the review in the *World*, perturbed (as many other readers have been) by a plot in which an artist, in search of the perfect form in woman and sculpture, falls in love with three separate generations of the same family.

Not surprisingly, poems of the period, most notably the 'In Tenebris' poems of 1895 and 1896 and 'Wessex Heights' of December 1896, display an uneasy blend between acute depression and highly strung instability. But by October 1897 much had changed. As Michael Millgate explains, Hardy's 'discovery of the bicycle, his abandonment of fiction, and his return to poetry seemed to be combining in a single movement of liberation and renewal'.[8]

Hardy revealed to Florence Henniker in September 1898 that he had begun to put together a collection of poems: 'Some of them have been lying around for many many years – with no thought on my part of publishing them' (*Letters*, II, 202). To puzzled critical reaction, Hardy himself supplied illustrations for *Wessex Poems*, which were published in December that year. 'Well: the poems were lying about, and I did not know quite what to do with them', Hardy explained unconvincingly to Gosse (*Letters*, II, 208), but the curiously idiosyncratic volume reads by contrast as a deliberate demonstration of the range of Hardy's verse, with perhaps less concern displayed for consistency of standard – both in the illustrations and in the poems themselves.

Further poetic production was spurred on by the outbreak of the Boer War on 12 October 1899. When news of the end of the war reached Max Gate on 2 June 1902, the Union Jack was flown and in general Hardy somehow felt reinvigorated by the start of a new century and a new reign. A new collection of verse, *Poems of the Past and the Present*, appeared in November 1901. More homogeneous than *Wessex Poems*, both in quality and expressed outlook, the volume won greater critical approval, and a second printing was ordered within weeks.

Though Hardy had abandoned writing novels he had not abandoned selling them, and increasingly adroit husbandry of his business prospects marked these years. Early in 1902 he had decided to cease using Harper Brothers as his British publisher and transferred his books to Macmillan, soon forming a high regard for the professional acumen of the chairman of the firm, Frederick Macmillan.

As the decade progressed Hardy became increasingly conscious of the attractiveness to readers of the idea of a topographical Wessex. Thus, whilst remaining distant from the majority of guide books and topographical studies which began to proliferate in the first decade of the century, he frequently sought at least covert means of encouraging them as a means of increasing his own sales. In October 1902 the half-title 'Wessex Novels' was added to Macmillan's new edition of *Tess*, and Hardy became increasingly involved with the researches of Hermann Lea, whose *Handbook* to the fictional Wessex appeared in 1905. Simultaneously Hardy was coming to be approached as an authority on all matters of folk mythology and dialect speech: he was consulted by Joseph Wright, for example, about entries in the *New English Dictionary*.

Part I of *The Dynasts*, Hardy's epic on the Napoleonic Wars, was published on 13 January 1904. Early reviews were lukewarm, perhaps largely because of the novelty of the genre. Hardy consistently suspected critics of theological bias, forgetting even his own recognition that the writing was of mixed quality. When the manuscript of Part II arrived at Macmillan a little over a year and a half later, commercial enthusiasm was limited.

Jemima Hardy died on 3 April 1904 and was buried at Stinsford a week later. Emma Hardy was not present at the ceremony, and grief is not suspected as a reason. But for Hardy the blow was a great one: 'The gap you speak of is wide, and not to be filled', he wrote to his friend, the banker Edward Clodd. 'I suppose if one had a family of children one would be less sensible of it' (*Letters*, III, 119). The bereavement did, however, cause a brief improvement in Hardy's marital relationship, though the lack of argument partly resulted from increasing lack of contact. Hardy the architect had designed Max Gate with some spaciousness, and Hardy the married man determined that he would make good use of it.

In August 1905 Hardy was approached by a young journalist, Florence Dugdale, and he gave her permission to visit Max Gate. Though it is not known whether this visit took place, she certainly met Hardy at Max Gate in January 1906. 'I do not think you stayed at all too long, and hope you will come again some other time', he encouraged her (*Letters*, III, 193). By the summer the relationship had deepened: Hardy gave Florence two photographs of himself in September; by the following April, as he sought to promote Florence's literary career, the restraints imposed by his own marriage were becoming increasingly irksome to him.

The final part of *The Dynasts* was finished in 1907 and published on 11 February 1908. 'It has dragged its slow length along through too many years already', Hardy told Desmond MacCarthy. 'This uses up all my energy – of which I have no superabundance' (*Letters*, III, 276). Secretly, however, he took much pride in the work, and in submitting the final instalment to a reluctant Sir Frederick Macmillan his pride outweighed his tact in terming the work 'the longest English drama in existence' (*Letters*, III, 277).

The Dynasts – eccentric in its conception, and uneven in its execution – is simultaneously at the centre and on the sidelines of Hardy's achievement. It chronicles the fortunes of the civilised Wessex world in the Napoleonic period, set, as seldom in the novels or poems, against the workings of a cosmology substantially apparent in its working but idiosyncratic or even occasionally vague in its structure. There is little tension between material and thesis, and an emphasis on the national rather than the personal; there is hence too little opportunity for Hardy's predilection – the human heart fluttering or shattering (love, in short) – which so motivates the personages of the fiction and absorbs the creator of the poems. The globe is too central and love too tangential to *The Dynasts*, and the literary technique employed is an idiosyncratically disconcerting blend of the real or semi-imagined with the literary – or even over-literary.

Sapping though the work on *The Dynasts* was, its completion had a major effect on Hardy's stature. The work's long-term importance, Professor Millgate comments, lies in Hardy's 'own increased confidence in his capacity to write effectively in a wide range of forms, and in the public perception of him henceforth as not merely a great writer but *the* great writer of his day'.[9] In November 1908 Hardy was offered a knighthood, but with a characteristic penchant for seeking the shadows he asked Asquith if it might be held over for a year, though the offer was not renewed. The death of Meredith on 18 May 1909 left Hardy in a clear position of pre-eminence amongst English authors, and he was persuaded to accept the presidency of the Incorporated Society of Authors left vacant by Meredith's decease. On 9 July 1910 Hardy's membership of the Order of Merit was announced. Emma was not present to see Hardy invested with it a few weeks later, asking Florence Dugdale to check that he was properly dressed.

Hardy's third volume of verse, *Time's Laughingstocks*, was published on 2 December 1909 in the middle of the Finance Bill crisis. On the whole more personal and less philosophical than its predecessor, it was favourably received by the critics, notwithstanding the inclusion of the low-life 'A Tramp-woman's Tragedy', which Hardy thought his most successful poem, and 'Panthera', based on a legend Hardy knew would shock his more orthodox readers.

At home, however, Hardy's problems were increasing. His relationship with his wife had now deteriorated substantially: the season of 1908 was the first for many years in which they did not rent a London flat together, and it was now difficult for him to accept social invitations, such as one to Clodd's for Whitsun 1908. 'The only scruple I have about it lies in my domestic circumstances', he explained, 'which, between ourselves, make it embarrassing to me to return hospitalities received, so that I hesitate nowadays to accept many' (*Letters*, IV, 21). This was not, in truth, Hardy's only scruple, for more and more he was organising meetings with Florence Dugdale of which Emma could neither know nor approve. Much gagging of a potentially harmful national press had to take place when a local paper reported how Clodd's boat had got stuck on a mud flat on the River Alde with Hardy and Florence on board – the latter's presence would have been unknown to Emma. The frustrations caused by the developing relationship caused low spirits and fine poems, a combination to be seen increasingly in the coming years, and well exemplified by one of the poems occasioned by the Florence affair, 'On the Departure Platform' in *Time's Laughingstocks*:

> We kissed at the barrier; and passing through
> She left me, and moment by moment got
> Smaller and smaller, until to my view
> >   She was but a spot;
>
> A wee white spot of muslin fluff
> That down the diminishing platform bore
> Through hustling crowds of gentle and rough
> >   To the carriage door.
>
> Under the lamplight's fitful glowers,
> Behind dark groups from far and near,
> Whose interests were apart from ours
> >   She would disappear,
>
> Then show again, till I ceased to see
> That flexible form, that nebulous white;
> And she who was more than my life to me
> >   Had vanished quite . . . .
>
> We have penned new plans since that fair fond day,
> And in season she will appear again –
> Perhaps in the same soft white array –
> >   But never as then!
>
> – 'And why, young man, must eternally fly
> A joy you'll repeat, if you love her well?'
> – O friend, nought happens twice thus; why,
> >   I cannot tell!

As Hardy's amanuensis, Florence came to be accepted by Emma almost as part of the household, and by 23 June 1910 Florence was well enough acquainted with the metaphorical mechanics and chemistry of Max Gate to be remarking that she admired Hardy more as an author than as a man. 'I am intensely sorry for her', Florence commented the same year, 'sorry indeed for both.'[10]

Hardy published a group of poems, 'Satires of Circumstance', in 1911 as well as substantially revising *Tess* for a new edition of his novels, the Wessex Edition, which began publication in 1912 and is now generally acknowledged as the definitive version of these works. Emma, whose confidence in her literary productions was growing, increased her own creative output. She completed an engaging autobiographical volume, *Some Recollections*, and had a collection of verse, *Alleys*, privately printed in Dorchester, where in April 1912 her muddled volume *Spaces* also appeared.

Hardy was becoming increasingly worried about Emma's mental stability. When Henry Newbolt and W. B. Yeats came to Max Gate in June 1912 to present Hardy with the Gold Medal of the Royal Society of Literature, Emma was allowed to sit beside Yeats at lunch (discoursing indeed on the merits of the cats seated beside her lunch plate) but was excluded from the subsequent presentation. With strikes marking a year of acute social unrest and the *Titanic* hitting an iceberg (commemorated by Hardy in 'The Convergence of the Twain'), the greatest personal blow for Hardy was yet to fall. On 27 November, following an alarming deterioration in Emma's condition, he was summoned to Emma's bedroom, now in the Max Gate garret, by the maid Dolly Gale. He arrived just in time to witness Emma's death.

'From her Lonely Husband, with the Old Affection', Hardy marked the card on Emma's funeral wreath. The old affection was now to release a remarkable poetic flood. 'One forgets all the recent years and differences', Hardy told Clodd, 'and the mind goes back to the early times when each was much to the other – in her case and mine intensely much' (*Letters*, IV, 239). The process was aided by the first of several revisits to Cornwall, as well as by the editing of Emma's diaries and recollections. A prodigious poetic consequence resulted, most of all in the 'Poems of 1912–13' which were to form part of the *Satires of Circumstance* volume, published in November 1914, that contained much work bitterly ironic, much deeply melancholic and much indisputably fine. The latter quality manifested itself particularly in the 'Emma' poems, which Hardy was to describe as 'the only amends I can make' (*Letters*, V, 37):

> Woman much missed, how you call to me, call to me,
> Saying that now you are not as you were
> When you had changed from the one who was all to me,
> But as at first, when our day was fair.
>
> Can it be you that I hear? Let me view you, then,
> Standing as when I drew near to the town
> Where you would wait for me: yes, as I knew you then,
> Even to the original air-blue gown!
>
> Or is it only the breeze, in its listlessness
> Travelling across the wet mead to me here,
> You being ever dissolved to wan wistlessness,
> Heard no more again far or near?
>
>   Thus I; faltering forward,
>   Leaves around me falling,
> Wind oozing thin through the thorn from norward,
>   And the woman calling.

With the collection of the stories in *A Changed Man and Other Tales*, published in October 1913 and considered by Hardy 'mostly bad' (*Letters*, IV, 300), Hardy's career in fiction had reached a tidy conclusion. His relationships were also being put in formal order: he probably proposed to Florence first in April 1913, and on 10 February 1914 they were married. 'We thought it the wisest thing to do, seeing what a right hand Florence has become to me', Hardy explained to Sir Sydney Cockerell, 'and there is a sort of continuity in it, and not a break, she having known my first wife so very well' (*Letters*, V, 9). For Florence such continuity was not always reassuring. The second wife found herself living with a husband commemorating the first: 'If I had been a different sort of woman, and better fitted to be his wife – would he, I wonder, have published that volume?', she wrote to Lady Hoare after *Satires of Circumstance* had appeared.[11]

The outbreak of the First World War did little for Hardy's morale. At first, the *Life* reports, 'To Hardy as to ordinary civilians the murder at Sarajevo was a lurid and striking tragedy, but carried no indication that it would much affect English life' (p. 393). When, however, the reality of the war became apparent, 'the contemplation of it led him to despair of the world's history thenceforward' (*Life*, pp. 365–6). There was much personal grief as a result of the death of his nephew Frank George, whom he had intended to be his heir, but there was also a significant addition to his poetic *oeuvre*, as several of Hardy's most anthologised poems date from the war years, especially 'Men Who March Away', 'In Time of "The Breaking of Nations" ' and 'The Oxen'.

Hardy's fifth volume of verse, *Moments of Vision*, was published on 30 November 1917. A more unified volume than any of its predecessors, and more wholly from a recent period of composition, it is also in the opinion of some critics Hardy's best. Originally entitled 'Moments from the Years' it contains a series of poems occasioned by the death of Hardy's sister Mary as well as many more on the Emma relationship. Clearly, the volume was an intensely personal one. 'I expect that the idea of the general reader will be that T.H.'s second marriage is a most disastrous one and that his sole wish is to find refuge in the grave with her with whom alone he found happiness', Florence gloomily reported to Cockerell. 'Well – all things end somewhere.'[12]

'I have not been doing much, – mainly destroying papers of the last 30 or 40 years, and they raise ghosts', Hardy told Sir George Douglas in May 1919 (*Letters*, V, 303–4). The impression of idleness was deceptive, for Florence had certainly by now been typing up the *Life* at Hardy's dictation for over a year, after a great re-ordering and deletion of papers. By November 1919 Hardy had completed the narrative up to 1918, and by 1922 Florence could report the book finished so far as was possible. Hardy's revisitation of the past decreased his appetite for the present. His short-term memory was beginning to become impaired, and in May 1919 he found attendance at the Royal Academy Dinner oppressive because of the large number of his contemporaries who were no longer able to attend. Junketings on Hardy's eightieth birthday, including messages from the King, the Prime Minister and the Lord Mayor of London, provided at least a temporary lifting of spirits. 'I have decided that it was worth while to live to be eighty to discover what friends there were about me up and down the world, and my judgement against the desirability of being so long upon earth is therefore for a time at least suspended', Hardy told A. C. Benson (*Letters*, VI, 24). Hardy's national standing was confirmed when on 20 July 1923 the Prince of Wales visited Max Gate.

In his last decade, however, Hardy was not to prove beyond new friendships. He corresponded with Siegfried Sassoon, for example, sent a letter of encouragement to Ezra Pound, was visited by Robert Graves, and by T. E. Lawrence – a new acquaintance, as a deleted passage in the *Life* makes clear – whom Hardy, like Florence, was particularly to value. A friendship which Florence at least could well have done without, however, was that with a young Dorchester girl, Gertrude Bugler, who acted in the adaptations of novels which had come to be staged annually in Dorchester by the Hardy Players, with the author's blessing and occasional minor assistance. When the Players performed *The Mellstock Quire* in the ruins of Sturminster Newton castle, Hardy took tea with the cast afterwards at his former home at Riverside Villa, and insisted that Gertrude Bugler should sleep in the room in which he had written *The Return of the Native*. Hardy's quirks were beginning to become onerous to Florence, whose own grip on existence, never characterized by gusto or vigour, was still weaker after an operation for cancer in September 1924. When plans were mooted for Gertrude Bugler to act the part of Tess in a dramatisation which was to transfer to London, Florence made a private and deeply felt intervention which ensured the abandonment of the plan. In August 1925 she tried to ensure that there would be no more Hardy plays in Dorchester.

Hardy was still highly active as a writer. January 1922 had found him ill in bed; for a while cancer was feared. But during this illness Hardy composed one of his most extensive comments on his writing, the 'Apology' which he later affixed to the volume *Late Lyrics and Earlier*, published on 23 May 1922. A new and perhaps less striking volume, *Human Shows, Far Phantasies, Songs, and Trifles* was sent off to Macmillan on 29 July 1925. 'I am weary of my own writing',

Hardy remarked, 'and imagine other people are too by this time' (*Letters*, VI, 359). But neither part of the statement was true. The first printing of the volume was almost immediately sold out, and Hardy continued to write poems, however unsprightly the sentiments expressed in them. Plans were afoot for the celebration of his ninetieth birthday (a day which he said he intended to spend in bed) and he himself composed a poem for his eighty-sixth, posthumously published in *Winter Words*:

He Never Expected Much
(or)
A Consideration
(A reflection) on My Eighty-Sixth Birthday

Well, World, you have kept faith with me,
    Kept faith with me;
Upon the whole you have proved to be
    Much as you said you were.
Since as a child I used to lie
Upon the leaze and watch the sky,
Never, I own, expected I
    That life would all be fair.

'Twas then you said, and since have said,
    Times since have said,
In that mysterious voice you shed
    From clouds and hills around:
'Many have loved me desperately,
Many with smooth serenity,
While some have shown contempt of me
    Till they dropped underground.

'I do not promise overmuch,
    Child; overmuch;
Just neutral-tinted haps and such,'
    You said to minds like mine.
Wise warning for your credit's sake!
Which I for one failed not to take,
And hence could stem such strain and ache
    As each year might assign.

Strain and ache were simultaneously on the increase and on the decline. In November 1927 Hardy declared that 'he had done all that he meant to do, but he did not know whether it had been worth doing. His only ambition, so far as he could remember, was to have some poem or poems in a good anthology like the *Golden Treasury*' (*Life*, p. 478). This Hardy had more than achieved. He was fulsomely acknowledged as the Grand Old Man of English Letters, and in a more comfortable financial position than ever his early musings could have predicted, let alone his parsimonious frugality require. On the other hand, physically he was ready to die. On 11 December he sat down at his writing table, but felt totally unable to work, 'the first time that such a thing had happened to him' (*Life*, p. 479). By Christmas Day he was unable to come down stairs – or, to his relief, to eat any Christmas pudding. A prolonged spell in bed was followed on 11 January 1928 by a heart attack which finally ended his life.

Obituary tributes made Hardy's perceived stature plain. 'The throne is vacant, and literature is gravely bereaved', wrote Edmund Gosse. 'The death of Thomas Hardy leaves English fiction without a leader', Virginia Woolf agreed.[13] Differences of opinion, however, surrounded the funeral. Was Hardy to be allowed the obscure country burial he had asked for, or the national spectacle his close friends and the nation demanded? The Dean of Westminster, pressurized, gave permission for Hardy's ashes to be buried in Westminster Abbey. Hence the unexpected role of a Dorset surgeon, F. L. Nash-Wortham, in excising Hardy's heart from his body and storing it in a biscuit tin until it could be placed in a burial casket and interred in Emma's grave. In death, as in life, Hardy was fulsomely divided.

Winter Words, Hardy's largely elegiac final volume of poetry, which he had been preparing for publication on his birthday, appeared on 2 October, posthumously.

2

'Nearest neighbours closest friends':*Hardy and the Romantics

In 'One We Knew (M.H. 1772–1857)' Hardy pays tribute to his grandmother, and the glimpse of a previous, Napoleonic, era which she gave him:

> She would dwell on such dead themes, not as one who
>   remembers,
>   But rather as one who sees.
>
> She seemed one left behind of a band gone distant
>   So far that no tongue could hail:
> Past things retold were to her as things existent,
>   Things present but as a tale.

Hardy inherited to the full this characteristic. Though born early in the Victorian era, he did not, eyewitnesses say, always live in it. In the end Hardy could declare to Siegfried Sassoon: 'I think I've had enough of Napoleon', but he was almost 87 by the time that he did so. 'Napoleon is a real man to him', T. E. Lawrence reported, 'and the country of Dorsetshire echoes that name everywhere in Hardy's ears. He lives in his period, and thinks of it as the great war.' Hardy's sense of 'his' time was curious. It was indeed in many ways the *first* part of the nineteenth century which interested Hardy as though it had been his own.[1]

Hardy's sense of preferred literature was also distinctive. As the texture of both Hardy's novels and his poems makes clear, it was essentially poetry rather than prose that

---

* From 'Prologue'.

32

influenced Hardy's ideas and fired his imagination. For
Hardy, the *Life* tells us, Scott the poet was preferable to Scott
the novelist (p. 51). The opinion may offend the modern
evaluator of Scott, but cannot surprise any student of the
published prejudices of Hardy. For two years in his twenties,
Hardy supposedly 'did not read a word of prose except such
as came under his eye in the daily newspapers and weekly
reviews', having already concluded that 'in verse was concentrated the essence of all imaginative and emotional
literature' (*Life*, p. 51).

Accordingly, this chapter takes a highly selective view of
Hardy and the literature of his time – a view convenient for
the position of this chapter in the volume. It surveys the
works of the Romantic poets, looks at several of Hardy's
best-known poems, and discusses the selective but crucial
issue of how Hardy modified what the Romantics and their
successors thought of as their purposes and achievements as
creative writers. In doing so, it argues that much of Hardy's
best and best-known verse has a significant part of its origin
in his debate with the literature of his time.

Hardy was far from unique in his response to his predecessors. In considering their *raison d'être*, Victorian writers
could not help but be overawed by the ideas and achievements of their forebears in the Romantic era. The Victorians
saw themselves not as themselves but as successors – often
successors oppressed by a sense of guilt and enfeebledness –
of the Romantics. The Romantic period had been dominated
by an extraordinary set of poets – principally Wordsworth,
Coleridge, Shelley, Keats, Blake and Byron – whilst its
achievements in the genre of prose fiction were distinctly
more limited. But these poets, so omnipresent to the
Victorians metaphorically, were in the more important literal
sense totally lost to them. By November 1827, when the
eighteen-year-old Tennyson went up to Trinity College,
Cambridge, Wordsworth and Coleridge were changed, both
as poets and as people, while Blake, Byron, Shelley and
Keats were all dead – and in three cases out of four with a
cruel prematurity. Poetic generations which should have
met failed to. Shelley's 'Adonais' suggests the predicament
in which a young poet of the period might have found
himself:

> Lost Echo sits amid the voiceless mountains
> And feeds her grief with his remembered lays
> And will no more reply to winds or fountains …

Tennyson's own biography bears the hypothesis out. 'Byron is dead', the fourteen-year-old prodigy, on hearing the news from Missolonghi, went out to carve in the neighbouring sandstone.[2] Over 60 years later, Hardy, staying near the Spanish steps in Rome, close to the house in which Keats had died, felt both loneliness and a historical quirk, as the *Life* (p. 195) reports:

> Hardy liked to watch of an evening, when the streets below were immersed in shade, the figures ascending and descending these steps in the sunset glow, the front of the church orange in the same light; and also the house hard by, in which no mind could conjecture what had been lost to English literature in the early part of the same century that saw him there.

With the Romantics died the viability of many of the ideas they had stood for, but not altogether their potency or attractiveness. 'Poets are the unacknowledged legislators of the World', Shelley famously concluded in his *Defence of Poetry*.[3] 'To a Skylark' develops the hypothesis. Shelley's bird, remote in situation, beautiful in song, listened to yet not necessarily regarded, undoubted – but not altogether definable – in its influence, is seen as having much in common with the artistic creator. It is

> Like a Poet hidden
>   In the light of thought,
> Singing hymns unbidden,
>   Till the world is wrought
> To sympathy with hopes and fears it heeded not.

The Victorians lacked such confidence – or shunned such arrogance. 'I only make men and women speak – give you the truth broken into prismatic hues, and fear the pure white light', Browning wrote, deliberately choosing a Shelleyan image to turn his ideological back on.[4] Poets could no longer have the same ideas because the fabric of the society around them was changing. Byron, in a typical burst of characteristic Romantic *contemptus mundi*, could declare in Canto IV of *Childe Harold*:

> There is a pleasure in the pathless woods,
> There is a rapture on the lonely shore,
> There is society, where none intrudes,
> By the deep Sea, and music in its roar ...

But for the Victorian, solipsism, isolationism were impossible. 'Poets we read not, / Heed not, feed not, / Men now need not / What they do', as Hardy's 'A Jingle on the Times' expresses it. Changes in society were forcing poets to respond. 'Tennyson, we cannot live in art', R. Chenevix Trench had reminded Tennyson at Cambridge,[5] and in Kingsley's novel *Alton Locke* (1850) the sagacious if somewhat sententious Dean Wynnstay explains his theory of the reason for the change:

> And be sure, if you intend to be a poet for these days . . . you must become a scientific man. Science has made vast strides, and introduced entirely new modes of looking at nature, and poets must live up to the age.[6]

As the next chapter will explain, scientific advance meant that the Victorian could no longer look at the landscape about him in the same way: the exciting Romantic vision, in Coleridge's 'Eolian Harp', of a 'one life within us and abroad' had given way to the Victorian nightmare expressed in the question of section LV of Tennyson's *In Memoriam* (1850): 'Are God and Nature then at strife?' For Coleridge, the poet's creative perception and understanding of the world about him brought a thrilling unity into man's experience; for Tennyson, by contrast, geological discoveries threatened a natural world incompatible with received theories of a love-based and lasting creation. The poet, in short, moved from being at the creating centre of a scheme of things to being a horrified and helpless onlooker.

The developing industrial townscapes removed emotional equilibrium yet one stage further: Wordsworth, who lived on

to see more of them than any of his contemporaries, could,
albeit with unconvincing optimism, talk in his 'Steamboats,
Viaducts and Railways' of 'Motions and Means, on land and
sea at war / With old poetic feeling'. For Matthew Arnold the
age was 'deeply unpoetical', an unfortunate perception for a
poet who realised that 'the *what you have to say* depends on
your age'.[7]

The overall effect of the shift in ideas and in society deter-
mined a fundamental change in poetic mood. Where the
Romantics could enthuse with brief-lived optimism, the
Victorians would recollect largely with a deepening of regret.
Tennyson's so-called 'high born maiden' figures (the phrase
taken from Shelley's 'To a Skylark') gradually move towards
absorption in society: from 'Mariana' through 'The Lady of
Shallott' to the lonely maiden of 'The Palace of Art', the poem
Tennyson wrote in response to Trench's injunction. The last
poem in the second volume of Tennyson's *Poems* (1842) is
subdued and ambiguous in tone:

The Poet's Song

The rain had fallen, the Poet arose,
  He passed by the town and out of the street,
A light wind blew from the gates of the sun,
  And waves of shadow went over the wheat,
And he sat him down in a lonely place,
  And chanted a melody loud and sweet,
That made the wild swan pause in her cloud,
  And the lark drop down at his feet.

The swallow stopped as he hunted the fly,
  The snake slipt under a spray,
The wild hawk stood with the down on his beak,
  And stared with his foot on the prey,
And the nightingale thought, 'I have sung many songs,
  But never a one so gay,
For he sings of what the world will be
  When the years have died away.'

The poet, turning his back on society, gains in isolation the
attention of the symbolic wild swan and lark, though the

content of his art is perhaps stronger on musicality than on reality or social relevance of message. Browning's Prologue to 'Asolando' (1889) is less visual, melodic, and emollient:

> The Poet's age is sad: for why?
>   In youth the natural world could show
> No common object but his eye
>   At once involved with alien glow –
>   His own soul's iris-bow.
>
> And now a flower is just a flower:
>   Man, bird, beast are but beast, bird, man –
> Simply themselves, uncinct with dower
>   Of dyes which, when life's day began,
>   Round each in glory ran.

Hardy's dialogue with the Romantics had begun to articulate itself at least as early as what the *Life* (p. 8) describes as 'the earliest discoverable of young Hardy's attempts in verse', the poem entitled 'Domicilium'. The *Life* describes these as 'Wordsworthian lines', and so indeed they are. The concern is with Hardy's birthplace, especially with the relationship between man and nature in it; and, by implication, the effect that Hardy's surroundings and his forebears (especially, again, his grandmother) have on his own personality:

> In days bygone –
> Long gone – my father's mother, who is now
> Blest with the blest, would take me out to walk.
> At such a time I once inquired of her
> How looked the spot when first she settled here.
> The answer I remember. 'Fifty years
> Have passed since then, my child, and change has marked
> The face of all things. Yonder garden-plots
> And orchards were uncultivated slopes
> O'ergrown with bramble bushes, furze and thorn:
> That road a narrow path shut in by ferns,
> Which, almost trees, obscured the passer-by.

As is immediately apparent, even more Wordsworthian than the subject is the style, a more than competent pastiche of Wordsworthian blank verse by a poet who claimed always to be influenced by the seminal essay which Wordsworth had prefaced to the second edition of his *Lyrical Ballads* (1800).[8] 'Domicilium' is, in a sense, Hardy's *Prelude* in miniature.

A second stage in Hardy's relationship with what appears to have been his early poetic master comes in 1868 with Hardy recording the reading of Wordsworth's poem 'Resolution and Independence' as one of three cures for despair (*Life*, p. 59). 'Resolution and Independence' is a magnificent poem, and the curious Hardy student might find much interest in detecting what aspects of it Hardy found so restorative. Certainly, Hardy's choice, in lighting on a poem which partly focuses on a poet changing his mind, is ironically proleptic of the change in Hardy's own attitude to the Romantics. 'We poets in our youth begin in gladness', Wordsworth's poet-narrator remarks, 'But thereof comes in the end despondency and madness.'

By the time of *Tess* Hardy has become distinctly icy. A swipe at Wordsworth, one of a number of allusions in the late novels to Romantic writers, double-handedly demands: 'Some people would like to know whence the poet whose philosophy in these days is deemed as profound and trustworthy as his song is breezy and pure, gets his authority for speaking of "Nature's holy plan" ' (iii). Tess is alleged to be no more convinced than the narrator, as an allusion to Wordsworth's 'Ode: Intimations of Immortality' reveals:

> for to Tess, as to not a few millions of others, there was ghastly satire in the poet's lines –
>
> Not in utter nakedness
> But trailing clouds of glory do we come.
>
> To her and her like, birth itself was an ordeal of degrading personal compulsion, whose gratuitousness nothing in the result seemed to justify, and at best could only palliate.   (li)

Despondency resulting from youthful identification with Romantic ideals, disillusion with the ideals of his poetic predecessors, is frequent in Hardy's verse. 'We are getting to the end of visioning / The impossible within this universe', he remarked in the first lines of a poem in his last collection of verse, *Winter Words*; and he was not reluctant, especially in later years, to expose the inadequacies of those who had inherited the Romantics' visionary gleam, as 'An Ancient to Ancients' makes plain:

> Where once we danced, where once we sang,
> Gentlemen,
> The floors are sunken, cobwebs hang,
> And cracks creep; worms have fed upon
> The doors. Yea, sprightlier times were then
> Than now, with harps and tabrets gone,
> Gentlemen!
>
> . . .
>
> The bower we shrined to Tennyson,
> Gentlemen,
> Is roof-wrecked; damps there drip upon
> Sagged seats, the creeper-nails are rust,
> The spider is sole denizen;
> Even she who voiced those rhymes is dust,
> Gentlemen!

'Shut Out That Moon' is an even more potent rejection of Romantic and conventionally poetic attitudes:

> Close up the casement, draw the blind,
> Shut out that stealing moon,
> She wears too much the guise she wore
> Before our lutes were strewn
> With years-deep dust, and names we read
> On a white stone were hewn.
>
> Step not forth on the dew-dashed lawn
> To view the Lady's Chair,
> Immense Orion's glittering form,
> The Less and Greater Bear:
> Stay in; to such sights we were drawn
> When faded ones were fair.

Brush not the bough for midnight scents
　That come forth lingeringly,
And wake the same sweet sentiments
　They breathed to you and me
When living seemed a laugh, and love
　All it was said to be.

Within the common lamp-lit room
　Prison my eyes and thought;
Let dingy details crudely loom,
　Mechanic speech be wrought:
Too fragrant was Life's early bloom,
　Too tart the fruit it brought!

If the second quoted stanza of 'An Ancient to Ancients' had been proficient in its imitation of Tennyson, this poem is even more so. 'An Ancient to Ancients' clearly sets out to parody early Tennyson, especially 'Mariana'. In 'Shut Out That Moon' the lushness of texture is a highly skilful imitation of later Tennyson poems, such as *In Memoriam, Maud* and *The Princess*, with some imitation of early Shakespeare comedies (especially *A Midsummer Night's Dream* and *The Merchant of Venice*) thrown in for good measure. The idea of the romantic wandering over a lawn is thoroughly Tennysonian, strongly recalling, for example, the great set piece of *In Memoriam*, xcv: 'By night we lingered on the lawn'. For an author who claimed that he despised the jewelled line as effeminate, Hardy here reveals himself, for a purpose simultaneously creative and destructive, as a brilliant exponent of it when required. The vocabulary too is highly imitative. 'Casement' is a word used over twenty times by Tennyson; and the image of dew, or words associated with it, is used over fifty times. The astronomical proficiency adds to the deftness of the Tennysonian pastiche. Orion is mentioned twice in *Maud* alone, once in connection with one of the hero's night-time walks.

The final stanza, in a harsh *bouleversée*, deliberately counterblasts the Tennysonian optimism and romanticism that has gone before. The personification typical of the first three stanzas, a poetic device by which objects are represented as people, is replaced by modernistic imagery and diction, symptomatic of a world in which, partly due to the influence of industrialism, people have become objects. The universe of the early stanzas closes down to the oppressive interior of a room whose lamp, rather than candle, sheds a harshly modern illumination. The language of the first six lines of the stanza is masterful in the nineteenth-centuryness of its overtones, deliberately jolting the reader into a realisation of the predicament of modern man, and the questionable relevance of ancient poetic methods and ideas to it. 'Common' has demotic overtones of an expanding proletariat; and 'loom', 'mechanic' and 'wrought' are suggestive of the new means by which it made its living. 'Dingy' (a word not to be found in Dr Johnson's *Dictionary* and never used by Tennyson) suggests the murky conditions in which the workforce were frequently forced to live, before perhaps being moved towards that 'prison' which the nineteenth century so distinctively added to its urban landscapes.

The strong contrast between Hardy's own perceptions and those of his predecessors is increased by a return in the final two lines to one of those predecessors' motifs. The perception that 'Too fragrant was life's early bloom' returns to the phraseology, and the ideas, of Matthew Arnold. The word 'Bloom' is something of an Arnoldian cliché, being particularly prominent in Arnold's elegiac lament for his fellow poet Arthur Hugh Clough in what is perhaps Arnold's best known poem, 'Thyrsis', with its repeated line 'The bloom is gone, and with the bloom go I'. Hardy is also here dealing with an Arnoldian idea: that the age in which the modern poet lived was deeply unpoetical. But Hardy's message (and resultingly his success) is very much the reverse of Arnold's. Where Arnold's poet figures flee from modernistic invention, Hardy is not afraid to ask to confront it; and where Arnold can function in only one poetic register, 'Shut out that Moon' shows how virtuosically Hardy can function in at least two.

Hardy's reaction to the writers of his time, and more especially the Romantics, shows through less allusively, yet perhaps more deceptively, in the poems he wrote directly about them. 'At the Pyramid of Cestius near the Graves of Shelley and Keats' is based on Hardy's visit to the graves of these poets in Rome in 1887. 'He was on the whole more interested in Pagan than in Christian Rome', the *Life* reports with deliberately judged provocativeness (p. 198), but the 'pilgrim feet' of the poem move towards neither of these interests: they are bound for reverential meditation over the graves of poets who are seen as all but deities, 'matchless singers' who possess 'immortal Shades'. The same religiose vocabulary is seen in another poem composed on the same holiday, 'Shelley's Skylark':

> Somewhere afield here something lies
> In Earth's oblivious eyeless trust
> That moved a poet to prophecies –
> A pinch of unseen, unguarded dust:
>
> The dust of the lark that Shelley heard,
> And made immortal through times to be; –
> Though it only lived like another bird,
> And knew not its immortality:
>
> Lived its meek life; then, one day, fell –
> A little ball of feather and bone;
> And how it perished, when piped farewell,
> And where it wastes, are alike unknown.
>
> Maybe it rests in the loam I view,
> Maybe it throbs in a myrtle's green,
> Maybe it sleeps in the coming hue
> Of a grape on the slopes of yon inland scene.
>
> Go find it, faeries, go and find
> That tiny pinch of priceless dust,
> And bring a casket silver-lined,
> And framed of gold that gems encrust;
>
> And we will lay it safe therein,
> And consecrate it to endless time;
> For it inspired a bard to win
> Ecstatic heights in thought and rhyme.

The claims for the poet here are obvious. He is capable of 'prophecies', of making the ephemeral 'immortal', and of 'ecstatic' achievements. The last word is significant, for it is also the word Hardy associates with the song produced by his darkling thrush; it is a word of acute religious overtones, associated with the soul being removed from the body. In essence, the poem seems to be supporting Romantic claims about the nature of the poet, and even to be prepared to think of him as semi- or quasi-divine. The experienced Hardy reader, however, is likely to want to detect a characteristic layer of irony and equivocality in the poem. *Can* dust be made immortal? Is the idea not a deliberately impossible one? The half-rhyme at the end of the second stanza, with the word immortality thus emphasized and appearing not quite to be in place, appears anxious to underline the point. In the following stanza the homeliness, almost bathos, of the vocabulary may on the one hand, with a characteristically Hardyan kind of RSPCA benevolence, lavish tenderness on the bird; but one wonders whether it is also intended to deflate the poet, to suggest an exaggeration of outlook on his part. We are almost into the tone of the 'Tit Willow Song' in Gilbert and Sullivan's *Mikado* of two years earlier.

The end of the poem has a similar instability of tone. On the one hand, the appeal to the 'faeries' and the emotional pressure evidently underlying the desire to officiate at a consecration is impressive; on the other hand, one has to sit back and reflect whether the vocabulary is not deliberately designed to draw attention to its own extravagance, and whether the agnostic and tentative Hardy really might presume to officiate at any ceremony of the sort. On the one hand, the poem glorifies Shelley; on the other, it appears to draw attention to the fact that the poet can be glorified – by himself and by others – overmuch.

Perhaps Hardy's most acute analysis of his disillusion with Romantic vision comes in a poem dated 9 October 1924 and entitled 'Nobody Comes'. The situation is quite an unexceptional one for Hardy, or indeed any poet, to write about: a reflection on the oddness of solitude. The poem is in a way a rewrite of Hardy's own poem 'The Sailor's Mother' and a reduplication of a situation common in Georgian poetry, for example the much anthologised and roughly contemporary 'Adlestrop' by the Georgian poet Edward Thomas or the less-well-known 'In Romney Marsh' by John Davidson. The immediate cause of Hardy's loneliness was the absence of his wife Florence, who was away undergoing an operation for cancer in London; but Hardy manages to turn the poem, as Thomas and Davidson interestingly do not, into an analysis of the predicament of the modern poet:

> Tree-leaves labour up and down,
>   And through them the fainting light
>   Succumbs to the crawl of night.
> Outside in the road the telegraph wire
>   To the town from the darkening land
> Intones to travellers like a spectral lyre
>   Swept by a spectral hand.
>
> A car comes up, with lamps full-glare,
>   That flash upon a tree:
>   It has nothing to do with me,
> And whangs along in a world of its own,
>   Leaving a blacker air;
> And mute by the gate I stand again alone,
>   And nobody pulls up there.

The key image here is perhaps the lyre, a symbol of the poet, and one particularly dear to the Romantic movement, whose characteristic sub-section of the image was the Eolian harp. Since Hardy's poem depends in part on a knowledge of the implications of this symbol, some background information is necessary. An Eolian harp has essentially the same mechanism as any other harp, but its mode of producing a sound is different. No human agent is required: the notes are produced by the wind, and differ in pitch and intensity in accordance with its strength. For the Romantics this little-known instrument could be turned into an image of the nature of poetic inspiration, and of the relationship between the poet and everything around him. The *locus classicus* for the exploration of these ideas is Coleridge's influential conversation poem 'The Eolian Harp'. First drafted on his honeymoon, the poem began as an ordinary love poem, but ended up as a kind of cosmic celebration, hymning the harmonious relationship of the individual with the universe:

O! The one Life within us and abroad,
Which meets all motion and becomes its soul,
A light in sound, a sound-like power in light,
Rhythm in all thought, and joyance everywhere ...

Hardy's *Literary Notebooks* show a keen interest in such ideas. 'The poet is in a great degree passive', Hardy noted. 'He aspires to be a sort of human Aeolian harp, ... welcoming every impression without attaching itself to any.'[9] A later note reflects what was probably Hardy's more authentic and characteristically ambivalent opinion:

> The realistic and poetical schools of painting. The two tendencies are indestructible – the struggle perennial ... Ever since it became full grown it has always oscillated between two endeavours – the endeavour of the artist now to forget himself in what he sees, and now to transfuse all the external world with his own thought and emotion.[10]

In part (and only in part, since it is a complex if apparently simple poem), 'Nobody Comes' is a dialogue based on these opposing ideas. It is, if you like, a sort of parody of the Coleridgean conversation poem, reaching a thoroughly un-Coleridgean conclusion via no conversation at all. Separated from his wife and from his friends, Coleridge composed in his conversation poem 'This Lime Tree Bower My Prison' a declaration of the extent to which the poet's facility for involving himself in the thoughts of others, and meditating on the glories of Nature, could raise the poet's spirits into a realisation that 'Nature ne'er deserts the wise and pure' and that 'No sound is dissonant which tells of Life'. The poem, like many another of Coleridge's, or indeed like many a Victorian novel, charts a growth from isolated loneliness to participation in a 'One Life within us and abroad'. The means, and the message, of 'Nobody Comes' are completely different. The poem gains its effect from a number of strong contrasts which build up an impression of disharmony: the first stanza is strongly contrasted with the second, rather as the shape of an internal Gothic arch is in tension with the slightly different shape of the arch which encases it. Thus the 'fainting light' of the first stanza contrasts with the 'lamps

full-glare' of the second; the 'crawl of night' contrasts with
the speed of the car; the telegraph, which 'intones', contrasts
with the poet who is 'mute'; and the isolation of a poet bereft
of supernatural aid contrasts with a telegraph network which
appears to be buzzing with extramundane interference.
Industrialism passes the poet by, and has reduced his
importance and his vision. The telegraph has a destination
and a message; the poet presents himself as having neither.
Illumination comes only from the car. But the lamps reveal
rather than understand; and their contact with Nature, represented by the tree, is only momentary. The car's chief effect is
as a pollutant rather than an insight, but the poem almost
suggests that the poet sees himself as the same, for he too is
in a world of his own, but without the means, either physical
or cognitive, of escape from it. In 'Dejection: an Ode'
Coleridge summed up something of the Romantic poet's
view of Nature:

> O Lady! we receive but what we give,
> And in our life alone does Nature live:
> Ours is her wedding garment, ours her shroud!
>   And would we aught behold, of higher worth,
> Than that inanimate cold world allowed
> To the poor loveless ever-anxious crowd,
>   Ah! from the soul itself must issue forth
> A light, a glory, a fair luminous cloud
>   Enveloping the Earth –
> And from the soul itself must there be sent
>   A sweet and potent voice, of its own birth,
> Of all sweet sounds the life and element!

In 'Nobody Comes' Hardy does not see himself as capable
of enlightening 'the poor loveless ever-anxious crowd' (a
typical piece of Romantic renunciation of society); rather he is
oppressed and restricted by the impedimenta of a large
industrialised society. There must have been a special reso-
nance in 1924 about the tree leaves labouring (an oddly
industrial word to use of a natural object), for it was in that
year that Ramsay MacDonald had formed the first Labour
government. The poet's instrument, the lyre, is now

associated not with the poet, but with the technological society and expanding proletariat which he is powerless to influence. The poem is less about a wife who has cancer than a concept of the poet which is dead.

The lyre image recurs in one of Hardy's best-known anthology pieces 'The Darkling Thrush', with which 'Nobody Comes' has much in common:

> I leant upon a coppice gate
>   When Frost was spectre-gray,
> And Winter's dregs made desolate
>   The weakening eye of day.
> The tangled bine-stems scored the sky
>   Like strings of broken lyres,
> And all mankind that haunted nigh
>   Had sought their household fires.
>
> The land's sharp features seemed to be
>   The Century's corpse outleant,
> His crypt the cloudy canopy,
>   The wind his death-lament.
> The ancient pulse of germ and birth
>   Was shrunken hard and dry,
> And every spirit upon earth
>   Seemed fervourless as I.
>
> At once a voice arose among
>   The bleak twigs overhead
> In a full-hearted evensong
>   Of joy illimited;
> An aged thrush, frail, gaunt, and small,
>   In blast-beruffled plume,
> Had chosen thus to fling his soul
>   Upon the growing gloom.
>
> So little cause for carolings
>   Of such ecstatic sound
> Was written on terrestrial things
>   Afar or nigh around,
> That I could think there trembled through
>   His happy good-night air

Some blessed Hope, whereof he knew
And I was unaware.

'The Darkling Thrush' and 'Nobody Comes' are remarkably
similar in situation and expression. A man isolated in a landscape, standing near the much-used Hardy symbols of trees
and a gate, in lighting conditions associated with failing
physical ability (the 'fainting light' of 'Nobody Comes', or the
'weakening eye of day' of 'The Darkling Thrush'), possesses a
melancholiness of mood from which an external force (the
thrush, the telegraph wires or the car) appears to offer at best
partial liberation. There are similarities of language (the word
spectral, for example, in both poems) as well as in the use of
the harp image. The harp of 'The Darkling Thrush' is,
however, an altogether more pathetic affair than that in
'Nobody Comes', distinguished forcefully by its broken
strings. The image is in many ways common enough, but one
cannot help wondering if Hardy was deliberately recalling
Keats's tomb in Rome, with its design by Severn after an idea
by Keats, showing a Greek lyre in *basso relievo*, with only half
the strings – Emma Hardy's *Diary 3* shows careful study of
the monument.[11] 'The Darkling Thrush' is an occasional
poem, intended to mark the ending of a century, and perhaps
to mark one aspect of that century in particular. Like
'Nobody Comes', much of its significance is in signalling the
end of a method of poetic composition, of an attitude to the
role of the poet, which Hardy now found untenable.

The significance of this attitude can hardly be overesti-
mated, for it appears to affect Hardy's response to the major
events of his life as well as to the literature he admired
during it. Of these events, perhaps the most significant was
the death of Hardy's first wife Emma, which set Hardy recol-
lecting the days of their courtship, and reflecting on his loss,
most of all in the magnificent 'Poems of 1912–13':

A Death-Day Recalled

Beeny did not quiver,
  Juliot grew not gray,
Thin Vallency's river

Held its wonted way.
Bos seemed not to utter
  Dimmest note of dirge,
Targan mouth a mutter
  To its creamy surge.

Yet though these, unheeding,
  Listless, passed the hour
Of her spirit's speeding,
  She had, in her flower,
Sought and loved the places –
  Much and often pined
For their lonely faces
  When in towns confined.

Why did not Vallency
  In his purl deplore
One whose haunts were whence he
  Drew his limpid store?
Why did Bos not thunder,
  Targan apprehend
Body and Breath were sunder
  Of their former friend?

This is a lament not so much for a wife as for a way of think-ing and a manner of writing. The central second stanza gives us a Romantic cliché: the country-lover immured in the town, as for example Coleridge's mention of Lamb as 'in the great City pent' in 'This Lime Tree Bower My Prison', or his refer-ence to himself as 'in the great city, pent 'mid cloisters dim' in 'Frost at Midnight'. But the cliché pitches us into a Romantic frame only the more to make us feel the absence of it else-where. Nature appears to have betrayed Emma, but not as much as it, and Romantic writing about it, has betrayed the poet: his impassioned plea in the last stanza is one without answer: this poet is unable to speak of a one life within us and abroad, and his sing-song ballad style is a deliberate con-trast to the exalted verse forms more characteristically used by the major Romantics for their reflections on the relationship between man and nature.

The same cast of mind less obviously underlies an even
more considerable piece in 'Poems of 1912–13':

The Going

Why did you give no hint that night
That quickly after the morrow's dawn
And calmly, as if indifferent quite,
You would close your term here, up and be gone
    Where I could not follow
    With wing of swallow
To gain one glimpse of you ever anon!

    Never to bid good-bye,
    Or lip me the softest call,
Or utter a wish for a word, while I
Saw morning harden upon the wall,
    Unmoved, unknowing
    That your great going
Had place that moment, and altered all.

Why do you make me leave the house
And think for a breath it is you I see
At the end of the alley of bending boughs
Where so often at dusk you used to be;
    Till in darkening dankness
    The yawning blankness
Of the perspective sickens me!

    You were she who abode
    By those red-veined rocks far West,
You were the swan-necked one who rode
Along the beetling Beeny Crest,
    And, reining nigh me,
    Would muse and eye me,
While Life unrolled us its very best.

Why, then, latterly did we not speak,
Did we not think of those days long dead,
And ere your vanishing strive to seek
That time's renewal? We might have said,

'In this bright spring weather
We'll visit together
Those places that once we visited.'

Well, well! All's past amend,
Unchangeable. It must go.
I seem but a dead man held on end
To sink down soon ... O you could not know
That such swift fleeing
No soul foreseeing –
Not even I – would undo me so!

The poem depends on a large number of contrasts and antitheses: the narrator loving his wife and yet not loving her, remembering her yet not remembering her, feeling calm and feeling distraught, feeling sure that things are 'unchangeable', yet upset that 'It must go'; and the style, in its alteration from the prosaic 'close your term here' to the more arch 'no soul foreseeing' – as well as in its beautifully judged variations in rhythm and line length – is finely calculated to reflect these instabilities. The greatest contrast of all, however, is between the powers attributed to the woman, and the complete lack of skills associated with the narrator, whose ability to fashion a poem as fine as this is never even hinted at, being altogether concealed by a persona of acute ordinariness.

Emma is throughout the poem recalled as someone mobile and sinuous, an impression aided by the large amount of animal imagery associated with her or with her environment: swallow, swan, beetle and horse. By contrast, the narrator's lack of movement, vision and knowledge is highly noticeable. He is, for example, unable to follow his wife (l. 5), he is unspoken to (ll. 9–10), 'unmoved' (l. 12), 'unknowing' (l. 12), and, in a final piece of irony, 'but a dead man'. Emma, in a cliché both Romantic and romantic, is viewed in stanza 4 in harmony with a natural backdrop at a moment of excitement in the past. In pointed contrast, stanzas 2 and 3 dwell on the miseries of the present, and the inability of the poet to alter or derive consolation from them. As in 'A Death-Day Recalled', it is the poet's lack of vision that is noticeable, his inability to shape things around him in accordance with the power of his own insights and imagination: he sees morning 'harden upon the wall', and the phenomenon remains but itself, unaltered: 'The yawning blankness / Of the perspective sickens me!'

Hardy's distinctive attitude to the role of the poet, his modification of the ideas he received from his nineteenth-century predecessors, perhaps shows itself most revealingly in the poems he wrote about contemporary authors, especially Barnes and Swinburne; in the poem he wrote to celebrate the three-hundredth anniversary of Shakespeare's death; and in perhaps the most famous poem he wrote about himself as a poet, 'Afterwards'.

Swinburne, born three years before Hardy, was amongst Hardy's favourite authors. His portrait was hung, along with those of Tennyson and Browning, above the fireplace in the Max Gate study, and a visit to his grave at Bonchurch on the Isle of Wight in March 1910 produced a poem by Hardy, 'A Singer Asleep', of exceptional lyricism. Swinburne is seen as 'peer in sad improvisations' of the waves beside which he lies buried, and distinguished enough in poetic achievement to have Sappho, 'she the Lesbian', as his 'singing-mistress'. But generous though the poem appears on the surface in its praise, there is a significant tentativeness and provisionality underlying it. The content, and the style, appear to speak of excess, and especially of youthful folly. Reference is made to 'The passionate pages of his earlier years', and when Hardy recalls his own contact with Swinburne it is, equally significantly, his youthful years that he thinks of. The stanza describing them is again something of a Romantic cliché, recounting (rather in the style of Yeats's similarly mannered 'Lake Isle of Innisfree') a visionary and poetic experience within the alien environment of the town:

> O that far morning of a summer day
> When, down a terraced street whose pavements lay
> Glassing the sunshine into my bent eyes,
> I walked and read with a quick glad surprise
>   New words, in classic guise ...

What Hardy sees Swinburne as accomplishing, and what position in society he sees him as occupying, are hedged around with ambiguity, not to mention half-heartedness; a fact all the more surprising given the spleen with which

Hardy defended Swinburne against the opposition and neglect of the press in a virulent letter to Florence Dugdale of exactly the same period (*Letters*, IV, 15–16). To stress Swinburne as some kind of educational descendant of Sappho is two-handed: for it is not only Sappho's lyricism that is mentioned, but also the self-destructive tendencies of her life.

As for how much, or exactly what, of Swinburne will live on, Hardy is again curiously half-hearted. True, stanza 5 argues that Swinburne's 'power … swells yet more and more' by comparison with the 'spindrift' abilities of some of his contemporaries; but those contemporaries are identified as Swinburne's critics, of whom Hardy's opinion was nothing other than highly contemptuous. Largely, the attention is directed towards whether or not Swinburne might live on in some physical form, yet here too the imaginings are noticeably tentative and would have seemed especially so to a contemporary audience: stanza 7 imagines that 'one might hold in thought' some nocturnal rendezvous between Swinburne and Sappho off the Isle of Wight; stanza 8 'dreams him sighing to her spectral form'. The poem ends not with a surprise, but with a sunset:

> I leave him, while the daylight gleam declines
> Upon the capes and chines.

The verb is carefully chosen, as if to underline the inadvisability of optimism or celebration. 'A Singer Asleep' recalls Swinburne , certainly; but what it claims for him is distinctly half-hearted.

When one turns to a poem about a contemporary whom Hardy knew more closely and, in personal terms, felt for more greatly, the same tentativeness is, oddly, even more apparent. The *Life* (p. 190) describes Hardy's attendance at the funeral in 1886 of his near-contemporary and quondam neighbour William Barnes:

> In October the Dorset poet William Barnes died. Hardy had known him ever since his schoolmastering time in South Street, Dorchester, next door to the architect under whom Hardy had served his years of pupillage. In 1864

Barnes had retired from school-keeping, and accepted the
living of Winterborne Came-cum-Whitcombe, the rectory
house being, by chance, not half a mile from the only spot
Hardy could find convenient for building a dwelling on.
Hardy's walk across the fields to attend the poet's funeral
was marked by the singular incident to which he alludes
in the poem entitled 'The Last Signal'. He also wrote an
obituary notice of his friend for the *Athenaeum*, which was
afterwards drawn upon for details of his life in the
Dictionary of National Biography. It was not till many years
after that he made and edited a selection of Barnes's
poems.

The account is blandly and coolly matter of fact, and there is
little significant uplift of tone in the poem:

> Silently I footed by an uphill road
> That led from my abode to a spot yew-boughed;
> Yellowly the sun sloped low down to westward,
> And dark was the east with cloud.
>
> Then, amid the shadow of that livid sad east,
> Where the light was least, and a gate stood wide,
> Something flashed the fire of the sun that was facing it,
> Like a brief blaze on that side.
>
> Looking hard and harder I knew what it meant –
> The sudden shine sent from the livid east scene;
> It meant the west mirrored by the coffin of my friend
> there,
> Turning to the road from his green,
>
> To take his last journey forth – he who in his prime
> Trudged so many a time from that gate athwart the land!
> Thus a farewell to me he signalled on his grave-way,
> As with a wave of his hand.

This is no grand classical elegy on the lines of Shelley's
'Adonais' or Arnold's 'Thyrsis'. The aim is very much at the
homely, and in pop a number of elements which the unkind

reader might by now wish to view as clichés: the evening setting, the poet's isolation in the country, the mildly portentous image of the gate, and the transient moment of ambivalent illumination. In style it is a deliberate tribute to Barnes: there is a noticeable use of *cynghanedd*, a form of consonantal patterning typical of the Welsh forms of poetic technique sometimes experimented with by the poet; but in subject matter and the kind of tribute it gives it is unusual and distinctive. There is affection for Barnes as a friend, but no mention at all of Barnes as a poet, let alone for what he achieved by being one: the nearest we get to praise of his accomplishments is the identification of him as a persistent trudger. Rather the poem, as though afflicted by embarrassment, avoids the issue, concentrating instead on the vague resurrectional possibilities that lend some comfort to the otherwise distressing experience.

For all his reading of the poetry of his time, then, Hardy is curiously and distinctively cautious and uncertain about what the role of the poet might be, and as such, his opinion is a noticeable contrast to the visionary views of his Romantic predecessors. It shows through in Hardy's view of the greatest of English poets, Shakespeare, as much as it shows through in Hardy's views of himself. When Hardy's celebration of the tercentenary of Shakespeare's death, 'To Shakespeare', is compared with Gerard Manley Hopkins's 'Shakspere' and Matthew Arnold's 'Shakespeare', clear distinctions emerge. All three set Shakespeare in the context of the universe, and in doing so disregard what happens on the stage; none of the poets mentions a single play or character; and none shows any interest in stagecraft or drama. Hopkins's tone is religiose, Arnold's Homeric, and Hardy's what might be described as in places studiedly banal. 'To Shakespeare' is not one of Hardy's more memorable poems, any more than the Arnold or Hopkins pieces can be regarded as flattering examples of their authors' work. But on the other hand, Hardy's style is significantly suited to the kind of attention which he wishes to pay to his subject: three of Hardy's six stanzas are concerned with Shakespeare's personality rather than his achievement, and what interests Hardy about that personality is its very ordinariness and inconspicuousness:

Bright baffling Soul, least capturable of themes,
Thou, who display'dst a life of commonplace,
Leaving no intimate word or personal trace
Of high design outside the artistry
    Of thy penned dreams,
Still shalt remain at heart unread eternally.

Through human orbits thy discourse to-day,
Despite thy formal pilgrimage, throbs on
In harmonies that cow Oblivion,
And, like the wind, with all-uncared effect
    Maintain a sway
Not fore-desired, in tracks unchosen and unchecked.

And yet, at thy last breath, with mindless note
The borough clocks but samely tongued the hour,
The Avon just as always glassed the tower,
Thy age was published on thy passing-bell
    But in due rote
With other dwellers' deaths accorded a like knell.

And at the strokes some townsman (met, maybe,
And thereon queried by some squire's good dame
Driving in shopward) may have given thy name,
With, 'Yes, a worthy man and well-to-do;
    Though, as for me,
I knew him but by just a neighbour's nod, 'tis true.

'I' faith, few knew him much here, save by word,
He having elsewhere led his busier life;
Though to be sure he left with us his wife.'
  – 'Ah, one of the tradesmen's sons, I now recall....
    Witty, I've heard....
We did not know him.... Well, good-day. Death comes to all.'

So, like a strange bright bird we sometimes find
To mingle with the barn-door brood awhile,
Then vanish from their homely domicile –
Into man's poesy, we wot not whence,
    Flew thy strange mind,
Lodged there a radiant guest, and sped for ever thence.

The poet described in the *Life*, in a word with significant
Romantic connotations, as a 'seer' (p. 368) is here examined
as a kind of Kafkaesque nondescript. Few had much
knowledge of or educated respect for him even in his own
dwelling place. 'I knew him but by just a neighbour's nod',
one townsman is made to remark.

The image takes us, perhaps significantly, straight to one
of Hardy's most celebrated anthology pieces, his vision of
what will be said about him after his death, the last poem in
Moments of Vision, 'Afterwards':

When the Present has latched its postern behind my
      tremulous stay,
  And the May month flaps its glad green leaves like
      wings,
Delicate-filmed as new-spun silk, will the neighbours say,
  'He was a man who used to notice such things'?

If it be in the dusk when, like an eyelid's soundless
      blink,
  The dewfall-hawk comes crossing the shades to alight
Upon the wind-warped upland thorn, a gazer may think,
  'To him this must have been a familiar sight.'

If I pass during some nocturnal blackness, mothy and
      warm,
  When the hedgehog travels furtively over the lawn,
One may say, 'He strove that such innocent creatures
    should come to no harm,
  But he could do little for them; and now he is gone.'

If, when hearing that I have been stilled at last, they stand
      at the door,
  Watching the full-starred heavens that winter sees,
Will this thought rise on those who will meet my face no
      more,
  'He was one who had an eye for such mysteries'?

And will any say when my bell of quittance is heard in
      the gloom,
  And a crossing breeze cuts a pause in its outrollings,

Till they rise again, as they were a new bell's boom,
   'He hears it not now, but used to notice such things'?

The poem presents Hardy not as a seer but as a countryman,
as a man-next-door. The most conspicuous feature of the
poem is its natural imagery: here is a poet who knows very
definitely what a nightjar is. As far as subject is concerned, it
is the ancient Anglo-Saxon poetic theme *par excellence*: as 'The
Seafarer' puts it:

ætercweþendra
lof ligendra lastworda best ... [12]

– what a man should most seek to obtain on this earth is the
praise of those who, living on, speak of him after his death.
In this sense, the title is perhaps a pun: not just 'Afterwards'
but also 'After-Words'. The poet recalled in 'Afterwards' (for
poet he just about appears to be) will be remembered, but
there is something altogether bathetic about the terms in
which he will be recalled. This duality in the subject matter is
reflected by a duality in the style: each stanza depends on a
contrast between three lines of Tennysonian euphoniousness
and Swinburnean lushness which then gives way to the ordinary, almost humdrum, style of the fourth line of each stanza
(especially those of stanzas 1 and 2), which are deflating in
their utterance as well as in their sentiment. The poet can
conjure beautiful lines certainly, but are these impressive to
Hodge, and do they affect his world? 'He could do little for
them, and now he is gone', we are told. The poet is thus
recalled as a noticer rather than as an achiever; and if his
poetic achievement is limited, his physical future is even
more so. The image of the eyelid's soundless blink and the
words 'mysteries' and 'rise' are perhaps echoes – deliberate
or otherwise – of the lesson from the funeral service in the
Book of Common Prayer (1 Corinthians 15). The 'bell of quittance' is thus not only an image representing the frail voice of
the poet, speaking onward in time, but also a poignant
reminder that for Hardy the agnostic no after-life is possible.
The poet's body cannot live on; his voice may perhaps do so,
but only with uncertainty and frailty. There is no physical
afterwards; and poetic after-words are limited in their effect.

Hardy's posthumously published collection of verse, *Winter Words*, ends with two personal poems largely concerned with the poet's role. 'He Resolves to Say No More' is something of a set-piece volume-ender, and perhaps suffers because of that; but its predecessor, 'We Are Getting to the End', forms a pertinent conclusion to this discussion:

> We are getting to the end of visioning
> The impossible within this universe,
> Such as that better whiles may follow worse,
> And that our race may mend by reasoning.
>
> We know that even as larks in cages sing
> Unthoughtful of deliverance from the curse
> That holds them lifelong in a latticed hearse,
> We ply spasmodically our pleasuring.
>
> And that when nations set them to lay waste
> Their neighbours' heritage by foot and horse,
> And hack their pleasant plains in festering seams,
> They may again, – not warely, or from taste,
> But tickled mad by some demonic force. –
> Yes. We are getting to the end of dreams!

The immediate cause of the poem is the acute despondency Hardy felt as a result of the horrors of the First World War, and its implications for those who believed that man might progress morally and ethically; but its relevance as a concluder to Hardy's last volume is greater than this. The image of the lark directs the reader straight to the Romantics, and the poem is in part Hardy's poignant lingering farewell to Romantic doctrine. From the beginning of his life, Hardy's response to his reading of the poetic literature of his time was a stimulus, and it remained so to the end. In the last analysis, Hardy's resultant concept of the writer, and of what the writer can achieve, underlies not only what Hardy writes, but also his ambivalent feelings about what he feels he can accomplish by writing it.

3

'Fellow earth-men surge and strive':* Hardy and Contemporary Society

Conventional theory suggests that literary forms develop their greatest amplitude when the nations that produce them are living through a period of heightened vitality, and that accordingly the dynamic of the Industrial Revolution made the reign of Queen Victoria the great period of the novel in Britain.[1] Certainly a new consciousness of society and the environment as active forces marks the Victorian novel. 'It is the habit of my imagination to strive after as full a vision of the medium in which a character moves as of the character itself', George Eliot explained to R. H. Hutton, who in turn (like many early critics) thought of Hardy as an imitator of Eliot and, in his review of *Far from the Madding Crowd*, defined its special appeal as a regional novel grounded in intimate knowledge of a functioning community.[2] 'Man is not alone but exists in society, in a social environment, and so far as we novelists are concerned, this environment is constantly modifying events', Emile Zola, also born on 2 June 1840, explained. 'That is just where our real task lies, in studying the interaction of society on the individual and of the individual on society.'[3]

The Industrial Revolution brought with it immense social problems, and novelists generally felt it their task to sensitise the social conscience of their readership. *Contemptus mundi* was outmoded. George Eliot, in 'A Writer's Notebook', explains the change of heart with a dismissive allusion to *The Earthly Paradise* and the Art for Art's Sake aesthetic of its author, William Morris:

* From 'A Sign-Seeker'.

Man or woman who publishes writings inevitably assumes the office of teacher or influencer of the public mind. Let him protest as he will that he seeks only to amuse, and has no pretension to do other than while away an hour of leisure or weariness – 'the idle singer of an empty day' – he can no more escape influencing the moral taste, and with it the action of the intelligence, than a setter of fashions in furniture and dress can fill the shops with his designs and leave the garniture of persons and houses unaffected by his industry.[4]

At its crudest, the instinct of the Victorian novel for analysing social conditions and stimulating reform is to be found in the so-called Condition of England novels of the late 1840s and early 1850s. 'I wish this summer ... to try and do some good – to examine a little into the condition of English working men', announces Lancelot Smith, the hero of Kingsley's *Yeast* (1848), to the squire's daughter, by name Argemone Lavington.[5] The novels generally dramatise the unacceptable gulf between rich and poor: 'We are to live as separate as if we were in two worlds; aye, as separate as Dives and Lazarus, with a great gulf between us', explains John in Gaskell's *Mary Barton* (1848), expressing in religious terms the seminal theory of 'two nations; between whom there is no intercourse and no sympathy' of Disraeli's *Sybil* (1845).[6] Political remedies, from Disraeli's Tory conservatism through to Christian Socialism and Chartism, generally receive some scrutiny in an effort to reconcile the harsh realities of economic imperatives (generally Malthusian in origin) with Christian moral law. *Hard Times* (1854) is the *locus classicus* for the conflict, with Mr Gradgrind attempting to prove 'that the Good Samaritan was a Bad Economist', but left only with a vision of what he himself might become: 'a white-haired decrepit man, bending his hitherto inflexible theories to appointed circumstances; making his facts and figures subservient to Faith, Hope, and Charity; and no longer trying to grind that heavenly trio in his dusty little mills'.[7]

Hardy, like Dickens and Eliot, was too considerable a creative artist to reproduce those didactic blueprints which are often at the bottom of the Condition of England novels: when reading Leslie Stephen's article 'The Moral Element in

Literature', Hardy copied into his *Literary Notebooks* Stephen's dismissal of 'the disguised pamphlets which are called novels with a purpose'.[8] But his work certainly does have a consciousness of social issues which this chapter, particularly with reference to the novels, will examine.

Reform was one of the overriding principles of Victorian society. Even before Victoria had come to the throne, the Reform Act had set the tone with its radical restructuring of the nation's psephological fabric. George Eliot's Mr Vincy proffers a much-quoted reaction:

> The doubt hinted by Mr Vincy whether it were only the general election or the end of the world that was coming on, now that George the Fourth was dead, Parliament dissolved, Wellington and Peel generally depreciated and the new King apologetic, was a feeble type of the uncertainties in provincial opinion at that time.[9]

A decade and a half later, with Peel again facing a crisis, this time over the Corn Laws, uncertainties in provincial opinion at Bockhampton there were not. Family opinions were Whig, becoming Liberal, and in them Hardy was soon schooled. 'Free Trade or Blood', Hardy chanted in 1845 as the crisis developed (*Life*, p. 501). A wooden sword, dipped in the blood of a pig recently and conveniently slaughtered, provided a confirmatory prop. Jude might not have approved.

Hardy maintained the family political sympathies, though this early incident probably represents his most public political act – it was indeed only the less-sensitive Florence who authorised its inclusion in the approved biography. When County Council elections were held for the first time as a result of the Local Government Act of 1888, Hardy encouraged Robert Pearce Edgcumbe to stand as the Liberal candidate. Writing to refuse (or rather attempt to postpone) the offer of a knighthood in 1908, he expressed admiration for Asquith's 'talents and courage in acting up to principles that I share' (*Letters*, III, 353). Hardy's sympathies for social reform were, in effect, considerable. 'I am against privilege derived from accident of any kind', Hardy once declared (*Life*, p. 213); and Alexander Macmillan, giving his objections to

The Poor Man and the Lady, which had contained much criticism of barriers of social class, concluded his comparison of Hardy's satire with that of Thackeray with this objection: 'He meant fair, you *"mean mischief"*.'[10]

Hardy thus learnt early that excessively overt support for political ideas and movements, especially those of a radical kind, prejudiced his chances of literary success. *Under the Greenwood Tree* is set in the 1840s, just before *Alton Locke* and just after the disturbances of *Sybil*. Arthur Shirley, the vicar of Stinsford on whose reforms much of the novel is based, had acute experience of local unrest: rick burnings, barricading of manor houses and the like. But the novel comments on the quietest of social processes, the removal of a parish's string choir. Only later, culminating in *Jude*, would Hardy begin again to address anything like an overt political theme, but always his own writing reflects an interest (however non-politically aligned) in those aspects of society which his contemporaries were engaged in reforming. Like the reformers, Hardy is constantly attentive to the lot of the underprivileged, and to the conditions and requirements of his society from its metaphorical cradle to its grave: its provision for the young, its attitude towards its women, its modification by industrialism, and its threatened destruction by war.

Education presented the young Victorian male with his best chance of transcending social class, and the intelligent Victorian female of ordinary social origin with one of her best chances of respectable employment. Hardy's two sisters, like his affianced cousin Tryphena, became teachers; his first assured novel *Under the Greenwood Tree* has a newly certificated teacher as its heroine, and his last novel *Jude* sets one of its scenes in that characteristic Victorian educational innovation, the teacher training college. Compulsory schooling to the age of ten was made general in 1880, though through a provision of the 1870 Education Act (which at last brought State, or Board, Schools into being and thereby afforded Hardy the architect many chances of employment) it had been anticipated in areas administered by the more progressive School Boards. In Conan Doyle's 'The Naval Treaty' (1894), Holmes tells Dr Watson that Board Schools are 'Lighthouses, my boy! Beacons of the future! Capsules, with hundreds of bright little seeds in each, out of which will spring the wiser, better England of the future.'[11] But in any case, the intelligent and educated amongst the working class, according to F. M. L. Thompson, regarded schooling for their children as normal well before it became compulsory. It is generally agreed that by 1870 somewhere between two-thirds and three-quarters of school-age children were at school, though, until 1891, school (and being clothed for it) had to be paid for.

Though the state was educationally behindhand, other agencies were not. Samuel Smiles, author of *Self-Help*, declared that home was 'the most influential school of civilization', and asserted that 'one good mother' was 'worth a hundred schoolmasters'.[12] He could hardly have found a more appropriate year for his pronouncement than 1843, the year in which Hardy and his mother agree the young boy first learnt to read, precipitating much maternal nursing of this talent. Jemima also saw to it that her son gained the maximum possible from the educational resources available outside the state domain. Educational institutions free of the state had been fostered by middle-class moralists and reformers since the later eighteenth century. Foremost amongst these was the Sunday School movement, initiated in the 1790s – Hardy finally became an instructor in the Stinsford school, along with one of the vicar's sons.

As has already been mentioned, Hardy was the first pupil to enter the newly built Stinsford National School started by Shirley and Julia Augusta Martin under the auspices of the Church of England National Society for Promoting the Education of the Poor (founded 1811). A visit by one of Her Majesty's Inspectors declared it a very creditable school, so it is hardly surprising that it gave such offence when Hardy was transferred to the voluntary school run by Isaac Last for the Nonconformist British and Foreign Bible Society (founded in 1808). In both schools, it should be noted, the education had religious respect as its hub: religious instruction was central to the curriculum, and the school day had a religious rhythm of prayers and hymns.

Isaac Last's name has a certain symbolic significance: for Hardy there was no formal education thereafter. Victorian reforms had but little affected the availability, or efficiency, of secondary schooling, whilst the universities were to him all but beyond reach. In a lecture which Horace Moule gave in Dorchester Town Hall on 15 November 1858 to the Working Men's Mutual Improvement Society he explained how recent changes at Oxford would open up the university to a wider middle-class public. But Hardy remained tantalizingly below such a social level. The Mayor's sons, Arthur and Francis Galpin, and the Moules' bevy of children, could proceed off to Oxford and Cambridge; so could Walter Lock, son of the local solicitor, and ultimately become Warden of Keble College. But for Hardy, despite his interests, and despite his ability, such a prospect was always going to be remote. This was perhaps acknowledged as early as 1854, when it was decided to leave Hardy with Last, who at the independent academy he had set up in 1853 offered technical instruction, rather than transferring the young boy to the more academic options of Hardye's Grammar School, and William Barnes's Classical and Mathematical School.

Thus it came about that Hardy's education was to end as it had begun: with a large measure of self-help. Texts were purchased, books were borrowed, advice was taken from available experts – Barnes and especially Moule. Alarm clocks were generally set early. The efforts were great, but so were the consequences. Upset when described as self-taught, Hardy greatly resented a reference to himself in a biographical study as '*Ce Saxon autodidacte*', self-aggrandisingly referring to himself in an angry and corrective marginal note as having been 'taught Latin and French at School and College'.[13]

Hardy's treatment of education reflects the texture of reform dominating his period. 'The class of folk that couldn't use to make a round O to save their bones from the pit can write their names now without a sputter of the pen, oftentimes without a single blot', remarks Olly in *The Return of the Native* (I, iii). Thus, unlike Poorgrass, Oak knows which way round to print the J and the E on a waggon, causing the rustics of *Far from the Madding Crowd* to regard him as 'a extraordinary good and clever man' (xv). Education is rapidly altering Hardy's Wessex, as a precisely defined reference to differing characters within the Durbeyfield family reveals:

Between the mother, with her fast-perishing lumber of superstitions, folk-lore, dialect, and orally transmitted ballads, and the daughter, with her trained National teachings and Standard knowledge under an infinitely Revised Code, there was a gap of two hundred years as ordinarily understood.   (iii)

Nor indeed is this distinction difficult to spot, for 'Mrs Durbeyfield habitually spoke the dialect; her daughter, who had passed the Sixth Standard in the National School under a London-trained mistress, spoke two languages; the dialect at home, more or less; ordinary English abroad and to persons of quality' (iii). Tess, so much a part of the past and of her natural environment in many ways, is different in this. Indeed, she is seen as a potential force for advancing this distinction: Hardy makes it clear in the novel, and made it even clearer in the manuscript, that her ambition had been to become a teacher.[14]

Hardy's treatment of education may also be said to reflect his own lack of opportunities for tertiary education, since the last two novels under consideration, *Tess* and *Jude*, both contain young men deprived of educational finish. Angel is 'the single one' of the Clare family whose 'promise might have done full justice to an academical training' (xviii), yet he is the only one who, because of the religious prejudice of his father, has not been allowed it. Mr Clare reflects the prejudices of his time, for it was only as the nineteenth century progressed that religious tests were abolished for university entrants and teachers, making Mr Clare's belief that a university education is to be used 'for the honour and glory of God' (xviii), however unreasonable, representative in its view of an alliance of education with the Established Church.

Earlier Victorian fiction – not least the Condition of England novel – had made something of a speciality out of the figure of the man who craved knowledge despite prevailing difficulties. Kingsley's *Alton Locke* and Eliot's *Felix Holt* are two examples. *Jude* began its complicated genesis with dangers of extending this didactic tradition. 'A short story of a young man – "who could not go to Oxford"', the *Life* reports (p. 216). 'There is something the world ought to be shown, and I am the one to show it to them.' The temptation to view the novel as a crusade is indeed offered. Jude who possesses 'a pretty zeal in the cause of education' (v, vi) joins an Artizans Mutual Improvement Society, offers a rival Commemoration as the university attends the Encaenia, and is driven to embittered graffiti by the university's failure to recognise his talent. 'I have understanding as well as you; I am not inferior to you', he chalks in disgust on the wall of Biblioll College. 'Yea, who knoweth not such things as these' (II, vi). The *Saturday Review* ('For the first time in English literature the almost intolerable difficulties that beset an ambitious man of the working class ... receive adequate treatment'),[15] clearly took the crusading point, and when Ruskin College, Oxford, was founded to help cater for working-class students the event may have owed something to the novel. Hardy, at any rate, appears to have believed so.[16]

Yet to see Hardy as a crusader for educational reform in his fiction would be to distort the tendencies of his art. A brief comparison with Dickens helps to make the point. Dickens's presentation of schools, so many of them Dotheboys Halls, belongs to his pre-reform period of writing. But Hardy, writing later, is concerned, as Phillip Collins has neatly pointed out, less with the process than with the consequences of education, less with the reforms required than with the ironic and unfortunate effects that such reforms can bring.

Hardy's novels commonly depend on a contrast between an under-educated community and a hero or heroine (or both) who are educated beyond that community's level. The education which causes least disruption in Hardy's novels is that which brings its recipient into least conflict with prevailing social conditions, retaining maximum compatibility of the individual with his or her environment. Too little education, as in the case of Henchard or so many of the rustics, can hinder achievement as well as enlightenment. Too much education, or the desire for it, as seen in Clym and Grace, can engender failure born of frustration or disillusion.

Oak provides, appropriately, a bench mark. Gabriel's library, '*The Young Man's Best Companion, The Farrier's Sure Guide, The Veterinary Surgeon, Paradise Lost, The Pilgrim's Progress, Robinson Crusoe*, Ash's *Dictionary*, and Walkingame's *Arithmetic*' (viii), provides staple rustic literary fare, with a healthy degree of emphasis on harnessing the physical and metaphysical environment. In the ingenuity of his dealings with threatened ricks and errant and bloated sheep, Crusoe himself would be proud of him. Elizabeth-Jane, possessing a mind constantly 'struggling for enlargement' (iv), sets out to provide herself with an education considerably more complex and arcane. By comparison with Oak's meagre textual apparatus, Elizabeth-Jane's room is characterised by 'the abundance of books lying everywhere' (xlii), and many of these educational works are to her of 'portentous obscurity' (xx). But the educational emphasis is however the same as that of Oak, and the reader unused to Hardy's thought patterns should not be blinded to the significance. 'She began the study of Latin, incited by the Roman characteristics of the town she lived in', we are carefully told (xx). In a town which 'looked Roman, bespoke the art of Rome, concealed dead men of Rome' (xi), Latin is the study that can best aid Elizabeth-Jane, the Newfoundland émigrée, in understanding and harmonising with her environment.

More commonly, however, Hardy focuses on educations less self-helping in their methods, more ironic and less desirable in their effects. 'Well, learning is better than houses and lands', remarks Robert Creedle in *The Woodlanders*. 'But to keep a maid at school till she is taller out of pattens than her mother was in 'em – 'tis a tempting o' Providence' (iv). The educational provisions and standards in Wessex are so limited that the educated in the novels frequently are outsiders (Fitzpiers, Wildeve, Farfrae) or have to become so. This is particularly true of the justifiable object of Creedle's remark, Grace, recipient of an expensive boarding school education arranged by her father. In chapter vi Giles drives Grace's mind out of Sherton, and the destabilizing effect of her education is soon apparent:

> The knowledge and interest which had formerly moved Grace's mind had quite died away from her. ... The fact at present was merely this, that where he was seeing John-apples and farm-buildings she was beholding a much contrasting scene: a broad lawn in the fashionable suburb of a fast city, the evergreen leaves shining in the evening sun, amid which bounding girls, gracefully clad in artistic arrangements of blue, brown, red and white, were playing

at games with laughter and chat in all the pride of life, the notes of piano and harp trembling in the air from the open windows adjoining.   (vi)

'Haven't I educated you for it', Mr Melbury makes clear when a prestigious offer of marriage is forthcoming (xxii). But for Grace, and for the reader, at the end of the novel the consequences of Melbury's educational efforts to make Grace maritally desirable are clear. Education often involves, and almost invariably entails, uprooting. 'I wish you had never, never thought of educating me', Grace announces, and continues with a carefully chosen metaphor from the novel's governing image pattern. 'I wish I worked in the woods like Marty South. ... Because cultivation has only brought me inconveniences and troubles. ... I have never got any happiness outside Hintock that I know of' (xxx).

Educational reformers, indeed, are ambiguous in the advantages they bring. Their idealism is impressive but unfortunate – at best misguided, at worst even hypocritical. Clym, 'because he went to school early, such as the school was', is 'become a real perusing man, with the strangest notions about things' (II, i). Clym, it is plain, wants to raise educational standards without any thought of the relationship between such standards and economic conditions. His vaunted plans 'for instilling high knowledge into empty minds' are as unspecific as they are unrealistic (III, v). Still worse, he lacks any recognition of Eustacia's suitability for the role he believes she will nicely fulfil, that of a matron in a boarding school. 'I, who was going to teach people the higher secrets of happiness, did not know how to keep out of that gross misery which the most untaught are wise enough to avoid' (V, i), he remarks with an ironically zealous and instructive conclusiveness. A failure as a teacher, Clym settles for a role as a preacher, one he considers less effective, a judgement that the novel's concluding tableau confirms, with Clym preaching as Egdonite stragglers pull heather, strip ferns and toss pebbles down the Rainbarrow slope.

Jude's educational idealism also lacks contact with reality of most kinds. As he strolls the countryside he recites what he has been able to knock off his reading list. 'Ha, ha, ha! Hoity-toity!', Arabella and her friends barrack, and in the end their leader is driven to resort to a visual aid (I, vi). But the pig's pizzle, though it may halt Jude, fails to draw him up short, just as surely as Sue's effect on the happiness of others fails to decrease her intellectual idealism. 'What do I care about J. S. Mill?', groans Phillotson in despair (VI, i), his libido erased by the intellectualism of his pupil-teacher-turned-wife-turned-turncoat, and the burdens of state-imposed school administration.

Perhaps only Angel could fail to agree, for Tess is largely right to regard him as 'an intelligence rather than as a man' (xix). Angel admits that 'I used to wish to be a teacher of men' (xxxiv), but his educational idealism is ironically associated with hypocrisy (like that of Clym) and misjudgement (like that of Jude). 'In the midst of my fine aims for other people, I myself fell', Angel confesses (xxxiv). Falling back on the language of education, he calls Tess Artemis and Demeter (xx); thinks of her as a text, 'as one deciding on the true construction of a passage' (xxxiv); and, on their wedding night, refers to her as 'the great prize of my life, my Fellowship', though this fellowship too has barriers to consummation (xxxiv). All these educational reformers are seen, or present themselves, as representatives of the future. But their performance in the present begs the question of the desirability of their reforming pasts.

The issue of the role of women, though it engaged the Victorians later than the reform of education, produced as far-reaching an effect in society. In the year of Hardy's birth, for example, votes for women were at best a marginal issue. By Hardy's fifties the literary symbol of the New Woman, educated, freethinking, and in many cases bicycle-riding too, provided a potent symbol of female emancipation. Herminia in Grant Allen's *The Woman Who Did* (1895) and Jessica in Wells's *The Wheels of Chance* (1896) exemplify the type, and Hardy's Sue has much in common with them. In 1927 Virginia Woolf exposed in a veiled form in her novel *To the Lighthouse* the petty tyrannies which Leslie Stephen, the mentor whom Hardy had once found so liberal, had exercised over his daughters. A year later, Stanley Baldwin's government gave the vote to all women aged over twenty-one.

Hardy's revered figure J. S. Mill, with his encouragement of the notions of individual liberalism, is again a central figure. The debates over the next thirty years added little to his classic text *The Subjection of Women* (1869) – indeed, in September 1895 Hardy could tell Florence Henniker that he still intended purchasing a copy. Mill, developing arguments partly derived from the pioneering eighteenth-century feminist Mary Wollstonecraft (wife of William Godwin and mother of Mary Shelley), held that equality for women must be regarded as an integral part of a modern liberal society, concluding:

> The social subordination of women thus stands out an iso-lated fact in modern social institutions; a solitary breach of what has become their fundamental law; a single relic of an old world of thought and practice exploded in every-thing else.[17]

The early Victorian ideal of womanhood had centred on marriage and the home: 'Man for the field and woman for the hearth; / Man for the sword, and for the needle she', explains the Prince's father in Tennyson's *The Princess* (1847).[18] A woman's role was to be passive and secondary to that of her husband; her chief task was reproduction. Her nature was frequently idealised. Rossetti, Tennyson and Browning all wrote in their separate ways of the perfect woman; and Patmore revered his 'Angel in the House':

> Her disposition is devout,
>   Her countenance angelical;
> The best things that the best believe
>   Are in her face so kindly writ
> The faithless, seeing her, conceive
>   Not only heaven, but hope of it.[19]

An analogy in prose can be found in *Pendennis* (1848–50) by Thackeray, whom Hardy recommended to his sister, with greater attention to her educational requirements than his own spelling as 'the greatest novellist of the day' (*Letters*, I, 5). Helen Pendennis is the 'most complete of all Heaven's sub-jects in this world', a representative of those 'angelical natures' in front of which 'the wildest and fiercest of us must fall down and humble ourselves, in admiration of that adorable purity which never seems to do or to think wrong'.[20]

Scientific orthodoxy supported traditional views of a woman's role, arguing that woman's place in society was the natural result of processes designed to strengthen her central function of reproduction. Even Havelock Ellis, a pioneer sexologist, an enlightened champion of women's emancipation and a perceptive early admirer of Hardy's fiction, could remark that 'Nature has made women more like children in order that they may better understand and care for children.'[21] Such views do much to explain the description of Sue's Melchester contemporaries in *Jude the Obscure*, of which Ellis was an enthusiastic early reviewer, 'every face bearing the legend "The Weaker" upon it, as the penalty of the sex wherein they were moulded, which by no possible exertion of their willing hearts and abilities could be made strong while the inexorable laws of nature remain what they are' (III, iii).

The epigraph to Part First – 'O ye men, how can it be but women should be strong … ?' – is plainly to be seen in an ironic light. For, however modern she may seem, Sue follows the all but universal destiny of other New Women of fiction of the period – Evadne in Sarah Grand's *The Heavenly Twins* (1893) or Hadria in Mona Caird's *The Daughters of Danaus* (1894) – towards breakdown, nervous prostration and conventional religion.

The history of women's rights in Hardy's time is one of attempts to thwart and disprove such physiological axioms by obtaining – chiefly via education, employment and suffrage – equality. 'Women feel just as men feel; they need exercise for their faculties, and a field for their efforts as much as their brothers do', Jane Eyre protests,[22] in the only novel by a Brontë sister that Hardy would admit to having read. 'Do I desire unreasonably much', echoes the trammelled Eustacia Vye, 'in wanting what is called life?' (IV, vi). Eustacia's question, as part of what so many Victorian women must have felt, deserves to have been rhetorical. But Hardy's irony, as usual, ensures that it is not.

The powerful campaigning presence of Emma Hardy must have caused flutters of anxiety amongst several members of the Dorset constabulary, but the same is hardly true of her husband: 'his interest in the Suffrage Cause is nil, in spite of "Tess"', Emma remarked, with a not altogether fair contempt.[23] However, suffragists and anti-suffragists could alike look in vain to Hardy for practical assistance with their cause. In December 1908 he refused to contribute to a suffragist newspaper, but eighteen months later refused to sign an anti-suffragist letter to *The Times*. To Millicent Fawcett he was prepared in 1906 to reveal that he had long been in favour of female suffrage, but he had little doubt that his unorthodox reasons for doing so would be likely to cause offence. The novels have little to say on the matter.

With education and employment, however, the situation is different. 'What women do know nowadays!', remarks the hollow-turner in the last chapter of *The Woodlanders*. 'You can't deceive 'em as you could in my time.' Queen's College London opened in 1848, the North London Collegiate School in 1850 and Cheltenham Ladies' College four years later; the Girls' Public Day School Company was founded in 1872 and from then on girls secondary day (or 'high') schools developed steadily. The universities were slow to admit women fully, but the foundation of two women's colleges at Cambridge (1869–72) and four at Oxford (1879–93) were significant steps.

Though Hardy, unlike George Eliot, exercised little influence and no guidance over such developments, his study of the unostentatious Elizabeth-Jane is an acute study of female educational ambitions. Elizabeth is, to be sure, self- rather than school-educated, but Hardy precisely defines her desires and the influences on them. How Elizabeth-Jane could 'become a woman of wider knowledge, higher repute – "better", as she termed it – this was her constant inquiry' (iv). A 'gratuitous ordeal' awaits her in the matter of her handwriting (xx). Asked by Henchard to pen a business agreement (perhaps itself a significant request), Elizabeth-Jane does so in a 'splendid round, bold hand of her own conception, a style that would have stamped a woman as Minerva's own in more recent days'. A second palaeographical reference, to Tennyson's *The Princess* – 'such a hand as when a field of corn / Bows all its ears before the roaring East' (xx) – is particularly significant. Tennyson's Princess Ida sets up a woman's university in one of her father's palaces, forcing a princely suitor to write a letter to her in an assumed lady's hand in order to obtain access. The allusion associates Elizabeth-Jane with a very particular movement, for *The Princess* was seen as Tennyson's contribution to the campaign for the foundation of Queen's College, and his poem formed the basis for Gilbert and Sullivan's *Princess Ida* (1884).

Not for nothing, indeed, is Elizabeth-Jane associated with predictors of the future, prophets and seers. Anxious to break down barriers of education, she breaks down barriers of class and gender too, siding with Nance Mockridge and the parlour maid, and (after a youth spent in male-supportive roles) allowing Henchard to become effectively her house-wife. 'Father, ... it is so kind of you to get this nice breakfast with your own hands, and I idly asleep the while', Elizabeth-Jane remarks (xli). But she knows that she gets up with a purpose, for it is she who now manages Henchard's affairs. 'She had her own way in everything now. In going and coming, in buying and selling, her word was law' (xlii). Nor is such behaviour altogether unparalleled in Casterbridge, as the example of Mrs Stannidge makes clear (vii).

This attention to female opportunities for, and perfor-mances in, employment is noteworthy. Victorian sexual stereotyping seriously restricted female opportunities for employment, especially amongst wives. By 1851 the number of married women actively employed had fallen to 25 per cent and it was only 10 per cent by the end of the century. Besides this, most female jobs were in low-paid occupations, such as the swede hacking to which Tess and Marian are reduced at the repressive establishment managed by Farmer Groby. A correspondent in the *Englishwoman's Review*, return-ing to his native land in 1904 after an absence of thirty years, found the change in this situation remarkable. 'In these days there is hardly an occupation, or even a profession, into which girls may not aspire to enter', he observed.[24] Shaw's *Mrs Warren's Profession* (1898) illustrates the point with a neatness born of didactic. Mrs Warren, mother of the play's heroine, is a member of the world's oldest profession; her daughter Vivie becomes a solicitor of another kind. As early as the first novel under consideration, *Far from the Madding Crowd*, Hardy is interested in women's performance in men's roles. Thereafter, Hardy's interest in women wearing the trousers, so to speak, can sometimes even be literal, as Eustacia's mumming appearance and Sue's donning of Jude's garments make apparent. Bathsheba, anxious to point out that her workforce now has 'a mistress instead of a master', warns slackers to beware:

> Don't any unfair ones among you … suppose that because I'm a woman I don't understand the difference between bad goings-on and good. … I shall be up before you are awake; I shall be afield before you are up; and I shall have breakfasted before you are afield. In short, I shall astonish you all.   (x)

But even at her first appearance in the Corn Exchange the rashness of the sentiment is plain: 'It had required a little determination – far more than she had at first imagined – to take up a position' (xii), we are told. Emma Hardy reported that her husband's views on the woman question were not generous on the female side, and Virginia Woolf complained, 'However lovable and charming Bathsheba may be, still she is weak; however stubborn and ill-guided Henchard may be, still he is strong. This is a fundamental part of Hardy's vision; the staple of many of his books.'[25] The novels largely justify the protests of both women. For though female experiments are tried, few are successful, the general explanation being not that Hardy's gender-reformers are too soon for their time but that a woman has instinctive powers of sympathy, and unavoidable limitations of physique, that make her unsuited for high office. 'I was a coward – as so many women are', Sue reflects (IV, iii). Jude can only agree. 'Strange difference of sex, that time and circumstance, which enlarge the views of most men, narrow the views of women almost invariably', he remarks (VI, x). The sentiment comes over with such force that the reader may be inclined instantaneously to agree – until he or she recalls that the sentiment comes oddly from one who has remarried Arabella.

As his own marriage deteriorated, Hardy became increasingly interested in the lot of the married woman (one should perhaps more correctly say the married person). The Matrimonial Causes Act of 1878 facilitated legal separation and maintenance for badly used wives, conditions for divorce for the well-to-do having already been eased by the Divorce and Matrimonial Causes Act of 1857. The latter piece of legislation is comprehensively (and pointedly) misrepresented by lawyer Beaucock in *The Woodlanders*:

> A new court was established last year, and under the new statute, twenty and twenty-one Vic., cap. eighty-five, unmarrying is as easy as marrying. No more Acts of Parliament necessary: no longer one law for the rich and another for the poor. But come inside – I was just going to have a nipperkin of rum-hot – I'll explain it all to you.
>
> (xxxvii)

For personal reasons, the divorce issue was one that occupied the Hardys particularly in the 1890s. Emma Hardy was invited to take Elspeth Grahame, wife of the creator of *The Wind in the Willows*, into her confidence. Mrs Grahame had once enjoyed a flirtatious relationship with Hardy; now she herself was experiencing what it was like to have a husband with attractions away from home. 'At Fifty, a man's feelings too often take a new course altogether', Emma Hardy advised. 'Eastern ideas of matrimony secretly pervade his thoughts, and he wearies of the most perfect and suitable wife chosen in his earlier life.'[26]

In *The Woodlanders* and *Jude* Hardy brought to the artistic centre of his narratives ideas on divorce which, though they had existed since at least the beginning of the century, shocked the serial reader. 'How long then ought the sexual connection to last?', Hardy's revered Shelley had asked in his *Notes on Queen Mab* – and answered, taking his cue from Godwin:

> A husband and wife ought to continue so long united as they love each other: any law which should bind them to cohabitation for one moment after the decay of their affection would be a most intolerable tyranny, and the most unworthy of toleration.[27]

In the utilitarian and liberal circles which surrounded such figures as J. S. Mill, John Chapman, George Eliot and G. H. Lewes such ideas flourished. Hence perhaps the Utilitarian vocabulary in which marriage is mentioned in the Preface to *The Woodlanders*, and hence also the provenance of the view advanced in the Postscript to *Jude* that 'a marriage should be dissoluble as soon as it becomes a cruelty to either of the parties'. Hardy saw the marriage laws as 'the tragic machinery' of *Jude*, and the same is equally true of *The Woodlanders*. Both books postulate a distinction between natural law and civil law, bitterly criticising the latter, whilst (especially in *Jude*) implicitly allowing the possibilities for cruelty in the former. The relationship of Jude and Sue is 'Nature's own marriage' (VI, iii), just as Grace and Giles are 'two whom nature had striven to join together' (xxxviii) – a union only therefore effected in the most impoverished and woodlandy of environments. Jude, adopting a prevailing image pattern of the novel, indicts 'the artificial system of things, under which the normal sex-impulses are turned into devilish domestic gins and springes to noose and hold back those who want to progress' (IV, iii).

The same image dominates the dénouement of *The Woodlanders*, where Timothy Tangs springs the man-trap towards which Grace symbolically moves after she has re-read the marriage service in a Prayer Book: 'Midway between husband and wife was the diabolical trap, silent, open, ready' (xlvii). Given this juxtaposition the reader who wonders, like Grace, 'whether God really did join them together' can be in little doubt – and the complacent reader is no doubt intended to be outraged. The similarity between the two novels explains how Hardy, in the words of the *Jude* Postscript, came to be given 'a large responsibility for the present "shop-soiled" condition of the marriage theme', whilst also showing the author only part-way to the more radical opinion expressed in a letter to Clodd, where modern views on marriage are described as merely 'a survival from the custom of capture and purchase, propped up by a theological superstition' (*Letters*, II, 92).

The distinction between civil (and intellectual) and natural (or instinctive) seen in Hardy's presentation of marriage is perhaps also the cardinal point in his presentation of women. With one exception, the novels under consideration have at the heart of their design a contrast between a woman who responds warmly to impulse and instinct (and is therefore

frequently sexually fallen), and one, often of greater intellectual accomplishment, who is sexually more chaste. Put
unflatteringly, Hardy tends to visualise the female sex as
offering a choice between brain and the female counterpart to
brawn. Though Hardy's ironic textures prevent too great a
sense of stereotype, this contrast is repeated in Bathsheba and
Fanny, Thomasin and Eustacia, Lucetta and Elizabeth-Jane,
and Arabella and Sue.

This dichotomy is not a surprising one, with a history in
Victorian fiction – and indeed way beyond. Where Hardy is
more bold is in his presentation of the fallen woman in *Tess*,
the one novel which lacks such a stereotypical dichotomy
simply because the heroine absorbs both prototypes in the
one personality. The fallen woman is now also the pure one;
just as, in the amalgamation of two other opposites, Tess is
simultaneously poor woman and lady.

With fallen women Hardy also did not lack precedent: a
recurrent theme in the Victorian novel is the seduction of
lower-class girls by the likes of Arthur Donnithorne in *Adam
Bede* (1859) or James Steerforth in *David Copperfield* (1849–50).
Gaskell's *Ruth* (1853) allows the student of Hardy to judge
just how boldly Hardy was deviating from previously
received notions of female morality. Ruth, a young dress-
maker, is seduced by Bellingham, but subsequently
befriended at a far-removed location by a deformed minister, Benson, and his sister, the aptly named Faith. Gossip in
the end finally reaches Wales. Society is outraged but finally
won round when Ruth agrees during an epidemic to act as
matron in the fever ward, where typhus conveniently claims
her. For Ruth, of course, read Tess; for Bellingham, Alec; and
for the Bensons (but for an Unfulfilled Intention), the Clares
– Gaskell's forays into snowdrop and camellia images
heighten the sense that Hardy was operating in well-charted
territory. But the moral thrust of the two texts is totally different. Ruth's destroyer, typhus, is less indictable, less
capable of a moral rebuke than the judge and the justicers
of Wintoncester. Furthermore Hardy is not afraid to confront sexuality head on. We never know when Arthur
Donnithorne seduces Hetty, but the same is hardly true of
Alec and Tess.[28]

Henry James complained of *Tess* that 'the pretence of sexuality is only equalled by the absence of it',[29] but that has not been the general experience. *Tess*, one early reviewer remarked, was 'peculiarly the Woman's Tragedy', historically a novel in which at last a major author, in another reviewer's words, left 'little unsaid',[30] a frank confrontation, as feminist critics have now in detail explained, of the tragic potential of female sexuality:

The air of the sleeping-chamber seemed to palpitate with the hopeless passion of the girls. They writhed feverishly under the oppressiveness of an emotion thrust on them by cruel Nature's law – an emotion which they had neither expected nor desired. The incident of the day had fanned the flame that was burning the inside of their hearts out, and the torture was almost more than they could endure. The differences which distinguished them as individuals were abstracted by this passion, and each was but portion of one organism called sex.   (xxiii)

Writing to H. W. Massingham to thank him for a sympathetic review of *Tess*, Hardy explained that he had long felt 'that the doll of English fiction must be demolished, if England is to have a school of fiction at all' (*Letters*, I, 250). Many such literary attempts at iconoclasm were being made, not least in the plays of Ibsen (which Hardy was attending in the 1890s), Shaw and even Wilde. But in the frankly surveyed sexuality of Grace, Tess, Arabella and Sue, Hardy undoubtedly made a contribution of historical as well as literary importance, a landmark in the re-examination of the woman's lot. Baldwin Brown's *The Home Life* (1866) had spoken of women 'who send forth husband or brother each morning with new strength for his conflict, armed, as the lady armed her knight of old, with a shield which he may not stain in any unseemly conflicts, and a sword which he dares only use against the enemies of truth, righteousness and God'.[31] Hardy refused to help keep the hands on the clock stationary. 'What solid bodies, what real existences', the novelist Margaret Oliphant commented in her review of *Tess*, 'in contrast with the pale fiction of didactic romance.'[32]

'We live in times of transition', remarks the narrator of Disraeli's last novel.[33] The society which Hardy generally presents is an agrarian one, and agrarian society felt the effects of Victorian transition particularly acutely, not least because of the effects of science. 'The most obvious and the most distinctive feature of the History of Civilization, during the last fifty years, is the wonderful increase of industrial production by the application of machinery, the improvement of old technical processes and the invention of new ones, accompanied by an even more remarkable development of old and new means of locomotion and intercommunication', observed Huxley in 'The Progress of Science, 1837–1887'.[34] But it was all too easy to recall the days only just gone by, and to feel that they might return. 'These modern inventions, this steam, and electric telegraph, and even the printing press, have but just skimmed the surface of village life', wrote Richard Jefferies in his study of rural life, *Hodge and his Masters* (1880). 'If they were removed – if the pressure from the world without, from the world around, ceased, in how few years the village and hamlet would revert to their original condition!'[35] Henry Hardy, who outlived his brother, proved the point. He frequently refused to wear a watch, preferring to tell the time by the sun, even in an age of railways and cars.

English agriculture had been in a relative decline since at least the seventeenth century; before the middle of the eighteenth-century it had probably ceased to provide the livelihood of a majority of the population. At the beginning of the nineteenth century the agricultural sector employed a third of the working population, and by 1831 it was a quarter. In the 1870s, freak conditions and an increase in imports marked the beginning of a long depression from which British farming had barely recovered in 1914. For all this, agricultural labouring, landless and propertyless, was far and away the largest single occupation of male Victorian workers. Such labourers earned far less than they could do in towns; and they received less in Dorset, a county regarded as particularly backward, than in any other English county. As a child Hardy knew a sheep-keeping boy who, to Hardy's horror, 'died of want – the contents of his stomach at the autopsy being raw turnip only' (*Life*, p. 335).

But this, Hardy admitted, was an extreme case even for that time: and conditions and pay since his childhood had much improved.

All these factors made agricultural workers an important political consideration, and Liberal plans to enfranchise them were partly self-interested. Hardy himself, invited in the early 1880s to contribute an article on 'The Dorsetshire Labourer' to *Longman's Magazine*, realised that he was in danger of a direct political pronouncement. 'Though a Liberal', Hardy wrote to John Morley, 'I have endeavoured to describe the state of things without political bias' (*Letters*, I, 119), though he did reveal his bias by sending copies of the essay to Gladstone and Morley. The article avoids the lurid. It sees the loss of intimacy between man and nature as the chief product of the increased mobility of the labourer, the latter being viewed, in the words of a lengthy letter to Sir Rider Haggard on agricultural conditions, written twenty or so years later, as one of the 'evils of instability' (*Life*, p. 337).

Hardy took the title for *Far from the Madding Crowd* from Gray's 'Elegy', a poem he particularly admired and which he associated with his native parish of Stinsford. The idea of being far from the city life was amongst the most persistent in his patterns of thought – and indeed habitation. Distinctions between rural and urban were habitual for him, a source of comedy (as in the poem 'The Ruined Maid') as well as a blueprint for fictional plot. In *Far from the Madding Crowd* 'God was palpably present in the country, and the devil had gone with the world to town' (xxii). Each Hardy novel has its disturbing invader from elsewhere – as often as not the North country – Troy, Wildeve, Farfrae, Fitzpiers, Alec and the engineman in *Tess*.

Furthermore, each novel tends to show modern life drawing closer. The approach of the railway, a symbolic link between, in the words of *Tess*, the 'secluded world and modern life' (xxx) is a convenient index of this. In *Far from the Madding Crowd* and *The Return of the Native* the permanent way does not yet threaten. But it has almost reached Casterbridge in *The Mayor* and Talbothays in *Tess*, where the 'steam feeler' of the railway engine finds the country 'uncongenial', and no object could have looked more foreign

to its 'gleaming cranks and wheels' than the unsophisticated
Tess (xxx). By the time of *Jude* the railway is omni-penetra-
tive: railway stations are 'the centre of town life now': they
welcome 'the modern vice of unrest' just as surely as the
Great Western Railway carries on it the hapless Young Father
Time (III, i; II, ii). Unemployment as well as instability come in
the railway's wake. 'What with this travelling without horses
that's getting so common', remarks a waggoner to the displaced Henchard in the penultimate chapter of *The Mayor of
Casterbridge*, 'my work will soon be done.'

   The Preface to *Far from the Madding Crowd* announces that
Hardy is presenting 'a modern Wessex of railways, the
penny post, mowing and reaping machines, union work-
houses, lucifer matches, labourers who can read and write,
and National school children'. *Far from the Madding Crowd*
begins the sequence of novels by presenting something
quite the reverse. The description of the great barn in
Weatherbury (xxii) is a self-consciously stylish set-piece, a
sort of hymn (as the religiose imagery of the description
makes clear) to stability. The barn represents and welcomes
'practices which had suffered no mutilation at the hands of
time'. It is akin to the shearers, for 'In comparison with
cities, Weatherbury was immutable ... nothing less than a
century set a mark on its face or tone.' It is the reverse of
the new church at Marygreen in the last of the novels, *Jude*,
which has been 'erected on a new piece of ground by a
certain obliterator of historic records who had run down
from London and back in a day' (I, i). As this progression
suggests, the novels generally chart that moment at which
such seeming immutability encounters transition. Clym
returns different to a heath that remains the same. Fitzpiers'
chemical experiment sets a new tone in Little Hintock:

> Almost every ... effect in that woodland place had hitherto
> been the direct result of the regular terrestrial roll which
> produced the seasons' changes; but here was something
> dissociated from these normal sequences, and foreign to
> local knowledge.   (vi)

Hardy examines the economic, social and personal implications of mechanisation. Casterbridge at the opening of *The*

Mayor is 'untouched by the faintest sprinkle of modernism' (iv). The town is a different proposition after the innovations pioneered by Farfrae – not least in its economic relationships. Hardy partly makes the point in the pendant of the wife-selling which begins the novel, in which 'the demand and response of real cash' utterly alters the atmosphere (i). The same will happen with Casterbridge. Just like the residents of Little Hintock, who help each other out without regard to reward 'well-nigh like one family' (xv), the Casterbridge populace 'still retained the primitive habit of helping one another in time of need' (xxvii). By the end of the novel, only the symbolically named Abel Whittle (wittol is the Old English word for fool) keeps the custom, travelling out to the primitive environs of the heath to help Henchard, just as Henchard had helped Whittle's mother.

The transition is studied acutely in twin scenes set in Lucetta's house, symbolically situated so that its windows afford a view of the market place, hence emphasising the tension between economic and personal relationships. In chapter xxiii Farfrae, deciding to court Lucetta, leaves the house to hire a young farm labourer and his father so that the young man shall not be parted from his sweetheart. Both Farfrae and Lucetta have moist eyes as they overhear the predicament which the labour market has forced upon the young man: 'I can't starve father, and he's out o' work at Lady-day.' But there is the world of difference between the moral Lucetta draws from the scene – 'If I had my wish, I'd let people live and love at their pleasure' – and the more economically shrewd, practical and selfish attitude which Farfrae takes to the old man: 'he'll not be very expensive, and doubtless he will answer my pairrpose somehow.' In the subsequent chapter new dresses arrive for Lucetta from London and a new seed drill in the market place. 'The romance of the sower is gone for good', Elizabeth-Jane correctly concludes: 'How things change!' Modernity brings disruption, displacement, unwelcome dualities: not for nothing do both women start to sigh for Farfrae in this chapter.

The threshing machine scene of *Tess* (chapters xlvii and xlviii) presents a more extended and personal study of the effects of mechanisation. Here is one of Tess's destroyers,

a 'red tyrant', a 'despotic', 'insatiable swallower'. Like
machine, like master. The diabolical engineman 'serves fire
and smoke', has 'the appearance of a creature from Tophet'
and is indifferent to all but his machine: 'Beyond its extent
the environment might be corn, straw, chaos: it was all the
same to him.' The unnaturalness of the machine draws much
of Hardy's attention – hence the 'long chimney running up
beside an ash tree' and the comparison of the threshed
produce to 'a yellow river, running uphill' – but it is the
engineman's lack of response to the natural that draws the
narrator's attention most, the mechanic being presented as
'hardly perceiving scenes around him, and caring for them
not at all'.

Of all the altars – metaphoric and otherwise – on which
Tess is sacrificed, this altar of industrialism is perhaps the
least attractive, though with characteristic irony Hardy
ensures that it is this experience that at last persuades Tess
that she should write to Angel. The migrations of labourers
depicted in the same phase of the novel are also seen as
unnatural, and compared to 'the tendency of water to flow
uphill when driven by machinery'. Such migrations, often
involving the dispossession of lifeholders (also a concern in
The Woodlanders) are seen as modern, regrettable and de-
stabilising: families 'who had formed the backbone of the
village life in the past, who were the depositaries of the
village traditions, had to seek refuge in the large centres.'
Again Hardy finds a strikingly symbolic tableau to render the
predicament visually memorable – the Durbeyfields pitching
their bedstead beneath the window of the d'Urberville aisle
in Kingsbere church before Tess encounters Alec recumbent
on a family tomb inside. Here as elsewhere *Tess* is typical of
Hardy's perennial concern with a way of life agrarian,
natural, passing.

British sense of identity, as seen in foreign policy and, most
of all, in the warfare such foreign policy entailed, constitutes
a fourth major aspect of the society which Hardy presents –
more frequently in verse than in prose. 'As the Roman, in
days of old, held himself free from indignity, when he could
say *Civis Romanus sum*', Palmerston famously proclaimed
over the Don Pacifico affair, 'so also a British subject, in

whatever land he may be, shall feel confident that the watchful eye and the strong arm of England will protect him from injustice and wrong.'[36] The Imperialist parallel is here implicit in the allusion to Rome, and its consequences were, in some eyes, to be morally unfortunate, as growing patriotism in the course of the century encouraged Podsnapian complacency. 'Mr Podsnap's world was not a very large world, morally; no, nor even geographically: seeing that although his business was sustained upon commerce with other countries, he considered other countries, with that important reservation, a mistake....'[37] The precept of fighting to defend what you believed in was central to the Victorian consciousness. 'Man is created to fight', Carlyle proclaimed, and *Tom Brown's Schooldays* (1857) shows how fully the principle was inculcated at schoolboy level: 'Fighting, really understood, is the business, the real highest, honestest business of every son of man.'[38]

Hardy early encountered the militarism necessary to support the extension of an expansionist foreign policy. The Volunteer Movement was rife in Dorchester and London in the days before Hardy turned to writing as a career. Hardy's lodgings at Westbourne Park Villas overlooked St Stephen's Church, Paddington, where the Rifle Volunteers met to be addressed by the vicar, Harvey Brooks, a man to whom Hardy was drawn by his Dorset connections. 'Volunteers!', Brooks explained, 'you are armed for the defence of a trust so sacred, that I cannot doubt the lawfulness of your position in the sight of God.'[39]

Bolstered by such attitudes, the Empire was ready to grow. In 1896, Lord Rosebery calculated that in the preceding twelve years an area 24 times the size of Great Britain had been added to the British Empire. With the appointment of the Radical Imperialist Joseph Chamberlain as Colonial Secretary in 1895 the expansion and development of the Empire became a major part of government policy for almost the only time in British history. Soon, the Empire was to cover a quarter of the land surface of the globe, and to colour it red. Kipling, unappointed laureate to the Empire, was understood (albeit mistakenly) to have enjoined the British populace to

> Take up the White Man's Burden –
>   Send forth the best ye breed –
> Go, bid your Sons to exile,
>   To serve your captives' need.[40]

'I contend that we are the first race in the world', Cecil
Rhodes claimed, 'and that the more of the world we inhabit,
the better it is for the human race.'[41] Nationalist sentiment
and the popularity of Empire reached a crescendo with the
celebrations for Victoria's Diamond Jubilee in 1897 and the
outbreak on 10 October 1899 of the Boer War, in which
Rhodes's tenet was militarily threatened on his own territory.
'The battles will be on a huge scale that's certain – and a terri-
ble ending it will all have', Emma Hardy reflected, with no
doubt as to where the moral right lay. 'The Boers fight for
homes and liberties – we fight for the Transvaal Funds, dia-
monds & gold.'[42]

Hardy's attitude to the wars he physically lived through
and imaginatively lived in was not a straightforward one.
The Napoleonic wars, of which many tales and veterans survived locally, consistently fascinated him. The most notable
products of this are *The Dynasts*, *The Trumpet-Major* and a
number of poems, including two sequences in *Wessex Poems*:
'The Sergeant's Song', 'Valenciennes' and 'San Sebastian'; and
'Leipzig', 'The Peasant's Confession' and 'The Alarm'. 'One
We Knew' hints at the reasons for this fascination. Hardy
recalls how his grandmother:

> told of that far-back day when they learnt astounded
>   Of the death of the King of France:
> Of the Terror; and then of Bonaparte's unbounded
>   Ambition and arrogance.
>
> Of how his threats woke warlike preparations
>   Along the southern strand,
> And how each night brought tremors and trepidations
>   Lest morning should see him land.

Napoleon attracted Hardy not only for his personal and military vim but also for his moral significance. Writing to Harley
and Helen Granville Barker on 29 December 1926 he spoke of
Napoleon as

the man who finished the Revolution with 'a whiff of grapeshot', and so crushed not only its final horrors but all the worthier aspirations of its earlier time, made them as if they had never been, and threw back human altruism scores, perhaps hundreds of years.   (*Letters*, VII, 54)

In Napoleonic Wessex Hardy found an ideal subject: an insular region threatened by invasion, with clashes of modern and ancient values, and rises and falls of powerful men. There is little doubt where his sympathies lay, and in the conflict of powerful personalities he saw material which he considered intrinsically literary – hence his early idea that a sequence of poems could be built up which would finally provide 'altogether an Iliad of Europe from 1789 to 1815' (*Life*, p. 110).

To those wars he lived through Hardy's attitude was more equivocal. 'I constantly deplore the fact that "civilized" nations have not learnt some more excellent and apostolic way of settling disputes than the old and barbarous one, after all these centuries', he told Florence Henniker; 'but when I feel that it must be, few persons are more martial than I, or like better to write of war in prose or rhyme' (*Letters*, II, 232). The 'War Poems' sequence in *Poems of the Past and the Present*, Hardy's response to the Boer War, assiduously avoids unthinking patriotism: 'I am happy to say that not a single one is Jingo or Imperial', Florence Henniker was told.[43] The much-anthologised 'Drummer Hodge' may be taken as representative. At first sight, it appears a satisfyingly glorificatory lament for a dead soldier, an attempt to commemorate ennoblingly the efforts of a youthful sacrifice. The poem's true textures are however more complex:

> They throw in Drummer Hodge, to rest
>   Uncoffined – just as found:
> His landmark is a kopje-crest
>   That breaks the veldt around;
> And foreign constellations west
>   Each night above his mound.
>
> Young Hodge the Drummer never knew –
>   Fresh from his Wessex home –

The meaning of the broad Karoo,
The Bush, the dusty loam,
And why uprose to nightly view
Strange stars amid the gloam.

Yet portion of that unknown plain
  Will Hodge forever be;
His homely Northern breast and brain
  Grow to some Southern tree,
And strange-eyed constellations reign
  His stars eternally.

The opening appears an unjustly dismissive ironic gesture –
'They throw in Drummer Hodge' – but the wary Hardy
reader may wonder if the irony extends further than this.
Young in years Hodge may be, but as drummer he is player
of the instrument of incitement to war. 'Hodge', the generic
term, mildly supercilious, for the country labourer, again
may be intended to attract sympathy for a young boy whose
individuality has been disregarded. On the other hand it is
distinctively an English term, perhaps disturbingly out of
context in a foreign military situation.

The first stanza revolves around rhythms at odds with each
other: the rhythms of war, with Hodge as their *primum mobile*;
and the rhythms of the skies of the southern hemisphere,
which assuredly do not have Hodge as their governing axis,
whatever the orotundity of the poem may try to hint to the
contrary. The opening line of the next stanza – 'Young Hodge
the Drummer never knew' – develops the ironic texture by
suggesting immediately that it is promoting sympathy for
opportunities lost. But who does know the meaning of the
earth and the stars? Is it fair to expect it in anyone, least of all
a soldier? Hodge becoming a tree, in a latterday Ovidian
metamorphosis, and being watched over by the stars, is the
consolation ostensibly offered at the end of the poem. But the
reader is no more fully persuaded that this is a situation that
is remotely probable; nor, even if possible, one from which
Hodge would necessarily draw any comfort; nor, least of all,
one that does anything other than point out that Hodge is
altogether an invader, an alien in an environment whose
rhythms are unaltered by his presence or otherwise. 'This

Imperial idea', Hardy reflected after the losses of the notori-
ous Black Week of December 1899, 'is, I fear, leading us into
strange waters' (*Letters*, II, 241). 'Drummer Hodge' perhaps
reads more than is commonly supposed as a poeticization of
this theme.

For all the guarded ambiguities of the 'War Poems' group,
the final poem, 'The Sick Battle-God', ends on a note of
optimism:

> Let men rejoice, let men deplore,
> The lurid Deity of heretofore
> Succumbs to one of saner nod;
> The Battle-god is god no more.

It was not of course to turn out that way. Calls to arms and
armaments marked the first decade of the century, even
though to Hardy it was 'an insanity that people in the 20th
Century should suppose force to be a moral argument'
(*Letters*, IV, 161). Britain declared war on Germany on 4
August 1914: 'The whole news and what it involved burst
upon Hardy's mind next morning, for though most people
were saying the war would be over by Christmas he felt it
might be a matter of years and untold disaster' (*Life*, p. 394).

Hardy studied the war poetry being written by what
would now be regarded as the great English practitioners of
the genre, especially Sassoon, whose *Counter Attack and Other
Poems* he particularly admired. Obviously, however, Hardy's
own poems are necessarily far different from the mainstream
of First World War literature. Owen and companions used
poetry as an exorcising of war; Hardy used it partly to keep
war out. 'He says he keeps from brooding over present affairs
by concentrating his mind on the poems he is writing',
Florence Hardy told Alda, Lady Hoare in May 1917,[44] but this
was not an attitude Hardy could feel altogether comfortable
with, as 'I Looked Up From my Writing' makes plain.

Though generally distrustful of his country's imperialistic
ambitions, Hardy appears to have decided that the fundamental blame for the onset of the war was German, and he
agreed to a government request to writers to do what they
could to support the British cause, with a number of set-piece
poems, all of them reprinted in the 'Poems of War and

Patriotism' section of *Moments of Vision*. But as Hardy confessed to Galsworthy, referring to 'The Whitewashed Wall', 'I cannot do patriotic poems very well – seeing the other side too much' (*Letters*, v, 275). A poem such as 'Men Who March Away' (Hardy's first response to the Cabinet's request for work, and published in *The Times* on 9 September 1914), however much anthologised, patently lacks the complexity of Hardy's best verse. Comparison with a poem such as Owen's 'The Send-Off' immediately reveals Hardy's handicap in having to contemplate the proposition – as Owen so tragically did not – from arm's length.

Even one of the best of the war-inspired poems, Hardy's armistice piece, ' "And There Was a Great Calm" ', is noticeable for the fact that little idea is given of who fought, or where, or why. For Owen and Sassoon and their contemporaries what partly fascinated and terrified about the war was its specificity, the horrifying fact that it was different from any other: new weapons, new numbers, new stalemate-ridden ways of fighting. But for Hardy, this was just the imaginative problem. Here was no Iliad of Europe, no focus-worthy great men, no globe-stretching route marches, no time-honoured methods of fighting or traditional styles of heroism – in short, no ready-to-hand epic. It is significant that Hardy's most quoted First World War poem actually derives from an experience the author had during the Franco-Prussian War over forty years previously, and was said by Hardy to be typical of his capacity 'for burying an emotion in my heart or brain for forty years, and exhuming it at the end of that time as fresh as when interred' (*Life*, p. 408).

In Time of 'The Breaking of Nations'

Only a man harrowing clods
  In a slow silent walk
With an old horse that stumbles and nods
  Half asleep as they stalk.

Only thin smoke without flame
  From the heaps of couch-grass;
Yet this will go onward the same
  Though Dynasties pass.

> Yonder a maid and her wight
> Come whispering by:
> War's annals will cloud into night
> Ere their story die.

The materials here are traditional, the execution professional in the extreme. Edward Thomas's 'At The Team's Head Brass' takes the same idea, but cannot manage the same compression, nor the concentrated ironic touches of language (the ambiguous 'harrowing'), situation (the lovers' selfish lack of awareness of anything but themselves) and imagery (couch-grass aids the dénouement of *Desperate Remedies* by its propensity for smouldering a long while and then bursting into violent flame). But the poem, as its genesis makes clear, is distinctive in that it is about every war, not one war in particular.

None of this is to say that Hardy did not consider the First World War's significance. If anything, he did so too much, and with a gloomy sense of finality. Florence subsequently told Cockerell that Hardy felt the horror of the war 'so keenly that he loses all interest in life',[45] and the *Life* announces that 'the war destroyed all Hardy's belief in the gradual ennoblement of man' (p. 398), an explanation, perhaps, of why the *Life* does not even mention the armistice. Virginia Woolf, declaring that 'in or about December, 1910, human character changed', perhaps dated the alteration eight or so years too early.[46] The war marks a watershed in Hardy's interrelationship with the society around him. That society was now to change immeasurably, acquiring an altered political, economic and cultural complexion. In came the party of the masses, but with it Modernism, a cultural system for the intelligentsia: 'when human relations change', Woolf went on to observe, 'there is at the same time a change in religion, conduct, politics, and literature'.[47] Hardy, into his eighties, was quizzically interested, but understandably did not possess the empathetic kind of interest that would have brought a significantly changed influence to his work. Thus he told Frederic Harrison that he suspected that he was of a Socialist way of thinking, but could not properly work out what the Socialist way of thinking really was (*Letters*, III, 304–5); just as, in thanking Ezra Pound for his *Quia Pauper*

Amavi, he made clear that, fine though the writing might be, the poet's attitude to his audience was modern in a way which Hardy was too old-fashioned to be able to accommodate (*Letters*, vi, 77–8). With the catastrophe of the First World War, the society of the present ceased in a way to be Hardy's society, the society that most interested him or that he wished most fully to interpret and understand. Rather, in the words of Robert Gittings 'the past now almost wholly absorbed him',[48] as 'Conjecture', published in 1917, suggests:

> If there were in my kalendar
>   No Emma, Florence, Mary,
> What would be my existence now –
>   A hermit's? – wanderer's weary?
>   How should I live, and how
>   Near would be death, or far?
>
> Could it have been that other eyes
>   Might have uplit my highway?
> That fond, sad, retrospective sight
>   Would catch from this dim byway
>   Prized figures different quite
>   From those that now arise?
>
> With how strange aspect would there creep
>   The dawn, the night, the daytime,
> If memory were not what it is
>   In song-time, toil, or pray-time. –
>   O were it else than this,
>   I'd pass to pulseless sleep.

The dual blows of the death of Emma and the death of a prewar civilisation may have induced a withdrawal from, and diminished interest in, contemporary society. But such a withdrawal was not in any way to be poetically unproductive.

4

'Yea, Great and Good, Thee, Thee we hail':* Hardy and the Ideas of his Time

'I have no philosophy', Hardy recorded in the *Life*, ' ... merely what I have often explained to be only a confused heap of impressions, like those of a bewildered child at a con-juring show' (p. 441). Few critics have believed Hardy – it has of course been academically convenient not to. But then Hardy himself could on other occasions be specific and infor-mative about the influences on him. 'My pages', he confessed to Ernest Brennecke in June 1924, 'show harmony of view with Darwin, Huxley, Spencer, Comte, Hume, Mill, and others (all of whom, as a matter of fact, I used to read more than Sch[openhauer])' (*Letters*, VI, 259). These contrasting quotations, the one deflective and denying, the other infor-mative and analytical, epitomise Hardy's bifurcated approach to the ideas of his time. He is knowing and unknowing, simultaneously intellectual and instinctive, derivative and original. This chapter hopes ultimately to get at the first trait of mind by way of an analysis of the second, with particular reference to the writers Hardy mentioned above. A tailor-made phrenology provides as five headings for this analysis the religious, the scientific, the free-thinking, the pessimist and the meliorist.

'Religion is the great business of life, I sometimes begin to think the only business', remarks a character in *Lothair*, Disraeli's *roman à clef* of 1870 in which a namesake and close relation of the vicar of Stinsford appears.[1] The Victorians were determined to Christianise the nation. But, split as they were into deep divisions of Dissenting versus Established Churches, and within the latter factions of High, Broad and

---

* From 'Chorus of the Pities (After the Battle)'.

Low, they were bitterly divided about how to approach the task. 'There never was a time in England in which there was more of religious controversy than at present', R. S. Smith, father of Hardy's friend Reginald Bosworth Smith, and vicar of the parish neighbouring Stinsford, pronounced.[2] Hardly anywhere could this controversy be avoided. In Westminster Abbey, at Palmerston's funeral service, which Hardy attended on 27 October 1865, all looked impressive and serene: 'I think I was never so much impressed with a ceremony in my life before,' Hardy wrote to his sister Mary (*Life*, p. 506). But only the year before, Pusey, on behalf of the High Church faction, had written to A. P. Stanley, the Broad Church Dean of Westminster whom Hardy saw in charge of this service, in highly inhospitable tones. 'I believe the present to be a struggle for the life or death of the English Church, and what you believe to be for life I believe to be for death; and you think the same reciprocally of me.'[3] Palmerston might have relished the set-to.

Hardy's religious life reflected the divided nature of his times, as indeed of his native county. For though nineteenth-century Dorset was one of the most Evangelical regions in the country, Stinsford was an isolated stronghold of remarkably advanced High Church practice, presided over by a vicar who had been at Oxford in the formative years of the High Church Tractarian movement. Much has been made of the symbolical significance of Matthew Arnold's baptism, with his father, champion of the Broad Church, standing beside his friend John Keble, chosen as godparent despite his High Church antipathy to Arnold's liberal views. Hardy's baptism contains a symbolism no less potent, both in social and religious terms. Initiated into the Church by Arthur Shirley, a great believer in that Church's authority, Hardy was given by his parents the name of the Christian religion's archetypal exponent of doubt. The tension was always to remain with him.

That Hardy was for many years an earnest Christian has never been doubted. He himself recorded that he was 'churchy; not in an intellectual sense, but in so far as instincts and emotions ruled. As a child, to be a parson had been his dream ... . He himself had frequently read the church lessons, and had at one time as a young man begun reading for

Cambridge with a view to taking Orders' (*Life*, p. 407). Though nothing more has proved discoverable about Hardy's ordination plans, it is possible from various sources to ascertain more of his religious sympathies, in particular of his troubled involvement with the Baptists through his fellow apprentice Bastow, and of what seems to have been an Evangelical conversion experience. The latter, datable from a Bible marking to 'Wednesday night April 17th/61, $\frac{1}{4}$ to 11', appears to have been brought about by Hardy's contacts with the Moule family, and with a nationwide Revival of remarkable potency which affected Dorchester in the early 1860s – according to the Archbishop of Canterbury of the day, nothing since the Day of Pentecost could justifiably be compared to it.

The twin pulls of Stinsford and Dorchester, High Church and Low, are remarkable for their apparent simultaneity, and produce a distinctive effect. They explain how Hardy could, paradoxically, find a sense of isolation or individuality by identification with communal values, and arrive at well-informed catholicity by the experience of contrary ideological extremes.

Hardy's poems on religious themes, such as 'The Oxen', 'A Sign Seeker', 'The Impercipient' and 'Afternoon Service at Mellstock', are much anthologised, and justly so. Such poems derive their effect not only from their stark contrasts of faith and doubt, tradition and innovation, individual and community, but also more particularly from the poignant and understated balance with which such opposites are retained in a closely felt and understood perspective: it was not only about Emma and her rivals that Hardy could write so effectively from the heart. An element of parody, of a reworking of an initial religious experience or work, is a common feature of such poems. 'Waiting Both', Hardy recalled, was a response to a sermon he had heard Henry Moule preach in Dorchester in the 1860s. The more famous 'The Darkling Thrush', for all its adoption of characteristic Hardy motifs, is probably at least in part a response to the poem for the twenty-first Sunday after Trinity in *The Christian Year* by the Tractarian leader John Keble: this collection was amongst the most popular books of the nineteenth century and Hardy's copy has marginalia against this particular poem in a volume which for a time he carried with him as a kind of *vade mecum*. There are elements of parody about 'The Oxen' too:

> Christmas Eve, and twelve of the clock.
>   'Now they are all on their knees,'
> An elder said as we sat in a flock
>   By the embers in hearthside ease.
>
> We pictured the meek mild creatures where
>   They dwelt in their strawy pen,
> Nor did it occur to one of us there
>   To doubt they were kneeling then.
>
> So fair a fancy few would weave
>   In these years! Yet, I feel,
> If someone said on Christmas Eve,
>   'Come; see the oxen kneel
>
> 'In the lonely barton by yonder coomb
>   Our childhood used to know,'
> I should go with him in the gloom,
>   Hoping it might be so.

Here is the adapted vision of the sentimental school of nineteenth-century hymn writers, a sort of English rural reworking of E. H. Sears's 'It came upon the midnight clear'. The language too is that of conventional hymnody: the 'meek mild creatures' recalls Charles Wesley's 'Gentle Jesus, meek and mild' or the more contemporary use of the word in Cecil Frances Alexander's 'Once in Royal David's City' (set to music by H. J. Gauntlett, who had been organist at one of the churches the young Hardy attended in London). Irony, however, distinctively characterises Hardy's vision. The suggestion that the humans have reduced themselves to the level of simple animals by forming a 'flock' draws attention to the point that the poem claims only to represent 'fancy', not fact: the narrator only admits that he would go off in search of the phenomenon, not, as too many sentimental readings of the poem have tended to believe, that he is at all confident of finding it.

The novels too involve reflection on, and reworking of, the religious fabric of Hardy's time. 'Who will deny', Walter Pater questioned in a famous review of 1888, 'that to trace the influence of religion upon human character is one of the legitimate functions of the novel?'[4] Religious stereotypes, as has long been realised, frequently underlie Hardy's character types, just as incidents from Hardy's religious youth provide a quarry for incidents in the novels – the dispute over paedobaptism with Bastow, for example, providing the basis for the opening of *A Laodicean*. *Under the Greenwood Tree*, as its Preface acknowledges, draws heavily on historical fact: the superannuation by Arthur Shirley of the Stinsford choir in which the Hardy family had given such service. The novel presents a characteristically Victorian contrast between the energy and reforming zeal of the new vicar, Parson Maybold, and the previous incumbent, Parson Grinham, who had been the type of eighteenth-century clerical indolence. As one of the choir remarks, the new vicar preaches 'about being good and upright till 'tis carried to such a pitch as I never see the like afore nor since' (II, ii). However, there are clear distinctions between the novel on the one hand, and historical fact and the usual attitudes of Victorian fiction on the other. Other nineteenth-century writers describing reforms in church music related the improvements to the conscientiousness of the clergy and the religious ferment of the age. Thus in George Eliot's 'Amos Barton' (1858) the determination of the newly arrived clergyman that the old set of singers should be dismissed is related to his Evangelical enthusiasm; and the new organ installed by the vicar in Jefferies's 'A Modern Country Curate' (1880) is described as the result of his Tractarian desire for renewal.

As diocesan records and personal papers make clear, Shirley's musical reform, like the introduction of a surpliced choir by his cousin W. C. Frampton at the nearby Dorset parish of Moreton, was a clear indication of his Tractarian ideals. Yet though Shirley's partisan churchmanship was readily apparent, any such sympathies in Hardy's presentation of Arthur Maybold remain completely unmentioned. 'Understand me rightly,' the vicar explains with a blush to Reuben Dewy, 'the churchwarden proposed it to me, but I had thought myself of getting – Miss Day to play' (II, iv). The choir regard this motive as scandalously irreligious: 'Then the music is second to the woman', one of their number concludes, ' ... and God A'mighy is nowhere at all' (II, v). Whereas Arthur Shirley displayed ecclesiastical allegiances which were potent and pervasive, Maybold's churchmanship is non-existent – a particularly noteworthy phenomenon, given Hardy's own detailed knowledge of ecclesiastical practice. Maybold's motives for reforming the choir, as well as for inspecting the school, are entirely secular and, unlike Shirley (whose plans for repewing at Stinsford strove sensitively to avoid any cause of social embarrassment), Maybold is presented as indifferent to giving social offence. The novel charts his social nemesis, as Hardy shows not only a lady's preference for a poor man but also her rejection of a vicar.

By the time of the final novels, Hardy's religious experiences seem at times to be providing the animus for his writing, *Tess* providing an exorcism of his Evangelical, as *Jude* of his Tractarian past. *Tess* reads like a parody of an Evangelical tract, in particular the most famous of them, Legh Richmond's perennially popular *The Dairyman's Daughter* (1809), sales of which reached two million. A pure-minded country girl of humble origins, Tess's initial character and circumstances have much in common with those of Richmond's Betsy; but, whereas Betsy is saved by her chance encounter with a preacher, an itinerant clergyman who 'held strange notions',[5] Tess is corrupted rather than redeemed by her contacts with the outside world. A parody of the Evangelical cautionary tale, *Tess* depicts not a young girl saved by Evangelicalism, but a heroine destroyed by exponents of it: Alec, converted by Mr Clare, and Angel, unable to shake off his early indoctrination. Likewise *Jude* apes the High Church *alter Christus* tradition, in which the believer becomes gradually more like Christ, as St Francis had. 'Yes, Christminster shall be my Alma Mater; and I'll be her beloved son, in whom she shall be well pleased', Jude announces (I, vi). But this modern-day Jerusalem offers only rejection. Christ and minster ironically cannot be linked at this location.

Almost as influential perhaps on Hardy's cast of mind as religious matters was scientific thought and advance. In Beatrice Webb's opinion, 'The belief in science and the scientific method ... was certainly the most salient element of the mid-Victorian Time-Spirit.'[6] Hardy's contact with scientific thought of the nineteenth-century, by which is meant principally geological and more particularly evolutionary studies, was of course non-specialised; but so too in a way were those studies themselves, modern works of science being then, as they are not now, predominantly accessible to the general reader. The two principal men of the scientific movement were, for Hardy, Darwin and Huxley, the one formidable as an amasser and original interpreter of evidence, and the other a lecturer and polemicist of exceptional ability.

Scientific advance has a threefold effect on Hardy. Gone for the Victorians was the easy-minded if precisely calculated theorem of Bishop Lightfoot that Man was created by the Trinity on 23 October 4004 BC at nine o'clock in the morning. Victorian chronological perspectives were lengthier. According to Darwin, in Chapter IX of *The Origin of Species*, Sir Charles Lyell (1797–1875) was the scientist who brought about this 'revolution in natural science', Lyell's *Principles of Geology* stressing 'how incomprehensibly vast have been the past periods of time'.[7]

In this, as in another respect, Hardy could not have lived at a more fortunate time. For the discoveries of science were happily at one with his own temperament, eager as it was to remind the infinitesimal of its larger context, and encouraged by the reading of formative years (not to mention interest in the fossil-chipping activities of the Dorset Natural History and Antiquarian Field Club and all the Roman-searching spadework in the Max Gate shrubbery) to stress a sense of perspective:

> If it be possible to compress into a sentence all that a man learns between twenty and forty, it is that all things merge in one another – good into evil, ... the year into the ages, the world into the universe. With this in view the evolution of species seems but a minute process in the same movement. (*Life*, p. 114)

Novels and poems are accordingly from the earliest full of such contexts: the 'roll of the world eastward' as seen from that 'shape approaching the indestructible' Norcombe Hill in Chapter ii of *Far from the Madding Crowd*, the twin interests of Swithin St Cleeve of *Two on a Tower* in Viviette and the 'ghastly gulfs' of the universe, and the confrontation of Knight and the trilobite in the cliff scene of *A Pair of Blue Eyes*:

> Separated by millions of years in their lives, Knight and this underling seemed to have met in their place of death. It was the single instance within reach of his vision of anything that had ever been alive and had had a body to save, as he himself had now.   (xxii)

Egdon, at the middle of the Wessex topography, occupies a similar centrality in terms of the fusion it provides for the author's chosen specialities: local knowledge, temperamental colouring and scientific background. The heath's vegetation seemed to belong to 'the ancient world of the carboniferous period', and even the landscape's 'trifling irregularities were not caused by pickaxe, plough, or spade, but remained as the very finger-touches of the last geological change' (I, i). All these things, the narrator tells us, 'gave ballast to the mind adrift on change, and harassed by the irrepressible new' (ibid.). Even when recalling the most personal event of his life, his romance with Emma, Hardy found it impossible not to view it within a geological context, replete with ironic potential, as 'At Castle Boterel' makes plain:

> As I drive to the junction of lane and highway,
>   And the drizzle bedrenches the wagonnette,
> I look behind at the fading byway,
>   And see on its slope, now glistening wet,
>   Distinctly yet
>
> Myself and a girlish form benighted
>   In dry March weather. We climb the road
> Beside a chaise. We had just alighted
>   To ease the sturdy pony's load
>   When he sighed and slowed.

What we did as we climbed, and what we talked of
    Matters not much, nor to what it led, –
Something that life will not be balked of
    Without rude reason till hope is dead,
        And feeling fled.

It filled but a minute. But was there ever
    A time of such quality, since or before,
In that hill's story? To one mind never,
    Though it has been climbed, foot-swift, foot-sore,
        By thousands more.

Primaeval rocks form the road's steep border,
    And much have they faced there, first and last,
Of the transitory in Earth's long order;
    But what they record in colour and cast
        Is – that we two passed.

And to me, though Time's unflinching rigour,
    In mindless rote, has ruled from sight
The substance now, one phantom figure
    Remains on the slope, as when that night
        Saw us alight.

I look and see it there, shrinking, shrinking,
    I look back at it amid the rain
For the very last time; for my sand is sinking,
    And I shall traverse old love's domain
        Never again.

Secondly, scientific discoveries radically altered human perception of the ethos of the natural world. William Paley, in his *Natural Theology* of 1802, a text book for Tennyson at Cambridge, and indeed one well into the twentieth century, ended an account of a country walk with the conclusion that 'It is a happy world after all. The air, the earth, the water, teem with delighted existence. In a spring noon or a summer evening, on whichever side I turn my eyes, myriads of happy beings crowd my view.'[8] Darwin's world picture was a different one: 'We behold the face of nature bright with gladness', he remarks in *The Origin of Species*, but 'We forget that the birds which are idly singing round us mostly live on insects or seeds, and are thus constantly destroying life; or we forget how largely these songsters, or their eggs, or their nestlings, are destroyed by birds or beasts of prey.'[9] 'To Outer Nature' records Hardy's reaction to this shift in the response to natural phenomena:

> Show thee as I thought thee
> When I early sought thee,
>   Omen-scouting,
>   All undoubting
> Love alone had wrought thee –
>
> Wrought thee for my pleasure,
> Planned thee as a measure
>   For expounding
>   And resounding
> Glad things that men treasure.
>
> O for but a moment
> Of that old endowment –
>   Light to gaily
>   See thy daily
> Iris-hued embowment!
>
> But such re-adorning
> Time forbids with scorning –
>   Makes me see things
>   Cease to be things
> They were in my morning.
>
> Fad'st thou, glow-forsaken,
> Darkness-overtaken!
>   Thy first sweetness,
>   Radiance, meetness,
> None shall re-awaken.
>
> Why not sempiternal
> Thou and I? Our vernal
>   Brightness keeping,
>   Time outleaping;
> Passed the hodiernal!

Again this aspect of scientific change accorded with Hardy's temperamental disposition, the Anglo-Saxon gloominess of his natural demeanour. Arthur Symons, with typical poetic insight, justly remarked that Hardy was a writer who was 'sorry for Nature, who feels the earth and the roots, as if he has sap in his veins instead of blood, and could get closer than any other man to the things of the earth.'[10] It accorded with Hardy's view of things from first to last to see life in Darwinian terms as a struggle for survival. The *Life* for December 1927 reflects back on Hardy's earliest memories and describes a scene with Hardy and his father in the garden at Bockhampton on a bitterly cold winter day:

> They noticed a fieldfare, half-frozen, and the father took up a stone idly and threw it at the bird, possibly not meaning to hit it. The fieldfare fell dead, and the child Thomas picked it up and it was as light as a feather, all skin and bone, practically starved. He said he had never forgotten how the body of the fieldfare felt in his hand: the memory had always haunted him.   (p. 479)

Novels and poems are packed with Darwinian perspectives. 'In a Wood' miniaturises the canvas of *The Woodlanders*:

> Heart-halt and spirit-lame,
> City-opprest,
> Unto this wood I came
> As to a nest;
> Dreaming that sylvan peace
> Offered the harrowed ease –
> Nature a soft release
> From men's unrest.
>
> But, having entered in,
> Great growths and small
> Show them to men akin –
> Combatants all!
> Sycamore shoulders oak,
> Bines the slim sapling yoke,
> Ivy-spun halters choke
> Elms stout and tall.

By the time of *Jude* the idea of the struggle for survival, of the extent to which the fittest are prepared to survive at the expense of the defenceless, has become a guiding structural principle. As though contributing to some operatic quartet, each of the principal characters is in turn provided with a view on the subject. 'Cruelty is the law pervading all nature and society', Phillotson remarks with such preciseness and directness that, perhaps for fear of outrage, Hardy excluded the passage from the serial edition (v, viii). 'Why should Nature's law be mutual butchery?', Sue expostulates after the sale of her two pet pigeons 'all alive and plump' (v, vi). For the young Jude, employment as a bird-scarer is an unwelcome education in the gap between the welfare of God's birds and the welfare of God's gardener: 'Nature's logic was too horrid for him to care for' (I, ii). But this is merely the matriculation ceremony in Jude's education: graduation by pig-killing awaits him.

Lastly, scientific advance had a considerable effect on the Victorians' tenuous grip on their belief in God. For Paley and his eighteenth-century ilk the study of nature invariably involved a greater respect for and understanding of God. Even Gideon Algernon Mantell's *Wonders of Geology* (1838), lent to Hardy by his friend Horace Moule after its appearance in the Moule household had scandalised Moule's clergyman father and suggested the arrival of the free-thinking volume in chapter xviii of *Tess*, tamely declared that 'every physical phenomenon which has taken place from first to last has emanated from the will of the deity'.[11] Only three-quarters of a century later, Hardy's friend Edward Clodd, chronicling recent scientific developments in his *Pioneers of Evolution* (1902), would reach exactly the opposite conclusion: 'There is no possible reconciliation between Evolution and Theology', he felt able to remark.[12]

In consonance with this idea, Hardy's presentation of nature frequently attempts to expose the divisions between nature and Christian or ecclesiastical morality. Tennyson's *In Memoriam*, sensing, after a reading of Lyell, that God and Nature might be at strife, attempted to reconcile them. 'Winter Night in Woodland' has no such intention:

> The bark of a fox rings, sonorous and long: –
> Three barks, and then silentness; 'wong, wong, wong!'

In quality horn-like, yet melancholy,
  As from teachings of years; for an old one is he.
The hand of all men is against him, he knows; and yet, why?
That he knows not, – will never know, down to his death-
    halloo cry.

  With clap-nets and lanterns off start the bird-baiters,
  In trim to make raids on the roosts in the copse,
  Where they beat the boughs artfully, while their
    awaiters
  Grow heavy at home over divers warm drops.
The poachers, with swingels, and matches of brimstone,
    outcreep
To steal upon pheasants and drowse them a-perch and
    asleep.

  Out there, on the verge, where a path wavers through,
  Dark figures, filed singly, thrid quickly the view,
  Yet heavily laden: land-carriers are they
  In the hire of the smugglers from some nearest bay.
Each bears his two 'tubs', slung across, one in front, one
    behind,
To a further snug hiding, which none but themselves are to
    find.

  And then, when the night has turned twelve the air
    brings
  From dim distance, a rhythm of voices and strings:
  'Tis the quire, just afoot on their long yearly rounds,
  To rouse by worn carols each house in their bounds;
Robert Penny, the Dewys, Mail, Voss, and the rest; till anon
Tired and thirsty, but cheerful, they home to their beds in
    the dawn.

The poem's landscape is a moralised tableau. Hardy's old-
stagers, the Stinsford choir, give the appearance of providing
a sentimental ending, new hope on a new day, and a heart-
warming carolled message of goodwill to all men. But the
ending is ironic, incapable of deflecting attention from what
has preceded it, even without the details that the carols are
'worn' (the manuscript had the more hopeful 'quaint') and

that the choir are unlikely to go thirsty to bed, given the
amount of contraband stashed in the locality (and the extent
to which, elsewhere in his *oeuvre*, Hardy had associated them
with smuggling). The fox of the first stanza and the birds of
the second are pitiable casualties of a harsh Darwinian
imperative – of the ability of the stronger to prey on the
weaker, with the added Huxleyan irony that it is man, supposedly possessed of a moral code above the animal, who is
here the predator. The bower towards which the smugglers
move is illegal yet undisturbed; the birds' roosts are
comparatively harmless yet ravaged.

In the novels, landscape likewise is presented not in any
furtherance of Paley's theories but rather as a disproof of
them. Tess at Talbothays enjoys an equivalent of Paley's
country walk: 'She heard a pleasant voice in every breeze,
and in every bird's note seemed to lurk a joy':

> And thus her spirits, and her thankfulness, and her hopes,
> rose higher and higher. She tried several ballads, but found
> them inadequate; till, recollecting the psalter that her eyes
> had so often wandered over of a Sunday morning before
> she had eaten of the tree of knowledge, she chanted: 'O ye
> sun and moon ... O ye stars ... ye Green Things upon the
> Earth ... ye Fowls of the Air ... Beasts and Cattle ...
> Children of Men ... bless ye the Lord, praise Him and
> magnify Him for ever!'   (xvi)

Tess's reaction, however, is interpreted as 'a Fetichistic utterance in a Monotheistic setting', and the novel as a whole is at
pains to place in antagonism contrasting interpretations of
natural fertility as nature's bounty or man's God-judged sin.
Sorrow is described ironically as 'that bastard gift of shame-
less Nature who respects not the social law' (xiv), whilst her
mother has only offended against the 'arbitrary law of society
which had no foundation in Nature' (xli). 'But for the world's
opinion', we are told, 'those experiences would have been
simply a liberal education' (xv). Chapter xiii ends with a set-
piece on the topic rather typical of the novel:

> On these lonely hills and dales her quiescent glide was of a
> piece with the element she moved in. Her flexuous and

stealthy figure became an integral part of the scene. At times her whimsical fancy would intensify natural processes around her till they seemed a part of her own story. Rather they became part of it; for the world is only a psychological phenomenon, and what they seemed they were. The midnight airs and gusts, moaning amongst the tightly-wrapped buds and bark of the winter twigs, were formulae of bitter reproach. A wet day was the expression of irremediable grief at her weakness in the mind of some vague ethical being whom she could not class definitely as the God of her childhood, and could not comprehend as any other.

. . . Walking among the sleeping birds in the hedges, watching the skipping rabbits on a moonlit warren, or standing under a pheasant-laden bough, she looked upon herself as a figure of Guilt intruding into the haunts of Innocence. But all the while she was making a distinction where there was no difference. Feeling herself in antagonism she was quite in accord. She had been made to break an accepted social law, but no law known to the environment in which she fancied herself such an anomaly.

Free-thinkers are the third kind of magician present at Hardy's figurative conjuring show. The label is loose but the cast of mind distinctive. According to Hastings' *Encyclopaedia of Religion and Ethics*, a copy of which Hardy owned, nineteenth-century philosophy, like nineteenth-century politics and the nineteenth-century novel, distinguishes itself by a concern with the concept of political and social freedom, the right of the individual to develop and discover his own identity unhindered. Thus John Stuart Mill was for Hardy 'one of the profoundest thinkers of the last century' and *On Liberty* one of Hardy's most treasured texts – the 'Individuality' section in the book was another of his three 'cures for despair' (*Life*, pp. 355, 59).

Hardy's free-thinkers are to be identified not only by this concern with the rights and distinctiveness of the individual but also by the courage with which they challenge all aspects of the ideological status quo. To quote a phrase from a passage of Matthew Arnold's 'Heine' much studied by Hardy, they are 'Dissolvents of the old European system of dominant ideas'.[13] Their cast of mind was empirical, questioning, agnostic, with all the implications of that word employed by its coiner, T. H. Huxley:

> Agnosticism, in fact, is not a creed, but a method, the essence of which lies in the rigorous application of a single principle. That principle is of great antiquity; it is as old as Socrates; as old as the writer who said, "Try all things; hold fast by that which is good"; it is the foundation of the Reformation, which simply illustrated the axiom that every man should be able to give a reason for the faith that is in him; it is the great principle of Descartes; it is the fundamental axiom of modern science. Positively the principle may be expressed: In matters of the intellect follow your reason as far as it will take you, without regard to any other consideration. And negatively: In matters of the intellect do not pretend that matters are certain which are not demonstrated or demonstrable.[14]

Few passages in Hardy more show his interest in this general aspect of nineteenth-century thought than the arrival of Jude in Oxford. The passage has a direct precedent – perhaps one Hardy wished to build on – in Thomas Hughes's popular *Tom Brown at Oxford*, for Tom on arrival walks the streets speculating on those in whose footsteps he is following. When Jude encounters the Christminster worthies in Part Second, Hardy is far more detailed and takes far greater liberties with historical fact. The 'Christminster' setting allowed Hardy greater ease of integration with the already-established Wessex topography, but the chief byproduct in this set-piece establishment of local intellectual tradition is the ability to emphasise individuals who have controversially challenged the received ideas of the Victorian era: Peel in his political *volte face* over the Corn Laws; Matthew Arnold in his views on culture and society; Newman, Keble and Pusey in their ideas on religion; and Browning, and more especially Swinburne, in their literary innovations.

The free-thinkers closest to Hardy influence his ideas, and especially his religious and philosophical ideas, in a number of ways. First, as regards Christianity they were iconoclastic. Leslie Stephen can perhaps be taken as the chief influence here: Hardy described him as the man 'whose philosophy was to influence his own for many years, indeed, more than that of any other contemporary' (*Life*, p. 102). Hardy's poem 'The Schreckhorn' likens Stephen to that Alpine peak 'in its quaint glooms, keen lights, and rugged trim'. Perhaps more concretely informative are Stephen's *Essays on Free Thinking and Plain Speaking* (1873) and *Agnostic's Apology* (1876), both from the period when Hardy was associated with him as editor. 'The one duty which at the present moment seems to be of paramount importance, is the duty of perfect intellectual sincerity', Stephen declares in the first of the *Essays*.[15] That duty involves a renunciation of orthodox Christianity, and a resulting pleasure in new-found intellectual freedom: 'Let us think freely and speak plainly, and we shall have the highest satisfaction that man can enjoy.'[16] For Stephen, the loss of orthodox views was not so much 'an abandonment of beliefs seriously held and firmly implanted in the mind, but a gradual recognition of the truth that you never really held them'. He perhaps encouraged Hardy to feel the same when, rather startlingly, he invited him to witness his renunciation of Holy Orders on 23 March 1875.

Hardy's free-thinkers replace orthodox Christianity with agnosticism. We commonly misunderstand agnosticism today as something passive and unaffirming, whereas for the Victorian it had a more positive and militant quality. Certainty and not doubt was the hallmark of many Victorian agnostics. As we have seen, for Huxley agnosticism was 'the rigorous application of a single principle': 'In matters of the intellect do not pretend that conclusions are certain which are not demonstrated or demonstrable.' If Huxley was an agnostic, Hardy might more aptly and literally be described as a 'not-knower': it is indeed significant that Hardy struck out the draft title 'The Agnostic' for one of his most famous religious poems, and replaced it with 'The Impercipient'. For there is nothing organised about Hardy's not-knowing as there is about Huxley's agnosticism. Huxley felt certain about what he could believe, but Hardy experienced no certainty at all. Commanding a lucid intellect and a scientist's habit of marshalling his ideas, Huxley was able to set clearly defined limits to his beliefs and doubts. Hardy, more artist than thinker, could not. Where there were no limits to his possible beliefs, there were equally no limits to his doubts. Although

there were few things which he could not believe, there were
likewise few things that he could.

A crucial influence on Hardy here may well have been
Herbert Spencer. Long before Spencer's death, let alone
Hardy's, Spencer had become an unfashionable and much-
ridiculed figure, 'the most immeasurable ass in
Christendom', as Carlyle proclaimed him.[17] Biographically,
however, Spencer and Hardy had much in common: an
underprivileged background leading to radical sympathies,
a technical training, and an autodidacticism leading to
varying degrees of literalness of mind. Thus Hardy faithfully
remained Spencer's champion, referring to Spencer's much
discredited *First Principles* (in much the way that he referred
to Mill's *On Liberty* or Wordsworth's 'Resolution and
Independence') as 'a book which acts, or used to act, upon
me as a sort of patent expander when I had been particularly
narrowed down by the events of life'.[18] An aspect of *First
Principles* that particularly appealed to Hardy seems
significantly to have been its concept of 'the Unknowable', a
profound yet unexplainable mystery at the back of the universe, from which all things proceed. Hardy was upset by
attempts to discredit the idea: 'I am utterly bewildered to
understand how the doctrine that, beyond the knowable,
there must always be an unknown, can be displaced', he
complained (*Life*, p. 400).

And this significant difference from the free-thinkers with
regard to agnosticism entails a further significant difference
from them with regard to the miraculous and supernatural.
Miracles were a totem to the Victorian controversialists.
'Miracle is to our time what the law was to the early
Christians', the hero of Mary Augusta Ward's bestselling
novel *Robert Elsmere* (1888) remarks: 'We *must* make up our
minds about it one way or the other.'[19] But make up their
minds about it the Victorians corporately – or indeed individ-
ually – could not. On the one hand, the author's uncle
Matthew Arnold could declare in italic and *Literature and
Dogma* that '*miracles do not happen*'; yet on the other, Hardy
could find him guilty (in a triumph of mixed metaphor) of
balancing dogma on its feet by hair-splitting (*Life*, p. 224).

Here the significance of Hume, the only eighteenth-century
figure on Hardy's list, becomes apparent. For Hardy seems

to have valued Hume not as an empiricist philosopher *per se*, but rather for a small part of his philosophical discourse, his scepticism about the miraculous. As Hardy's poem 'Drinking Song' puts it

> Then rose one Hume, who could not see,
> If earth were such,
> Required were much
> To prove no miracles could be:
> 'Better believe
> The eyes deceive
> Than that God's clockwork jolts,' said he.

The source is 'Of Miracles' in Hume's *Inquiry Concerning Human Understanding*, which later goes on to assert that 'no testimony for any kind of miracle has ever amounted to a probability, much less to a proof'.[20]

But for all that Hardy may have revered Hume's sceptical intellect, the attitude was not one that he slavishly followed. Hardy's imagination is heavily reliant on the interference of the supernatural, whether it be through portentous coincidence or disconcerting appearance. 'I am most anxious', Hardy once told William Archer, 'to believe in what, roughly speaking, we may call the supernatural – but I find no evidence for it!' He would willingly give ten years of his life to see a ghost, he remarked, but then eighteen years later claimed actually to have observed one, an eighteenth-century-clad gent fond of Stinsford church and in favour of a Green Christmas.[21] 'When a man falls he lies', 'A Sign-Seeker' regrets; yet at the same time Hardy's poetry peoples villages, towns, houses, cliff tops and, for preference, churchyards with multitudes of the still-speaking dead. There are, indeed, at least nine of them murmuring mildly throughout 'Friends Beyond'. 'How long halt ye between two opinions?', Hardy had pencilled in his 1861 Bible. But for Hardy the final choice between Humean scepticism and human gullibility always remained avoidable.

Hardy's free-thinkers also encouraged him to see the Christian religion as but one amongst many religions, and far from necessarily pre-eminent amongst them. More than any other factor, anxiety about the Christian religion's claims about its own exclusiveness seem to have been responsible for Hardy's doubt. Hardy's markings in his religious books, so informative about the shades of his belief, appear at first remarkably unforthcoming about the reasons for his doubt. *At first*, that is, because in fact a marking that relates with remarkable particularity to the onset of Hardy's doubts was later erased by him with such zeal that much of the paper surface has been removed, and only forgery detection techniques have been able to reclaim the original marking. This is a single word, doubt, and a date, 11 September 1864, against an otherwise still extant marking of Isaiah 44–5.

This text, with its exclusive claim that 'I am the Lord, and there is none else, there is no God beside me' appears much to have troubled Hardy, and with good reason. According to Stephen in the *Agnostic's Apology*, 'the one thing certain is, that all creeds have perished'.[22] Everywhere in the freethinking writers, as well as very prominently in the poetry of his revered Swinburne, Hardy could observe attempts to place Christianity and other religions, especially Hellenic ones, side by side, and to indulge in comparative evaluation. '"Pagan self-assertion" is one of the elements of human worth, as well as "Christian self-denial"', Mill's *On Liberty* declared, in a passage which Hardy marked in his copy of the text.[23]

Hardy's writings follow suit, and with increasing virulence. The barn scene in chapter xxii of *Far from the Madding Crowd* deliberately develops a correspondence between Weatherbury's church and its barn, thus emphasising a natural religion which rivals the traditions of ecclesiastical Christianity. The barn expresses not a 'worn-out religious creed' which is 'founded on a mistake' but practices which have suffered 'no mutilation at the hands of time' (xxii). Not surprisingly, the editing Leslie Stephen found the scene 'excellent'.[24]

Later novels, emboldened, employ a contrast between Hebraic and Hellenic religion as a founding structural and ideological principle. Thus Clym's repressive Hebraism triumphs over the more joyful Hellenism of Eustacia; Angel has 'been so unlucky as to say to his father, in a moment of irritation, that it might have resulted far better for mankind if Greece had been the source of the religion of modern civilization, and not Palestine' (*Tess*, xxv); and *Jude* constantly reverts to struggles between Christian self-denial and pagan self-assertion, not least in the scene where Sue reveres her pagan statuary to the accompaniment of readings from Swinburne and others. On Egdon pagan impulses seem 'in some way or other to have survived mediaeval doctrine' (*The Return*, VI, i), whilst in *The Woodlanders* we are reminded of Marty South's 'ancestral goddess' Sif, and of the 'ante-mundane Ginnung gap believed in by her Teuton forefathers' (iii). As Hardy's sense of Wessex develops, so does his sense that it might possibly be a region somehow as yet untouched by the emissaries of Augustine.

Having dealt with the twin oppositions of faith and doubt, it is necessary to turn to the inevitable opposition of pessimism and optimism, or meliorism, as it is probably better to call it. *The Times* for 12 January 1928 in its obituary had no doubt in acclaiming Hardy as 'the greatest writer of his time'. It was equally clear about the character and antecedents of his philosophy:

> His philosophy, no abstract or *dilettante* theorizing, but an energetic conviction permeating his work from first to last, was too stern and melancholy to arouse flippant applause. He had embraced with sad-eyed acquiescence the metaphysical doctrine of SCHOPENHAUER and VON HARTMANN, that the life of man is the product and the wind-driven derelict of a blind Will, immanent in the Universe, but careless, because unconscious, of human happiness or human progress. It is a form of pessimism less than any other likely to tempt the cheerful genius of these islanders. ... HARDY nevertheless succeeded, not in converting many to his view of life, but in extorting respect for his interpretation of it, and he succeeded by virtue of a personal quality in himself, remote from cynicism or pedantry.

Accuracy and inaccuracy are both usefully prominent here. That Hardy had a single philosophy permeating his work from first to last, and that this philosophy was almost imitatively derived from pessimistic German sources, are assertions which nowadays command little support. Quite apart from Hardy's own disclaimers on the subject, of which one may properly be wary, there is the simple fact that Hardy knew little German, that an English translation of Schopenhauer's *World as Will and Idea* was not published until 1883, and that Hardy's notes on this German pessimistic school date from the late 1880s and early 1890s, by which time his career as a novelist was all but over. *The Times* reveals itself as just that: belonging in its assessment to a generation of readers accustomed to Hardy as active only as poet, and more generous in its estimation of *The Dynasts* than subsequent generations have allowed.

For the enthusiast of *The Dynasts*, however, and of those poems (sometimes perhaps of dubious merit) which develop its schema (mostly to be found in *Poems of the Past and the Present*), this obituary offers with succinct clarity a summary of the salient features of the philosophy in question: a blind will, immanent in the universe, and unconscious of human affairs or progress. Even more usefully, however, the obituary recognises that Hardy's 'personal quality' was essential for the successful modification and transmission of the ideas of his time. The obituary thus gives us an interesting historical and critical document: a one-sided view of Hardy from a particular period and viewpoint; and, at the same time, and in more concealed form, an essentially right-minded and more lasting assessment of Hardy's literary personality.

For Hardy's pessimism has in the end a far more Anglo-Saxon and emotional than Germanic and philosophical quality. 'The ideas which have animated Mr Hardy's books were already present in his mind and conversation, and were the result of temperament and observation, rather than of "influence"', Gosse correctly told the troublesome F. A. Hedgcock in 1909.[25] In the final analysis, there is but a very short difference in effect between the more thoroughly worked-through perceptions of the German school and the more thoroughly lived-through early influence of Jemima and her relations. In a sense, Hardy progresses little beyond the early notebook *aperçu*: 'Mother's notion, and also mine: that a figure stands in our van with arm uplifted, to knock us back from any pleasant prospect we indulge in as probable';[26] for here indeed is a notion of a frustrating will imaginatively far more potent than anything to be found in philosophical translations, and capable of influencing, even in inversion, as early and as powerful a poem as 'Hap' of 1866:

> If but some vengeful god would call to me
> From up the sky, and laugh : 'Thou suffering thing,
> Know that thy sorrow is my ecstasy,
> That thy love's loss is my hate's profiting!'
>
> Then would I bear it, clench myself, and die,
> Steeled by the sense of ire unmerited;
> Half-eased in that a Powerfuller than I
> Had willed and meted me the tears I shed.
>
> But not so. How arrives it joy lies slain,
> And why unblooms the best hope ever sown?
> – Crass Casualty obstructs the sun and rain,
> And dicing Time for gladness casts a moan. ...
> These purblind Doomsters had as readily strown
> Blisses about my pilgrimage as pain.

By the later years, Hardy's pessimism, at first a heady influence, and at one stage perhaps a Germanic affectation, can slacken into a debilitating and delimiting cast of mind. 'I, who could go anywhere, at any time of the year, go nowhere', he wrote with a touch of pride to one correspondent in 1906.[27] The attitude took its toll on Florence, for all that she occasionally managed to make light of it in correspondence. 'He is now – this afternoon – writing a poem with great spirit: always a sign of well-being with him', Florence told Cockerell in December 1920.[28] 'Needless to say', she added, 'it is an intensely dismal poem.' Max Gate conversations could become reduced to a minimum:

FH: It's 12 days since you spoke to anyone outside the house.
TH (*triumphantly*): I have spoken to someone.
FH (*surprised*): Who was it?
TH: The man who drove the manure cart.

FH (*much impressed*): What did you say?
TH: Good morning.[29]

Arguably (a debate to which the final chapter will return), the same reducing tendency can stereotypically affect poems, especially those of the later years, 'The Sunshade' being something of a *cause célèbre* in the debate:

> Ah – it's the skeleton of a lady's sunshade ,
>   Here at my feet in the hard rock's chink,
>   Merely a naked sheaf of wires! –
> Twenty years have gone with their livers and diers
>   Since it was silked in its white or pink.
>
> Noonshine riddles the ribs of the sunshade,
>   No more a screen from the weakest ray;
>   Nothing to tell us the hue of its dyes,
>   Nothing but rusty bones as it lies
> In its coffin of stone, unseen till to-day.
>
> Where is the woman who carried that sunshade
>   Up and down this seaside place? –
>   Little thumb standing against its stem,
>   Thoughts perhaps bent on a love-stratagem,
> Softening yet more the already soft face!
>
> Is the fair woman who carried that sunshade
>   A skeleton just as her property is,
>   Laid in the chink that none may scan?
> And does she regret – if regret dust can –
> The vain things thought when she flourished this?

Reasons for Hardy's pessimism, his tendency to see the skull beneath the skin are – quite apart from the influence of the German philosophers – not hard to find. *Tess* refers to 'the chronic melancholy which is taking hold of the civilized races with the decline of belief in a beneficent Power' (xviii): 'We are the generation who have had to see "the spring sun shine out of an empty heaven, to light up a soulless earth"', the mathematician and philosopher W. K. Clifford pronounced;

'we have felt with utter loneliness that the Great Companion is dead.'[30] In the last analysis, one has to admit that there were ample grounds for gloom in what Hardy had inherited, read, lived through – some might add lived with – and that he was by providence provided with a temperament adequately blessed, when the occasion arose, for the exploitation of them all.

This is, however, no excuse for avoiding the more optimistic side of Hardy's ideology, his belief in progress which, partly because less understood, receives less attention. Hardy copied into his *Literary Notebooks* a quotation from Frederic Harrison:

> *The 19th Century.*   We are on the threshold of a great time. ... "We shall see it, but not now". The Vatican with its syllabus, the Mediaevalists at all costs, Mr Carlyle, Mr Ruskin, the Aesthetes, are all wrong about the nineteenth century. It is not the age of moneybags and cant, soot, hubbub, and ugliness. It is the age of great expectation and unwearied striving after better things ... .[31]

Perhaps in later years nothing made Hardy look quite so old-fashioned as his belief in advance: T. E. Lawrence, reporting to Robert Graves on one of his visits to Max Gate from army camp, commented on 'an unbelievable dignity and ripeness about Hardy':

> he is waiting so tranquilly for death, without a desire or ambition left in his spirit, as far as I can feel it: and yet he entertains so many illusions, and hopes for the world, things which I, in my disillusioned middle-age, feel to be illusory. They used to call this man a pessimist. While really he is full of fancy expectations.[32]

Hardy's belief in progress is less temperamental than circumstantial and has two chief origins. Scientific advance, and in particular the theory of evolution, naturally entailed optimism about man's future: 'Onward and ever onward, mightier and forever mightier, rolls this wondrous tide of discovery', G. H. Lewes enthused in his *History of Philosophy*: with George

Eliot to contend with across the breakfast table few can have begrudged him the stimulus.[33] To some minds, even the vigorous and well informed, it appeared that science might be able altogether to abolish human misery. Thus 'A time will come when science will transform [the world]', wrote Winwood Reade in *The Martyrdom of Man* (1872). 'Disease will be extirpated; the causes of decay will be removed; immortality will be invented. Man will then be perfect.'[34]

There was also a philosophical background to this belief in progress. For Hardy, this existed principally in his familiarity with the theories of Auguste Comte, the founder of Positivism, or the religion of humanity. Positivism saw itself as succeeding theology and replacing the catholic and revolutionary spirits. Comte held that 'The highest progress of man and of society consists in gradual increase of our mastery over all our defects, especially the defects of our moral nature.'[35] To encourage this he envisaged the creation of a Positivist liturgy and calendar which would introduce Positive ceremonies for birth, marriage and death and opportunities for the worship of great men of different ages and cultures, especially Caesar, St Paul and Charlemagne. He also suggested the foundation, under his leadership, of a Western European republic, for which he proposed an international coinage and for which he designed a flag which would have Positivism's scientific motto '*Order and Progress*' on one side and its moral and aesthetic motto '*Live for Others*' on the reverse.

For all that this design suggests that Comte may not have been possessed of a particularly pictorial imagination, his ideas enjoyed a substantial following in the nineteenth century. Hardy's mentors, especially Stephen and Moule, were much interested in Comte, and the precedent was powerful. 'No person of serious thought in these times could be said to stand aloof from Positivist teaching and ideals', Hardy told one correspondent (*Letters*, III, 53), and added in the *Life*:

> If Comte had introduced Christ among the worthies in his calendar it would have made Positivism tolerable to thousands who, from position, family connection, or early education, now decry what in their heart of hearts they hold to contain the germs of a true system.   (pp. 150–1)

Though Hardy stopped short of card-carrying Comtism, he retained many of its ideas. In 1876, he had copied well over a hundred quotations from Comte into his *Notebooks*, and the influence shows in *The Return of the Native* where Clym, 'acquainted with ethical systems popular at the time' of his stay in Paris (III, ii), attempts to convert the Egdon masses, not least in his final, highly Positivist sermon, which Hardy characteristically surrounds with much irony. In *Tess*, Angel reels off the Positivist clichés. Religion must be reconstructed: humanity, not God, should be the focus of reverence and attention. No wonder that Hardy's friend Frederic Harrison, leader of the English Positivists, and therefore perhaps not the most impartial of critics, should tell the author that 'To me it reads like a Positivist allegory or sermon.'[36] But again the irony, which the partisan Harrison was perhaps not the party most suited to notice, is all pervasive. Positivism prided itself on its practicality, and it is the untheorising Tess who more strongly represents the Positivist motto of 'Live for Others', especially in the course of her relationship with Clare. 'Her mood of long-suffering made his way easy for him, and she herself was his best advocate', we are told (xxxvii): the ideological Angel triumphs at the expense of his more deserving partner.

Just as poetry was of special importance to Comte, so too it is in Hardy's poetry that the influences of Positivism are most apparent. Comte held that nineteenth-century poets must now 'adequately portray the new man in his relation to the new God'.[37] Two poems in *Satires of Circumstance*, 'A Plaint to Man' and 'God's Funeral', do just this. Following significantly after Hardy's elegy on Swinburne they mark the death of orthodox religion and look forward to a new moral and religious dispensation:

> The truth should be told, and the fact be faced
> That had best been faced in earlier years:
>
> The fact of life with dependence placed
> On the human heart's resource alone,
> In brotherhood bonded close and graced
>
> With loving-kindness fully blown,
> And visioned help unsought, unknown.

Proposing that poetry should be used extensively in Positivist solemnities, Comte looked to artists 'to construct types of the noblest kind, by the contemplation of which our feelings and thoughts may be elevated'.[38] Here too Hardy conformed, offering types of the noblest kind (albeit unexpected ones) in order to elevate thoughts and feelings in a quasi-liturgical manner:

The Blinded Bird

So zestfully canst thou sing?
And all this indignity,
With God's consent, on thee!
Blinded ere yet a-wing
By the red-hot needle thou,
I stand and wonder how
So zestfully thou canst sing!

Resenting not such wrong,
Thy grievous pain forgot,
Eternal dark thy lot,
Groping thy whole life long,
After that stab of fire;
Enjailed in pitiless wire;
Resenting not such wrong!

Who hath charity? This bird.
Who suffereth long and is kind,
Is not provoked, though blind
And alive ensepulchred?
Who hopeth, endureth all things?
Who thinketh no evil, but sings?
Who is divine? This bird.

Lastly, more than a hint of Positivism can be found in that other *rara avis*, as it were: Hardy commenting extensively on the nature of his art in the remarkably undiffident Apology prefixed to *Late Lyrics and Earlier*. In a sentence where the earnestness is responsible well-nigh for the evanition of syntax, Hardy's philosophy of 'evolutionary meliorism' is expounded. Pain should everywhere 'be kept down to a minimum by loving-kindness, operating through scientific knowledge'. Having assimilated scientific advance, religion and reason may perhaps now be reconciled through 'the interfusing effect of poetry': the Comtean goals of order, progress, altruism and the perfection of the moral nature are amongst the implied benefits resulting. The thought processes here are thoroughly Positivist, and not for nothing are both Harrison and Comte amongst the authorities cited.

The First World War, as Hardy knew even at the time of writing this dying-swan-like Apology, called all such prospects in question.

Christmas : 1924

'Peace upon earth!' was said. We sing it,
And pay a million priests to bring it.
After two thousand years of mass
We've got as far as poison-gas.

The aftermath of the war brought an altered *zeitgeist*. 'The mould in which the Victorian age cast its hopes is broken. There is no law of progress', Dean Inge could declare in his second series of *Outspoken Essays* (1922), favoured reading with the Hardys in the author's last decade.[39] Even before writing the Apology to *Late Lyrics and Earlier* Hardy could fear that evolutionary meliorism and related philosophies had and would accomplish little. Hence the reflection in the *Life* on Hardy's eightieth birthday:

Though my life, like the lives of my contemporaries, covers a period of more material advance in the world than any of the same length can have done in other centuries, I do not find that real civilisation has advanced equally. People are not more humane, so far as I can see, than they were in the year of my birth. Disinterested kindness is less.   (p. 435)

But, as T. E. Lawrence's remark made clear, Hardy, for all that he might fear in his darkest moments that a new Dark Age threatened, certainly remained full of sympathy, if not also minor hope. To quote 'God's Funeral' out of context, 'I did not forget / That what was mourned for, I, too, long had prized.' Hope, and – to use a Hardy nonce word – unhope, existed side by side.

For the ideas of his time, then, Hardy directed readers principally to Darwin, Huxley, Spencer, Comte, Hume, Mill, Schopenhauer and others. Cataloguing alternatively by subject, this chapter has laid these and associated intellectual influences out as religious, scientific, freethinking, pessimistic and meliorist. Where finally does the bewildered child stand in relation to this analysed conjuring show?

Hardy might have approved of pursuing the matter by reference to story and to art. Augustus John's sketch for his famous Hardy portrait shows Hardy against a blank background, much in the manner of John's equally superb portrait of Hugh Walpole. The final oil shows a change of mind, with the Max Gate bookcases providing a backdrop. 'The walls of Hardy's study, where I painted him, were piled to the ceiling with books, mostly of a philosophical nature', John recalled.[40] In the finished portrait, John seems magnificently to have sensed, and to wish to draw our attention to, Hardy's relationship with his reading. The subject is closely interested in those books – they are pictorially *and* intellectually his background – but at the same time the lighting stresses that he is also completely independent of them: interested (of course), amused (because worldy wise), sometimes bad-tempered (because the reading can be misleading), but most of all detached, somehow altogether transcendent.

In the end, readers may prefer to take John's pictorial assessment of Hardy's reading to Hardy's own. The bewildered child image is a creation of Hardy's modesty, and indeed of his wry sense of humour, which John puts firmly in perspective. Hardy was no intellectual innocent. Bemused he may have been, unconcluding he may have been, but lacking in theories he was not. Hardy's impressions are not the impressions of child, but those of a mature, receptive and manipulating artistic thinker.

5

'How shall we ply, then, / Our old mysteries?'*
Hardy and the Other Arts

Hardy had a keen interest in the arts. He was amateurly as adept with the paint brush as with the violin bow, and professionally qualified as an architect. Hardy's interest in these other arts can be discussed in ascending order of competence.

Hardy was passionate about music. 'He was of ecstatic temperament, extraordinarily sensitive to music', the *Life* records, giving several anecdotes of Hardy's childhood exploits as a fiddler at country dances, and revealing that, aged 80, on hearing an anthem by Croft sung in Exeter Cathedral, he felt that he would like to be a cathedral organist more than anything else in the world (pp. 19, 434). This is not, however, to say that Hardy's understanding of music was altogether orthodox, as was, say, that of George Eliot. Hardy appears to have known no Bach, little Mozart, less Beethoven, some Grieg and less Wagner. Though he went to concerts with some enthusiasm, he was not a structured attender of the orthodox repertoire: 'I gathered from the general conversation that his love was for the old tunes. He never discussed classical music', Vera J. Mardon noted when she was summoned to Max Gate as an accompanist in Hardy's later years.[1] With opera, the situation was slightly different and, as we shall see, there are grounds for saying that Hardy, as artist as well as listener, was less musical than he was operatic. Most of all, however, as Vera Mardon discovered, Hardy was of course a folk musician and, partly through being a folk musician, well versed through juvenile experience in the music of the country church. Before examining Hardy's knowledge and use of various kinds of music

* From 'A Jingle on the Times'.

more closely, it may be useful to see just how prominently music featured in Hardy's creative processes and thought patterns.

Hardy tends to see his autobiography in terms of significant musical moments. His parents' first encounter is to the accompaniment of church music ('A Church Romance'), just as his neglect of Emma, or his lack of appreciation of his home, has acute musical associations ('On the Tune Called the Old 104th' and 'The Self Unseeing'); people remembered often become melodies or instruments recalled, as in 'To My Father's Violin'. Hardy's perceptions of experience are, in short, frequently registered through a musical ear. Coming from the century which saw the emergence of the orchestral and choral conductor, Hardy saw things with a musical director's eye. The openings of *Under the Greenwood Tree* and *Far from the Madding Crowd* are kinds of tone poem – evocative descriptions frequently realized in musical terms – just as the wind playing over Egdon Heath has all the variety of a massed nineteenth-century chorus (*The Return*, I, vi); and the wanderer around the waterways bordering Casterbridge 'might hear singular symphonies from these waters, as from a lampless orchestra':

> At a hole in a rotten weir they executed a recitative; where a tributary brook fell over a stone breastwork they trilled cheerily; under an arch they performed a metallic cymballing; and at Durnover Hole they hissed. The spot at which their instrumentation rose loudest was a place called Ten Hatches, whence during high springs there proceeded a very fugue of sounds.   (*The Mayor of Casterbridge*, xli)

Hardy's landscapes can often seem a kind of *Lied von der Erde*: one critic has indeed suggested that Mahler's deep feeling for nature and his stark questioning of man's destiny invite comparison with Hardy, though from any disciplined Viennese musical school to autodidactic Dorchester seems a far enough distance in many other respects.

This is not least because Hardy's musical language is, like his musical experience, largely folk in character. In the terms of the musical historian, Hardy's novels are Nationalist *avant la lettre*. In advance of Vaughan Williams and his school,

Hardy has a collector's feel for folk songs, something of a Cecil Sharp-like enthusiasm for transcribing them, and a willingness to let their texture and patterns stand at the centre of his art. In *Far from the Madding Crowd* the 11th Dragoon Guards play 'The Girl I Left Behind Me' as Troy leaves Fanny, and his regiment Casterbridge (x); 'The Soldier's Joy' forms the climax of the harvest supper (xxxvi); and 'Jockey to the Fair' is twice associated with Oak (vi, viii). Tess is seduced in fog, governing symbol of the comparable narrative of the folksong 'The Foggy Foggy Dew', a snatch of which Suke Damson sings to entice Fitzpiers into spending the night with her.

Out of Hardy's association with the family string group comes his acquaintance with ecclesiastical as well as folk music, and indeed his life-long enthusiasm for it. Church musicians are often Hardy's subject – in *Under the Greenwood Tree* no less than in the fine group of poems about the Stinsford choir (such as 'The Dead Choir', 'The Rash Bride', 'The Choirmaster's Burial' and 'Winter Night in Woodland') and odd curios such as 'Barthélémon at Vauxhall' and 'The Chapel Organist'. In the poems stanza forms often follow hymn models, frequently to ironic effect.

Likewise in the novels, high-key scenes often take place to the accompaniment of church music. The attention of George Somerset in chapter 1 of *A Laodicean* is taken by a tune unaltered by the Victorian composer W. H. Monk (also the much-criticized re-arranger in 'Apostrophe to an Old Psalm Tune'). *Far from the Madding Crowd* ends with just the kind of hymn that would have been popular at the Tractarian churches Hardy frequented in the London of the 1860s, two of which were renowned for the high quality of their music and one of which even for a time employed the famous hymn composer H. J. Gauntlett. This is Newman's 'Lead, Kindly Light', one of Hardy's three favourite hymns, as the *Life* reveals (p. 291). To the strains of this melody Bathsheba reconsiders her errant past: 'All the impassioned scenes of her brief experience seemed to revive with added emotion at that moment, and those scenes which had been without emotion during enactment had emotion then.' Oak, choir member and, in the American first edition, churchwarden to boot, promptly arrives, however, and the future appears more certain. 'Remember not past years', the background

choir distantly advises (an offstage technique to be discussed
again below) and past differences are soon forgotten, amidst
a stream of references to lost disciples and the Song of
Solomon. The technique reaches its apogee in *Jude*. Here
indeed the hero is temporarily inspired by a contemporary
hymn ('At the Foot of the Cross'), an attitude less shared by
the composer himself, who, in search of another kind of distorted viewpoint (and in fulfilment of a Hardy cliché which
commonly parallels love of drink and love of religion)
decides he will desert hymnody for the wine trade. With an
irony less detailed and more swingeing, the psalm 'God is
loving unto Israel' accompanies the discovery of the corpses
of Little Father Time and his siblings.

Such scenes are, odd as it may sound, operatic rather more
than they are ecclesiastical: they have the quality of the Easter
Hymn in Mascagni's *Cavalleria Rusticana*, the technique of the
offstage band or chorus so beloved of Rossini, Verdi and the
Italian operatic school. Hardy's operatic experience, especially in early life, was more extensive and influential than
has generally been recognized. In the nineteenth-century
dispute between the Italian and German traditions, Hardy
was very definitely on the side of Verdi rather than of
Wagner.

Hardy's knowledge of Verdi may have begun even before
his time in London: the *Dorset County Chronicle* for 16
February 1860 advertised with enthusiasm the first performance in Dorchester of Verdi's *Il Trovatore*, given on a tour by
the English Opera Company. After arrival in London, Hardy
attended performances by the company, and also went two
or three times a week to the opera at Covent Garden and Her
Majesty's. The Victorian canon of Verdi was largely confined
to *Ernani*, *Rigoletto*, *Il Trovatore*, *La Traviata*, *Un Ballo in
Maschera* and *Aida*. Hardy seems to have reflected Victorian
taste in making *Il Trovatore* his favourite, as the poems 'An
Ancient to Ancients' and 'The Dead Man Walking' suggest.
'Whenever he heard any music from *Il Trovatore*', the *Life*
reports, 'it carried him back to the first year when he was in
London' (p. 476). Aged 87, with middle-period Verdi rather
out of fashion, Hardy was pleased to note that his opinion
that *Trovatore* was 'good music' was shared by the composer
Ethel Smyth (*Life*, p. 477). Verdi's adoption, late in his career,

of a new musical language also moved Hardy in the *Life* to, by his standards, an extensive comment on the similarities between that composer and himself:

> It may be observed that in the art-history of the century there was an example staring them in the face of a similar modulation from one style into another by a great artist. Verdi was the instance, 'that amazing old man' as he was called. Someone of insight wrote concerning him: 'From the ashes of his early popularity, from *Il Trovatore* and its kind, there arose on a sudden a sort of phoenix Verdi. Had he died at Mozart's death-age he would now be practically unknown.' And another: 'With long life enough Verdi might have done almost anything; but the trouble with him was that he had only just arrived at maturity at the age of threescore and ten or thereabouts, so that to complete his life he ought to have lived a hundred and fifty years.'
>   But probably few literary critics discern the solidarity of all the arts. (pp. 320–1)

There is certainly an artistic solidarity between the theatrical and melodramatic textures of Verdi's operas and Hardy's novels – a kinship perhaps startlingly apparent when *Tess* was turned into an opera by Frederick d'Erlanger (the eruption of Vesuvius on the night of the first Italian performance did not prevent transfer to Covent Garden). Hardy and Verdi have much in common in the bold strokes of their imagination and narrative technique: the texture of a Hardy novel is frequently Italianately operatic, just as (as the *Life* almost brings itself to acknowledge) the similarities between both artists extend to the way in which at the end of their rejuvenating careers they pare down their effort, and refine the pliability and suggestibility of their technique.

Suggestive for Hardy (Mrs Yeobright, Drusilla Fawley; Tess, Fanny; the d'Urberville coach, the two haunting brothers of King's Hintock Court) are Verdi's overpowering and stifling parents (Azucena, Germont, Rigoletto), his sacrificial women (Violetta, Gilda) and his predilection for the curse (*Rigoletto*, *Trovatore*). Improbability is less important than exploration of sharp Gothic contrasts and exploitation of ironic potential. Revelation of inner character takes place at a

heightened melodramatic moment through the manifesta-
tion of some special skill: the troubador's song in *Trovatore*;
or, for Hardy, Oak on the ricks, Knight on the cliff, Somerset
on baptismal doctrine. Scenes in the novels are frequently
like the arias and ensembles of Italian opera. They catch the
characters in a deeply experienced moment and then
suspend time, so that sleepwalking (Angel) or even
sleeptalking (Azucena, Clym) do not seem out of place. Such
scenes have a tendency to present themselves as tableaux,
with broad oil-brush strokes of irony, much use of overhear-
ing/looking, a heavy element of choral commentary, and
multiple offstage effects – often in exceptional meteorologi-
cal and/or topographical conditions. The last act of *Rigoletto*
provides a good example. Both artists, of course, have a
common debt and reverence for Shakespeare, but both are
too similar in their poetic heightening of character and situation for there not to be a direct link. Of course Gilda must
sing as she dies, just as Violetta does, and Manrico and
Leonora sing of their love above the plainchant of the
Miserere mei – just as Jude, to a similar accompaniment of
dramatic and choric offstage effects, must, in highly operatic
moments, preach to the crowd at the Commemoration, or
recite his final catechism. 'My art', said Hardy, 'is to intensify
the expression of things, ... so that the heart and inner
meaning is made vividly visible' (*Life*, p. 183). It was an aesthetic he may well have found more in Verdi than in any
other artistic source.

Hardy's artistic interests owe much to the autodidactic
years of his study in London:

> His interest in painting led him to devote for many
> months, on every day that the National Gallery was open,
> twenty minutes after lunch to an inspection of the masters
> hung there, confining his attention to a single master on
> each visit, and forbidding his eyes to stray to any other. He
> went there from sheer liking, and not with any practical
> object; but he used to recommend the plan to young
> people, telling them that they would insensibly acquire a
> greater insight into schools and styles by this means than
> from any guide books to the painters' works and manners.
> (*Life*, p. 53)

In 'An Indiscretion in the Life of an Heiress' (perhaps representing a borrowing from Hardy's first novel *The Poor Man and the Lady*) Egbert Mayne visits galleries for personal rather than artistic reasons, as part of his campaign to win friends and influence people: 'He examined Correggio to criticize his flesh shades. ... Benozzo Gozzoli was better worth study than Raffaelle, since the former's name was a learned sound to utter, and all knowledge got up about him would tell' (II, i). If at times there is a similar insecure pretentiousness about Hardy's artistic references, especially in the early novels, there is equally no doubt that, as Hardy's career developed, his artistic interest exerted an influence on the kind of fiction he wrote, the skill with which he wrote it, and the way that audiences were encouraged to perceive it. Thus Macmillan, advertising reprints of *Wessex Tales* and *The Woodlanders* in 1892 in the endpapers of other fiction, chose to stress the painterly side of Hardy's achievement by the inclusion of a quotation from *The Times*:

> There is hardly a novelist, dead or living, who so skilfully harmonises the poetry of moral life with its penury. Just as Millet could in the figure of a solitary peasant toiling on a plain convey a world of pathetic meaning, so Mr Hardy with his yeomen and villagers. Their occupations in his hands wear pathetic dignity, which not even the encomiums of a Ruskin could heighten.

As well as the continental Old Masters so frequently referred to in the text, and the subject of several studies, Hardy is also held to have been much influenced by mid-Victorian genre and narrative painting, and some ingenious parallels have been suggested. But as Professor Millgate goes on to caution, this is often 'perhaps only to say that Hardy, like so many contemporary painters, was working deliberately in terms of moral fable'.[2] Certainly, in later books the nature of the artistic influence is altered: more home-grown and modernistic influences replace the conventional Dutch and Italian. The Social Realism movement in Victorian painting centred on a group of artists employed by the *Graphic* (founded in 1870) and the *Illustrated London News*. A leading figure in it was Hubert Herkomer, who was to contribute

several of the illustrations for *Tess* when it appeared in the
Graphic, and who also painted a portrait of Hardy. The movement was, of course, much influenced by the Realist work of
Courbet and his French school, and it in turn exerted much
influence on Van Gogh during his English years. Subjects
were chiefly urban, in presentation devoid of sentiment, and
not without a whiff of social instructiveness – *Hard Times*
(now in the Manchester City Art Gallery) is perhaps the most
famous.

The Mayor of Casterbridge, which began serialisation in the
Graphic in 1886, probably shows the influence of the style:
Henchard carrying the tools of his trade walking on a road in
search of work, the furmity woman at the fair, Elizabeth-Jane
at work on the fishing nets, and the informative treatment of
the Mixen Lane slums – all these have something of the feel
of set pieces of the Social Realist school. The presentation of
rural life is noticeably less picturesque than is, say, *Far from
the Madding Crowd*, and this is representative of Hardy at this
time in his career. Hardy's essay 'The Dorsetshire Labourer'
of 1883 is also representative of the change in perspective,
noting how, 'like the men, the women are, pictorially, less
interesting than they used to be'. The same decline in the
old Dutch glow, and greater emphasis on the unsentimental
and unpictorial marks subsequent novels, especially *The
Woodlanders*, *Tess* and *Jude*. One of Hardy's favourite illustrations was indeed from the latter novel, Hatherell's *Jude at the
Milepost*, as unromantic a representation of proletariat misery
as any propagandist could ask for, hung with pride in the
Max Gate study.

Hardy's interest in modern artistic movements seems to
have increased after *The Mayor*. As if rather arrivistically to
announce this interest he sent a presentation copy of *The
Woodlanders* to the President of the Royal Academy, Sir
Frederick Leighton, and his friendships with artists – notably
Sir Hamo Thornycroft (and, after 1889, his temptingly
mouthed wife Agatha), Sir Lawrence Alma-Tadema, Alfred
Parsons and William Powell Frith – began to blossom. Frith
himself acclaimed *The Woodlanders* for many things, not least
its 'truth to nature',[3] but the novel shows Hardy turning
towards a sphere of influence far removed from Frith's conventional mid-Victorian style, as seen in his *Derby Day*, which

in earlier times Hardy had much admired. Shortly before finishing *The Woodlanders* Hardy recorded:

> After looking at the landscape by Bonington in our drawing room [given to Mrs Hardy by T. Woolner RA, the sculptor] I feel that Nature is played out as a Beauty, but not as a Mystery. … I want to see the deeper reality underlying the scenic, the expression of what are sometimes called abstract imaginings.
> The 'simply natural' is interesting no longer. The much-decried, mad, late-Turner rendering is now necessary to create my interest. (*Life*, p. 192)

Responsible for this change was Hardy's contact with the French Impressionist school and, perhaps even more, with the eccentric English genius they admired, J. M. W. Turner (1775–1851). Hardy had much reflected on the impressionist work he had seen on a visit to the Society of British Artists Exhibition in December 1886:

> The impressionist school is strong. It is even more suggestive in the direction of literature than in that of art. … their principle is, as I understand it, that what you carry away with you from a scene is the true feature to grasp; or in other words, *what appeals to your own individual eye and heart in particular*. (*Life*, p. 191)

The influence is soon palpable. The manuscript of *The Woodlanders*, at the visit in Chapter ii of the barber to Marty South, likens the scene to a 'post-Raffaelite' picture. The emendation is designed to be much more *à la mode*, offering now 'an impression-picture of extremest type'. The Preface to *Tess* confirms the new trend, for here the novelist confidently announces that 'A novel is an impression, not an argument', and the way in which the subsequent characterisation, description and atmospheric effects of this novel have affinities with the work of the Impressionists has already been extensively studied.[4]

Hardy had long been familiar with Turner – there is indeed a reference to him as early as *A Pair of Blue Eyes* (xiii). But, like Beethoven, later Turner took time to become appreciated, and as Hardy grew older he reflected his age as well as his Age, as his interest in Turner's more eccentric later compositions increased. Hardy particularly enjoyed the Turner exhibition at the Royal Academy in early 1889:

> Jan. 9. At the Old Masters, Royal Academy. Turner's water colours: each is a landscape *plus* a man's soul.... What he paints chiefly is *light as modified by objects*.... He said, in his maddest and greatest days: 'What pictorial drug can I dose man with, which shall affect his eyes somewhat in the manner of this reality which I cannot carry to him?' – and set to make such strange mixtures as he was tending towards in 'Rain, Steam and Speed', 'The Burial of Wilkie', 'Agrippina landing with the ashes of Germanicus', 'Approach to Venice', 'Snowstorm and a Steamboat', etc. (*Life*, pp. 225–6)

Turner's local effects on Hardy appear to have been slight, though the description of the Flintcomb Ash birds in *Tess* (xliii) appears to have been inspired by one of the paintings Hardy mentions here, *Snowstorm*.[5] Turner's importance for Hardy seems rather to have been of an aesthetic nature, to have given him increased confidence in developing a theory of the primacy of the artist's individual viewpoint. Perhaps, indeed, Turner, like Verdi, provided Hardy with a role model of an artist able to keep changing his style as he aged. In 1906 Hardy reflected that he preferred late Turner to early because 'When a man not contented with the grounds of his success goes on and on, and tries to achieve the impossible, then he gets profoundly interesting to me' (*Life*, p. 354). Turner's quirkiness and determination to branch out on new courses provided a precedent for Hardy to develop his own: thus he adroitly defended the historical locations of *The Dynasts* by remarking that it was 'sometimes necessary to see round corners, down crooked streets, and to shift buildings nearer each other than in reality (as Turner did in his landscapes)'.[6] In short, Hardy's development of Turner as a kind of protecting aesthetic precedent, and ideological patron before his time, allowed Hardy the confidence to develop ideas that had always been congenial to him, to emphasize the primacy of the artist's viewpoint, and to stress that art should be seen as impression not argument.

Hardy's involvement with architecture was very much of his time. With the growth in the population, the economy and the demand for buildings came the emergence of the architect as a recognisable and discrete professional. The Institute of British Architects, founded in 1834, in 1837 acquired a royal charter of incorporation; Hardy received the Institute's silver medal in 1863 and was elected an honorary fellow in 1920. The Architectural Association was likewise founded in 1847: Hardy was proposed as a member by Blomfield in 1862, and the next year won first prize in their competition for the design of a country mansion.

Hardy's writings frequently reveal his involvement with his former profession. *The Poor Man and the Lady*, *Desperate Remedies* and *A Pair of Blue Eyes* all have an architect as their hero. The lines of the buildings in Chief Street, Christminster, in *Jude* are 'as distinct in the morning air as in an architectural drawing' (III, ix), and architectural terms recur: 'Viewed sideways, the closing line of [Eustacia's] lips formed, with almost geometric precision, the curve so well known in the arts of design as the cima-recta, or ogee' (*Return of the Native* I, vii), just as Lucetta is to fling herself 'on the couch in the cyma-recta curve which so became her' (*Mayor of Casterbridge*, xxii). When Hardy was unduly driven back on his personal resources, the architectural element tended to grow in proportion. Thus *Jude*, the novel into which Hardy feared he had put too much of himself, has a mason as its hero; and *A Laodicean*, into which Hardy, fearing death, put more of the facts of his own life than he otherwise might, has yet another architect (and, indeed, more architectural matter than any other Hardy novel).

Charles Fowler, in the *Architectural Magazine* for 1835, wrote that 'The present enlightened period in architecture is woefully distinguished as having no character of its own nor any pretension beyond that of adopting the various styles that have prevailed in all ages'; the Victorian period, Nikolaus Pevsner more baldly explains, 'was the age of historicism in architecture'.[7] The most favoured historical style soon became the Gothic: 'It was always a principle that anything later than Henry the Eighth was Anathema', Hardy would recall of his early architectural years.[8] Thomas Rickman in his seminal *Attempt to Discriminate the Styles in*

English Architecture (1819), which Somerset recommends to
Paula, had not only established the periods and terms of
Gothic architecture that are still used today, but had also
given currency to the idea that Gothic was a national – and
indeed a pre-eminent – architectural style. Hence his criticism
of Wren, 'a man whose powers, confessedly great, lead us to
regret he had not studied the architecture of his English
ancestors with the success he did that of Rome'.[9]

The passion for Gothic was, however, given most force,
and an ideological basis, by the contrasting characters of
A. W. N. Pugin (1812–52) and John Ruskin (1819–1900). 'On
comparing the Architectural Works of the last three Centuries
with those of the Middle Ages', Pugin remarks in his
Contrasts (1836), 'the wonderful superiority of the latter must
strike every attentive observer.'[10] The work goes on
to provide contrasting plates, showing in a manner witty,
spirited and unfailingly partisan, modern and mediaeval
manifestations of the same building: the imposing Gothic
gateway of Christ Church, Oxford, for example, below the
less-impressive contemporary entrance to King's College,
London. Ruskin, more analytically, offered in chapter 6 of
volume II of *The Stones of Venice* (1851–3) an essay on 'The
Nature of Gothic', in which he argued that 'the characteristic
or moral elements of Gothic are the following, placed in the
order of their importance:

1.	Savageness	4.	Grotesqueness
2.	Changefulness	5.	Rigidity
3.	Naturalism	6.	Redundance.'[11]

To at least some of these terms it will be necessary to return.
Both in this work and in *The Seven Lamps of Architecture*
(1849) Ruskin drew attention to the Gothic buildings of
Verona and Venice, showing a new delight in the different
textures of materials, and, especially, in their colours. Thus
Ruskin, rather in the style of Pugin, showed in contrasting
illustrations in *The Stones of Venice* the dullness of a mono-
chrome, uniform Regency Classical stone surface compared
with a mediaeval wall in Northern Italy, which had a colour
that was inbuilt – a 'constructional polychromy', as it came
to be known.

In the Gothic architecture of the so-called High Victorians, who flourished in the 1850s and 1860s, polychromy became the main concern, achieved not only by applying paint, but also by combining different building materials. The repeal of the brick tax in 1850 and the increased availability of railway transport enabled architects to employ bricks (and especially coloured bricks) far more frequently. Hardy's interesting little contrast piece 'Architectural Masks', with its 'villa' of 'blazing brick' reflects the taste. In a less rarified genre, the Operative Bricklayers Society, founded in 1848, issued in the early 1860s a membership certificate depicting the triumph of bricklaying in Antiquity (with the Tower of Babel) and modern times (in London and Rome), all set in a framework of ornamental polychrome brickwork: at roughly the same time Hardy was writing his prize winning essay 'On the Application of Colored [*sic*] Bricks and Terra Cotta to Modern Architecture', unfortunately now lost, but clearly of a Ruskinian nature, and, as its prize winning status suggested, to the taste of the architects' official body.

Around the early 1860s, the more advanced architects began to weary of subservience to Gothic. They preferred to choose their style of architecture more freely, resulting in what has been termed High Victorian Eclecticism, or 'Progressive Eclecticism'. Styles of the past should be studied, carefully combined and adapted to the needs of the nineteenth century, varying the choice of styles from building to building, and employing not only Gothic and Classical designs but also imitations of Elizabethan, Jacobean and, most especially, Queen Anne. This anti-Gothic rebellion germinated in the office of G. E. Street, whose assistant Norman Shaw was soon to set up partnership with another adherent of Queen Anne, W. E. Nesfield. 'The Gothic Revival is dead', Shaw was later to declare.[12]

Hardy had been presented with books by both Shaw and Nesfield as his Architectural Association prize, and his novels reflect the shift in taste for which this pair were in the end to be heavily responsible. The provincial Jude, naively and newly arrived in the stonemasons' workyard at Christminster, 'did not at that time see that mediaevalism was as dead as a fern-leaf in a lump of coal; that other developments were shaping in the world around him, in which

Gothic architecture and its associations had no place' (*Jude the Obscure*, II, ii). Sue is to put him right: 'You ought to have learnt Classic', she tells him. 'Gothic is barbaric art, after all. Pugin was wrong, and Wren was right' (V, vi). Hence the house that George Somerset is to build for Paula at the end of *A Laodicean* is to be 'eclectic in style' (VI, v); and Hardy's own house at Max Gate, with its mixture of neo-Gothic and Classical ingredients, shares this predilection.

A further characteristic of Victorian architecture particularly relevant to Hardy should lastly be mentioned. Restoration involved about as much of a Victorian architect's time as the design of new buildings – more so in the case of the most pre-eminent Victorian restorer, Sir George Gilbert Scott, from whose hands Hardy had received his prize medal in 1863, and whom he was also to meet when Scott agreed to show a group of architectural students around Westminster Abbey. The mere term 'restoration' now can produce a sneer, being sometimes applied to what would nowadays be regarded as works of rebuilding, redesigning, or even total destruction. Writing in 1906 and looking back over the previous three-quarters of a century Hardy concluded that: 'If all the mediaeval buildings of England had been left as they stood at that date, to incur whatever dilapidations might have befallen them at the hands of time, weather and general neglect, this country would be richer in specimens to-day than it finds itself to be after the expenditure of millions in a nominal preservation during that period.'[13] But few knew better than Hardy that it was easy to criticise with the benefit of hindsight. The restorers were generally men of conviction, architectural and religious. They felt not only that they must preserve buildings in danger of collapse and unsuited for proper worship, but also that they were the first generation of architects to understand the Gothic. Unfortunately, however, their training led them to look for a sense of completeness and perfection in a work of architecture: they failed to understand that this was something which few mediaeval buildings, by their very nature, possessed. Ruskin, in *Seven Lamps of Architecture*, condemned this kind of restoration, and slowly a change of mind ensued. By 1877 the Society for the Protection of Ancient Buildings had been founded. By late 1889 Hardy was sending information to it, and in 1906 he prepared for them his own expiatory 'Memories of Church Restoration'.

Hardy worked principally for four architects. With John Hicks, the work was chiefly church restoration, almost exclusively in the Gothic style. The office undertook work on at least twelve local churches during Hardy's first period of employment, in one case (St Mary's, Bridport) winning the subsequent approval of Sir Nikolaus Pevsner. The London practice of Blomfield was also predominantly church-based: responsibilities given to Hardy seem to have been minor and records are scant, so that it is uncertain if Hardy was responsible for any more than minor details in the two projects with which he may definitely be associated: All Saints, Windsor, and the Radcliffe Infirmary Chapel in Oxford.

With Hardy's return to Hicks's office in 1867, and his work for Crickmay when Crickmay took over the practice after Hicks's death, it becomes far more possible to analyse Hardy's particular architectural style, and more drawings which may definitely be assigned to his hand exist. These include churches at West Lulworth, St Juliot and, in particular, Turnworth. With Crickmay too, Hardy began to diversify the kinds of building he worked on. His *Architectural Notebook* shows involvement with several projects in the Weymouth area, including schools, an eye infirmary, and some domestic work, principally on the Greenhill Housing Estate on the town's eastern edge. Hardy's last period of employment was with T. Roger Smith, assisting with the preparation for a competition for designs of London Board Schools. It seems to have been a design that was largely Hardy's own work that won the competition for Smith;[14] but, intent now on writing, Hardy declined Smith's offer of further work, though giving his surname to the hero of the novel he was currently writing, *A Pair of Blue Eyes*, and sending that hero on an architectural assignment to Bombay, where Smith himself had undertaken commissions in the 1860s.

The Builder, titling its obituary notice of Hardy 'The Master Craftsman', implied that Hardy the one-time articled assistant, continued to write with an architect's eye and pen: surprisingly, no full scale study of the topic has yet been published. The architect, after due regard to his brief and the available site, generally places the new in the context of the old, selecting overall style after considering the relationships between the building and its environment, and the building and those who are to use it. To say that Hardy's novels have much regard to buildings, their relationships with their occupiers and their environs does not make them outstandingly architectural or unique in a century which (merely to think of famous titles) could produce *Barchester Towers, Bleak House, The Mill on the Floss* and *Wuthering Heights*. None the less, it would be wrong not to note with what fulsome architectural detail Hardy enters into this tradition, as also to fail to record that the novels repeat the technique of 'Architectural Masks' in suggesting that the differing architectural styles of buildings can lead to moral conclusions about the nature of their inhabitants.

The reader, like Oak, is introduced to the Weatherbury of *Far from the Madding Crowd* via its buildings, in set-piece descriptions whose Ruskinian prejudices carefully prepare for the bias of the novel as a whole. Chapter viii opens with a description of Warren's Malthouse; chapter ix with a depiction of Bathsheba's manor house (based on Waterston Hall, where Hardy's father had undertaken work). For Ruskin, Naturalness was one of the elements of the Gothic: 'the Gothic did not arise out of, but developed itself into, a resemblance to vegetation. ... It was no chance suggestion of the form of an arch from the bending of a bough, but a gradual and continual discovery of a beauty in natural forms which could be more and more perfectly transferred into those of stone, that influenced the heart of the people, and the form of the edifice'.[16] Hardy in 'The Abbey Mason', the poem about the invention of the Perpendicular style which he dedicated to John Hicks, whimsically visualises rain as primarily responsible for the new style: the mason 'did but what all artists do, / Wait upon Nature for his cue'. Little analysis of the architectural style of the Malthouse is given the reader: what is seized on is its integration with the natural world around it: 'Warren's Malthouse was enclosed by an old wall inwrapped with ivy', the chapter immediately announces, and this close relationship between the constructed world and the natural world is soon extended to the occupier, an aged man 'now sitting opposite the fire, his frosty white hair and beard overgrowing his gnarled figure like the grey moss and lichen upon a lifeless apple tree'.

The manor house too has its moss encrustation, but here its naturalness ends. Pugin, with his extravagant moral fervour for Gothic, had declared that all Classical architecture was 'false'.[17] Hardy, capitalising on this prejudice, seems generally to place his women of doubtful morality in non-Gothic buildings – thus Lucetta Templeman's High Place Hall is precisely placed as Palladian and, 'like most architecture erected since the Gothic age', is 'a compilation rather than a design' (*Mayor of Casterbridge*, xxi).

Bathsheba's dwelling conforms to this pattern. It 'presented itself as a hoary building, of the early stage of Classic Renaissance as regards its architecture, and of a proportion which told at a glance that, as is so frequently the case, it had once been the manorial hall upon a small estate around it, now altogether effaced as a distinct property, and merged in the vast tract of a non-resident landlord, which comprised several such modest demesnes' (*Far from the Madding Crowd*, ix). A paragraph of more detailed and precise architectural description follows, including 'coped gables with finials and like features still retaining features of their Gothic extraction'. The architectural analysis ends with the speculation that the present front of the building was once its back, the transformation having been occasioned by its conversion into use as a farm. 'Reversals of this kind, strange deformities, tremendous paralyses', Hardy concludes by way of perhaps gratuitous architectural generalisation, 'are often seen to be inflicted by trade upon edifices – either individual or in the aggregate as streets and towns – which were originally planned for pleasure alone.' Bathsheba's falseness of feeling, unnaturalness and isolation, which give the narrative its momentum and part of its moral framework, are all here adumbrated: the architectural detail is used as a clear moral indicator.

This, as it were, architectural ground plan seems to have pleased Hardy enough for its elements to have been retained and extended in *The Woodlanders*. Mr Melbury, that self-torturing and ambivalent social climber possessed of 'a certain sense of exultation in the very sense of that inferiority he affected to deplore' (iv), inhabits a dwelling which, like

Bathsheba's, is Classical in style and possessed of a fundamental duality: where formerly carriages had entered products of the wood are now stacked. The syntax highlights the
ambivalence:

> The house was of no marked antiquity, yet of a well-
> advanced age; older than a stale novelty, but no canonized
> antique; faded, not hoary; looking at you from the still dis-
> tinct middle distance of the early Georgian times, and
> awakening on that account the instincts of reminiscence
> more decidedly than the remoter, and far grander, memor-
> ials which have to speak from the misty reaches of
> mediaevalism.   (iv)

On either side of this ambiguity are the dwellings of the two
invaders of the woodland, Mrs Charmond and her lover
Fitzpiers, and the dwellings of the dispossessed Giles. The
house of the unnatural Mrs Charmond, 'the wrong sort of
woman for Hintock – hardly knowing a beech from a woak'
(xxxiv), was probably based by Hardy on Turnworth House,
well known to him from his architectural work on the nearby
church. Its site is 'vegetable nature's own home', making it,
by Ruskinian canons, perfectly suited for blending in with
the Gothic. But instead the house is (like Bathsheba's)
Elizabethan in style. At war with the national instinct inside
in its pervasively French fittings, it is manifestly at war with
nature without. The dampness of the spot is 'a stimulus to
vegetation', and unlike the integration of greenery and wall
at Warren's, 'an endless shearing of the heavy-armed ivy
went on, and a continual lopping of trees and shrubs' (viii).

Where Mrs Charmond's house is foreign inside, Fitzpiers'
rented accommodation is foreign without – and here Hardy
refines the *Far from the Madding Crowd* paradigm: 'The cottage
and its garden were so regular in their plan that they might
have been laid out by a Dutch designer of the time of William
and Mary' (*Woodlanders*, xvi). The house suits Fitzpiers in that
it is simultaneously foreign and *à la mode*: the original of the
kind of style imitated by Shaw and Nesfield ('Dutch William'
or 'Low Dutch' being two of the labels first being put on it).
Ruskin identified a 'wildness of thought, and roughness of
work' as essential to Gothic.[18] Fitzpiers' dwelling is removed

from such naturalness by carefully defined tiers. Behind his manicured and regimented garden, with its 'spheres of box resembling a pair of school globes' (xvi) is his house, and 'Over the roof of the house could be seen the orchard on yet higher ground, and behind the orchard the forest trees, reaching up to the crest of the hill' (ibid.).

The stratification is all the more noticeable because of its contrast with Winterborne, who inhabits dwellings ever more natural, moving, in a kind of inversion of Ruskin, from building to bower to bough. The striking and characteristic tableau in which Grace first sees Giles depicts him in Sherton market place, beneath a ten feet high apple tree which is 'like an ensign' (v). A sign of Giles's trade, it here acts also as a symbol of his naturalness and his out-of-placeness. It also prefigures what his home will become when he frequently revisits it after Mrs Charmond has ordered its demolition in the poignant chapter xxvi: 'The apple trees still remained to show where the garden had been. . . . Apples bobbed against his head, and in the grass beneath he scrunched scores of them as he walked.' As Giles falls into meditation, the trees become his resting place – 'half-sitting, half-leaning against one of these inclined trunks' – only to be again interrupted by the invader figure as Mrs Charmond overturns her phaeton on the road nearby. This natural home anticipates Giles's next home, the cot utterly removed from the corruptions of modern society, keeping company with animals, 'neighbours who knew neither law nor sin' (xli), before he self-denyingly passes this over to Grace, retreating to 'a dwelling too slight even to be called a hovel' (xlii) – ironically paralleled by Hardy to the lumber room, full of man-made artefacts, in which Felice has attended Fitzpiers.

Hardy is of course, as would be expected of the Victorian architect, attentive to the materials of his characters' dwellings as much as to their constructional style. *Tess*, drawing heavily on Hardy's architectural past, perhaps furnishes the best example of this. The description of ancient locales makes use of Hardy's architectural experience (for example the region around 'Woolbridge Abbey', where Hardy had undertaken a commission for Hicks), just as in the Sandbourne housing estate, with its 'lofty roofs, chimneys, gazebos and towers' bordering a region of 'enormous Egdon waste' (lv), more than a reminiscence of Hardy's work on the Greenhill estate at Weymouth may be involved. In a novel charting the impact of ancient upon modern, the treatment of architectural materials significantly helps to shape the reader's response at critical moments. With Tess's arrival at The Slopes, coloured brick makes an immediate and gaudy debut:

> The crimson brick lodge came first in sight, up to its eaves in dense evergreens. Tess thought this was the mansion itself till ... the house proper stood in full view. It was of recent erection – indeed almost new – and of the same rich red colour that formed such a contrast with the evergreens of the lodge. Far behind the corner of the house – which rose like a geranium bloom against the subdued colours around – stretched the soft azure landscape of The Chase – a truly venerable tract of forest land, one of the few remaining woodlands in England of undoubted primaeval date, wherein Druidical mistletoe was still found on aged oaks. ... All this sylvan antiquity, however, though visible from The Slopes, was outside the immediate boundaries of the estate. (v)

Victorian brickwork – Hardy's speciality – is thus early assimilated into the novel's use of the colour red, with its associations of blood, danger and sexual and criminal shame; indeed 'polychrome' is a word used in the one of the novel's most celebrated symbolic set-pieces, the unnatural meeting of Angel and Tess in the Talbothays garden, where the word's man-made overtones deliberately contrast the natural colours of the weeds the word is used to describe (xix).

The novel's final chapter gives almost a reduplication of an illustration in Pugin's *Contrasts*. The opening perspective of Wintoncester is presented in the first paragraph as a kind of Puginesque ideal, a sort of lower plate from *Contrasts* suggesting ironically that in this city the ancient manages to live on uninterrupted: 'in the sloping High Street, from the West Gateway to the mediaeval cross, and from the mediaeval cross to the bridge, that leisurely dusting and sweeping was in progress which usually ushers in an old-fashioned market-day' (lix). The description is continued in the fourth paragraph from the end, with the 'more prominent buildings showing as in an isometric drawing'; but what follows in the ensuing passage is the equivalent of one of Pugin's distastefully offputting top plates. The first of Pugin's illustrated contrasts had shown as the bottom plate 'Catholic Town in 1440', the foreground of the same town in the illustration above despoiled by a modern prison on the radial plan. Hardy copies the technique exactly, and gives characteristic prominence to the ingredient materials:

> Against these stretches of the country rose, in front of the other city edifices, a large red-brick building, with level gray roofs, and rows of short barred windows bespeaking captivity, the whole contrasting greatly by its formalism with the quaint irregularities of the Gothic erections. It was somewhat disguised from the road in passing it by yews and evergreen oaks, but it was visible enough up here. The wicket from which the pair had lately emerged was in the wall of this structure. From the middle of the building an ugly flat-topped octagonal tower ascended against the east horizon, and viewed from this spot, on its shady side and against the light, it seemed the one blot on the city's beauty. Yet it was with this blot, and not with the beauty, that the two gazers were concerned.

The interpretative crux of the last paragraph – how to understand the President of the Immortals – has perhaps deflected attention away from what might be a more remarkable aspect of the novel's ending: the final chapter is moved along as much by architectural description as it is by anything else – a distinctive strategy.

Hardy's architectural training also explains his choice of settings and the way he treats them. The published works of the Brandon brothers – Hardy briefly worked for the older Brandon in 1870 – had been largely not only a glorification of Gothic but, more particularly, a recommendation of the insufficiently recognised merits of the English parish church. This they attempted to set right in the two volumes of *Parish Churches* (1848) no less than in their *Analysis of Gothic Architecture* (1847), which Hardy studied – both publications voluminously supplied with drawings made by the Brandons themselves. 'Personal inspection of the old churches of

England', the brothers advised, 'is the *only mean*, by which it can be possible now, either to appreciate the genius of our medieval architects, or to sympathize with the spirit which animated them.'[19]

With 'Drawing Details in an Old Church', 'Copying Architecture in an Old Minster' and 'While Drawing in a Churchyard' Hardy makes almost his own poetic genre-piece out of following the Brandons' advice. Novels as well as poems show a propensity for settings in churches or church-yards. Though there are fewer church scenes in *Far from the Madding Crowd* than in the three novels which precede it their weightiness is noticeable. Fanny, in a late addition to the manuscript, mistakes All Saints' and All Souls' (xvi). Oak has his comparably decisive final encounter with Bathsheba in Weatherbury churchyard, where he has also ascertained the unsuitability of Troy (xxix), and had his first meeting with Fanny (vii). Here too Troy 'almost for the first time in his life … wished himself another man' as a result of the aquatic ravages of the gargoyle on Fanny's grave (xlvi). Lengthily described in what seems almost a self-sufficient grammar of ornament, the gargoyle represents just that kind of detail that will have been Hardy's responsibility as an architect's assist-ant; characteristically he turns it into something more; in the words of one critic 'this charade – one of many in the novel – epitomizes much of Hardy's attitude to life and of his method of expressing it'.[20]

The same emotional and thematic prominence marks the church scenes of *Jude the Obscure*: Jude listening to Psalm 119 as he watches Sue in the Cathedral-church of Cardinal College (II, iii); Jude and Sue witnessing a wedding in one church in the Aldbrickham locality and then painting the Ten Commandments in another; Sue fleeing to the Church of St Silas (modelled by Hardy on a Blomfield design he knew well, St Barnabas in the Oxford suburb of Jericho); and, finally, in a re-use of the *Far from the Madding Crowd* strategy, Jude and Sue's dramatic final encounter in Marygreen Church.

Restored churches or churchyards tend to play a pre-dictably prominent part. The relocation of graves, which Hardy had experienced particularly gruesomely when super-vising work on Old St Pancras Churchyard for Blomfield

(*Life*, pp. 46–7), resurfaces wryly in 'The Two Men', humorously in the 'Memories of Church Restoration' in *Personal Writings*, and skittishly in the spirited parody-piece in Common Metre 'The Levelled Churchyard'.

Most particularly, however, it was the restoration of his native church of Stinsford, or 'Mellstock', that would involve Hardy personally and affect him emotionally. Hardy's family had been involved with the upkeep of Stinsford for many years. Though he was too young to remember the sweeping restoration of the early 1840s, its imaginative recreation forms a central part of the narrative of *Under the Greenwood Tree*; and he was probably deputed by Hicks to undertake the restoration work of 1868, involving a new roof, window alterations and the addition of a vestry. In April 1909 Hardy joined the Stinsford Church restoration committee, advising that all work should be in accordance with 'the only legitimate principle for guidance', namely 'to limit all renewals to *repairs for preservation*, and never to indulge in alterations' (*Letters*, IV, 18). In the subsequent decade, returning to the architectural notebook he had used in the 1860s, he advised on the refurbishment of the font, and again in the next decade, two years before his death, advised the vicar on the restoration of the church bells.

Arthur Shirley, who supervised both the nineteenth-century restorations of the church, sought to introduce to Stinsford the newest High Church practice – in fabric no less than in music or schooling. The changes are reflected in 'Afternoon Service at Mellstock (Circa 1850)':

> On afternoons of drowsy calm
>   We stood in the panelled pew,
> Singing one-voiced a Tate-and-Brady psalm
>   To the tune of 'Cambridge New'.
>
> We watched the elms, we watched the rooks,
>   The clouds upon the breeze,
> Between the whiles of glancing at our books,
>   And swaying like the trees.
>
> So mindless were those outpourings! –
>   Though I am not aware

That I have gained by subtle thought on things
Since we stood psalming there.

The poem, seemingly thrown-off, is precise in its frame of reference. The musical point is a clear one: 'Cambridge New' was used at Stinsford for the Tate and Brady version of Psalm 78, which discusses a man's responsibility for passing his faith on to the next generation. The poem deals with a fabric and a set of customs (as much as with a viewpoint) now outmoded. Everywhere there is unwelcome alteration. Tate and Brady the Tractarians replaced by plainchant. Stained glass the Victorian restorers preferred to the clear glass which once made the natural vistas of this poem possible; and, in conformity with best High Church practice, Shirley removed the Stinsford box pews, replacing them with benches. The poem builds up a powerful feeling of vulnerable loneliness and erosion partly by an accumulation of precisely observed contemporary detail.

What Hardy seems to have resented most in restoration work, as his fictional presentations of Mellstock Church make clear, is a concern with buildings at the expense of people. In two poems about new or restored churches, 'The Church and the Wedding' and 'Whispered at the Church Opening', new building work is associated with dearth of historical and personal sentiment. Hardy's own views on the topic are clear – indeed they may partly explain how he came to desert architecture for a calling he felt had more human interest. The argument that 'The human interest in an edifice ranks before its architectural interest, however great the latter may be' is developed in 'Memories of Church Restoration' at some length:

> The protection of an edifice against renewal in fresh materials is, in fact, even more of a social – I may say a humane – duty than an aesthetic one. It is the preservation of memories, history, fellowship, fraternities.[21]

'At the end of the lecture', the *Life* reports, 'great satisfaction was expressed by speakers that Hardy had laid special emphasis on the value of the human associations of ancient buildings ... since they were generally slighted in paying regard to artistic and architectural points only' (p. 356). As with artefacts, so with buildings, it was human associations that Hardy valued most – as the beautifully paced 'Old Furniture' makes poignantly clear.

That most of all Hardy's training in Victorian architecture exerted an influence on his style has been noticed by no one more explicitly than Hardy himself. Commenting on the adverse reception of *Wessex Poems*, the *Life* explains:

> years earlier he had decided that too irregular a beat was bad art. He had fortified himself in his opinion by thinking of the analogy of architecture, between which art and that of poetry he had discovered, to use his own words, that there existed a close and curious parallel … . He knew that in architecture cunning irregularity is of enormous worth, and it is obvious that he carried on into his verse, perhaps unconsciously, the Gothic art-principle in which he had been trained – the principle of spontaneity, found in mouldings, tracery, and such-like – resulting in the 'unforeseen' (as it has been called) character of his metres and stanzas – that of stress rather than of syllable, poetic texture rather than poetic veneer; the latter kind of thing, under the name of 'constructed ornament', being what he, in common with every Gothic student, had been taught to avoid as the plague. He shaped his poetry accordingly …
> (p. 323)

The occasion for this uncharacteristically forthright pronouncement was the critical reception of Hardy's poetry, in particular *Wessex Poems*, and the realisation, in 1919, that one of the most hurtful assessments of Hardy's poetic style, published anonymously and containing the suggestion that 'On Sturminster Foot-Bridge' was as musical as a milk-cart, had in fact been written by a well-informed critic friendly to Hardy, the essayist Robert Lynd. The revelation caused one of the few explosive items of correspondence to be found in the *Collected Letters* (v, 318–19; *Life*, pp. 323–4).

Quite what Hardy meant by this 'Gothic art principle' embodied in his work can best be analysed by reference to the architectural writings of his time. In the first instance, theorists of Gothic stressed that convention and uniformity should always be second to function and individuality. In *True Principles*, Pugin based part of his preference for Gothic architecture on practicality. A building should be designed after due regard had been given to its internal requirements. Thus a building was likely to be irregular because its individual functions demanded it: a variety of functions could never be squeezed into a symmetrical frame. 'Modern English Architecture' by H. H. Statham, an article which Hardy carefully noted, though declaring that 'it is now ebb-tide with the medieval period', held that in looking forward to post-Gothic Revival styles function should still be held paramount. 'The law of modern architectural design', Statham maintained, was to 'commence first from the basis of practical consideration.'[22] In 'Heiress and Architect', a poem Hardy dedicated to Blomfield, the immediate concern of the 'deeply skilled' architect is with the practicality of the design for its final occupants:

> 'Whatever it be,'
> Responded he,
> With cold, clear voice, and cold, clear view,
> 'In true accord with prudent fashionings
> For such vicissitudes as living brings,
> And thwarting not the law of stable things,
> That will I do.'

Conversely in Hardy's first published work, 'How I Built Myself a House', it is the client who, in this humorous *jeu d'esprit*, considers the building's functions, and the architect who shows himself oblivious to the individuality of his client's requirements. When Hardy came to build himself a house, the eclectic exterior owed much to the particularity of the internal requirements: the building, in copybook Pugin fashion, had been designed, as Michael Millgate explains with some particularity, from the inside out.[23] Ruskin, analysing 'CHANGEFULNESS or Variety', the second characteristic of Gothic, explains that Gothic builders never allowed ideas of outside symmetries and consistencies to interfere with the real use and value of what they did. 'If they wanted a window, they opened one; a room, they added one; a buttress, they built one; utterly regardless of any conventionalities of external appearance.'[24]

Michael Millgate, with the benefit of living in Max Gate, notes exactly this Gothic characteristic: 'The failure of the various parts of the front elevation to balance one with another is a direct consequence of Hardy's concern to give each window precisely the size, shape, and location demanded by the function of the room to which it belonged and by the arc of the sun at different periods of the year.'[25] The novels, and more especially the poems, have a Gothic art principle in that they care about effectiveness more than about purity of form, about individual requirements, not stultifying convention, with consequences for senses of proportion and decorum which it will be necessary to return to later.

A second essential element of the 'Gothic art principle' is imperfection. The individual workman expresses his unique personality, unhindered by the consciousness that personality is imperfect. Ruskin illustrates this argument at some length in considering the first characteristic of Gothic, Savageness. An old cathedral front for Ruskin expresses 'signs of the life and liberty of every workman who struck the stone; a freedom of thought, and rank in scale of being ... which it must be the first aim of all Europe at this day to regain for her children'. Imperfection is inherent but not shameful; for Ruskin not only concludes that *'the demand for perfection is always a sign of a misunderstanding of the ends of art'*, but also unveils the 'universal law, that neither architecture nor any other noble work of man can be good unless it be imperfect'.[26]

This Gothic doctrine of imperfection is essential to any understanding of Hardy's written style – and indeed, Hardy might have added, to any assessment of his artistic achievement – Browning's 'Rabbi Ben Ezra', with its rationale of human imperfection, was one of the pieces he asked to have read to him on his deathbed. Ruskin, further defining 'Savageness', explains how Gothic architecture necessarily avoids mathematical precision; Hardy, examining what was for him the self-defining 'uniqueness' of Gothic, speaks of 'deviations from exact geometry' which cannot be reproduced.[27] Thus Hardy's style is consistently characterised by what we may call, to use Hardy's own term, its 'cunning irregularity', knowingly and regularly acquired. Seeking to set himself up more solidly as a professional writer following the success of *Far from the*

Madding Crowd, Hardy read a number of authors ranging from Defoe to Newman as a stylistic study. The work confirmed his Gothic prejudice: 'Am more and more confirmed in an idea I have long held ... ', he noted. 'The whole secret of a living style, and the difference between it and a dead style, lies in not having too much style – being – in fact, a little careless, or rather seeming to be, here and there. It brings wonderful life into the writing ...' (*Life*, p. 108).

A poem of the 1890s provides a useful example of this 'living style':

Wessex Heights
(1896)

There are some heights in Wessex, shaped as if by a
    kindly hand
For thinking, dreaming, dying on, and at crises when I
    stand,
Say, on Ingpen Beacon eastward, or on Wylls-Neck west-
    wardly,
I seem where I was before my birth, and after death may
    be.

In the lowlands I have no comrade, not even the lone
    man's friend –
Her who suffereth long and is kind; accepts what he is
    too weak to mend:
Down there they are dubious and askance; there nobody
    thinks as I,
But mind-chains do not clank where one's next
    neighbour is the sky.

In the towns I am tracked by phantoms having weird
    detective ways –
Shadows of beings who fellowed with myself of earlier
    days:
They hang about at places, and they say harsh heavy
    things –
Men with a wintry sneer, and women with tart
    disparagings.

Down there I seem to be false to myself, my simple self
    that was,
And is not now, and I see him watching, wondering
    what crass cause
Can have merged him into such a strange continuator as
    this,
Who yet has something in common with himself, my
    chrysalis.

I cannot go to the great grey Plain; there's a figure
    against the moon,
Nobody sees it but I, and it makes my breast beat out of
    tune;
I cannot go to the tall-spired town, being barred by the
    forms now passed
For everybody but me, in whose long vision they stand
    there fast.

Here is 'cunning irregularity' on an extended scale. The
diction incorporates the biblical ('her who suffereth long and
is kind') the conversationally casual ('Say, on Ingpen Beacon
eastward'), the modernistically industrial ('mind-chains do
not clank where one's next neighbour is the sky'), and the
arrestingly idiosyncratic ('such a strange continuator as this').
This rhythm too is idiosyncratic. The lines are unusually
long, and vary between those with an exceptionally strong
pulse (as in the first stanza) and those almost prosaic in their
lack of emphasis (as in the last two lines of stanzas 4 and 5).
Rhythmically, the poem seems on occasion as though it is
about to fall apart, though the first stanza, and the balancing
last stanza (not printed here) provide a restraining metrical
frame. The rhyme scheme conforms to the same principle, the
overall *aabb* being strongly challenged by contrasts between
masculine and feminine endings, rhyme and half-rhyme. The
poem is not only an example of cunning irregularity writ
large, but also an embodiment in verse of Gothic art principles. Ruskin's check-list for the ingredients of Gothic is fully
met here: there is not just the already mentioned savageness
and variety, but also a naturalness which appears 'uncon-
strained by artistical laws', a 'Grotesqueness', a 'Rigidity' (by
which Ruskin meant energy) and lastly a 'Redundance', an

effect achieved by the 'accumulation of ornament' and animated by 'a magnificent enthusiasm, which feels as if it could
never do enough to reach the fullness of its ideal'.[28]

In many ways Ruskin's 'The Nature of Gothic' provides
one of the best stylistic companions to Hardy's work that the
analytical reader could wish for; for it is not only the poems
but also the novels that constantly show themselves capable
of Gothic analysis. As has often been noticed, Hardy's idiosyncrasy of style and technique often accounts for his most
startling successes. The 'Poems of 1912–13' offer many examples. In 'After a Journey' there is the quaint image of the stars
closing their shutters and the dictional oddity of the 'unseen
water's ejaculations', just as in 'The Voice' it is, as F. R. Leavis
has noted, the sudden and unexpected change to a quite different stanza form that clinches the poem's emotional effect.

In the novels, Gothic features are similarly prominent. 'On
the whole', *The Athenaeum* remarked in its review of *Desperate
Remedies*, 'the chief blemish of the book may be found in the
occasional coarseness to which we have alluded, and which
we can hardly further particularize, but which, startling as it
once or twice is, is confined wholly to expressions ...'.[29] The
major novels provide corresponding features, in extravagance of allusion, extremity of incident (the glow-worm-lit
gambling scene of *The Return*), and bizarreness of diction
(Angel's 'how can forgiveness meet such a grotesque –
prestidigitation as that!' in the confession scene of *Tess*
(xxxv)). Critical assessment of such features has however
developed. Such Gothic irregularities cannot now be dismissed without debate as to whether they are not local point-
ers to some part of Hardy's overall structural or thematic
plan, and hence dismissed at the reader's peril.

And here indeed is the central dilemma in any consideration of the influence of Hardy's architectural training on his
literary career. For, if it is undoubted that Hardy's second
career owed much to his first, it is undecided whether that
influence was entirely beneficial. Victorian Gothic, and its
Eclectic successors, have been perenially controversial. Even
Ruskin could see danger in the Gothic taste for accumulation
of idiosyncratic ornament; Gladstone, writing fifty-odd years
later, had more experience and less reserve:

There is [one] circumstance in architecture which terrifies me, and that is ... redundant ornamentation. There are a great many new buildings in London ... [in which] the architect had either a horror or a dread of leaving bare a single square foot of wall, as if [doing so] were something indecent.[30]

Hardy reached the zenith of his architectural practice in what was the height of the Gothic craze, at the time of the so-called 'Modern Gothic', analysed and discussed by Henry Goodhart-Rendel in a 1949 RIBA lecture, 'Rogue Architects of the Victorian Era'. These architects (William Butterfield, E. B. Lamb, S. S. Teulon, F. T. Pilkington, E. Bassett Keeling and Thomas Harris) represented Victorian Gothic at its brashest and most idiosyncratic. Harris defined 'Steam power and electric communications' as 'entirely new revolutionary influences'. 'So must it be in Architecture', he concluded, justifying how his contemporaries felt a need for 'an indigenous style of our own.'[31] This style was controversial at best. One critic found Teulon's designs 'original, but in some points rather deficient in reserve'; another found the whole Rogue School mere 'architectural rant', defined as 'the perpetual forcing into notice of the personality of the architect'.[32] The school had a characteristic emphasis on self-expression, achieved via idiosyncrasy of style, particularly in emphasis on ornament, with a resulting unease of relationship between the parts of the building and the whole.

The student of Hardy's writing, let alone the observer of any of his architectural productions, cannot help noticing what Hardy has in common with these so-called Rogue Architects. Bassett Keeling's much-criticised design for the Strand Music Hall – with its roof of wrought iron and zinc, and its cast iron columns with copper foliations on their capitals – was the architectural talking point of 1864 – and, conveniently for Hardy, just round the corner from Blomfield's office. It was attacked by conventional Gothic architects – Gilbert Scott and his school – for 'eclecticism ... eccentricity ... vulgarity ... and ... coarse hugeness'.[33] But it seems to have exerted a peculiar fascination over Hardy, who studied carefully its descriptions in the *Builder* and *Building News*.[34]

Hardy's architecture, like that of the Rogue Gothics, is distinctive not only in the quantity of its attention to the individuality of its parts but also in respect of how fully those parts blend into the whole. The corbels at Turnworth and the turrets of the Greenhill Housing Estate (echoed in the turrets with which Hardy ornamented Max Gate: 'two hideous low-flanking turrets with pointed roofs of blue slate', as A. C. Benson described them),[35] are conscious of their own distinctiveness, but not always confident of their contribution to the overall plan: the parts are unconscious of the whole. This is most true of the little owl sketched in Hardy's architectural notebook, and found on a pillar at Turnworth: it is unusual, individual, but altogether out of place: unassimilated in an overall plan and unconscious of its own, highly unecclesiastical failure to fit in. The failure is one of consciousness of proportion within an overall idea of plan – like the over-heavy details of the Turnworth font, which looks as though the weight of its Ruskinian leaf-mould will cause it to fall over. Each reader needs to decide for himself how far this architectural habit is carried over into literary practice, how much *Jude* should be considered as a series of polychromatic episodes rather than a homogeneous whole, or poems like 'Wessex Heights' and 'In Tenebris I–III' regarded as self-indulgently eccentric, as their lines, seeming almost overgrown, tumble off the end of the page.

For T. S. Eliot, however, the fault of excessive self-expression that conventional Gothic architects objected to in the Rogues became in *After Strange Gods* the basis for a criticism of Hardy as a whole:

> He seems to me to have written as nearly for the sake of self-expression as a man well can; and the self which he had to express does not strike me as a particularly wholesome or edifying matter for communication. He was indifferent even to the prescripts of good writing: he wrote sometimes overpoweringly well, but always very carelessly; at times his style touches sublimity without ever having passed through the stage of being good ... .[36]

Eliot's swingeing criticism (which he subsequently regretted) is in part the Modernist reacting against the Victorian: the

Gothic values that Hardy had espoused Eliot puts to the pen. That impression of carelessness that for Hardy was something to cultivate is for Eliot a subject of condemnation; that Ruskinian tenet that the artist should not be afraid to express himself because the imperfection at the heart of him was grounds for glorification not embarrassment is here dismissed.

Hardy's response to the architecture of his time is, then, of a different kind from his response to contemporary art and music. His interest in the latter was keen but essentially amateur, and could therefore remain independent and selective. By contrast, his experience of architecture was professional, and the consequences of his thorough training were not easy to avoid. Response to Hardy's architecture, and its influences, remains, like response to Victorian architecture as a whole, more than usually a matter of taste. The balanced student may reasonably wish to conclude that if Hardy's architectural training assuredly influences some of the best of Hardy's writing, it might also be accountable for some of the worst.

6

'Time / Part steals, lets part abide':* The Critics of Thomas Hardy

Hardy's critical fortunes have been various. To chart their chronological development is instructive, and readers are recommended to accounts by the witty and balanced Richard H. Taylor in Norman Page's excellent anthology *Hardy: The Writer and his Background* (1980) and the drier, wide-ranging erudition of Charles Lock's *Thomas Hardy: Criticism in Focus* (1992). This chapter takes a topical rather than temporal approach, and examines seven points that have proved consistent cruxes in attempts at assessing Hardy. These are Hardy and experience; Hardy and texts; Hardy and theme; Hardy and tradition; Hardy and genre; Hardy's modesty; and Hardy and reputation. There is no attempt at a comprehensive survey of all that has been written about Hardy. But at the same time most major surveys will be mentioned – and some particularly recommended for the interested student.

More than many other authors, Hardy has excited attempts at discovering the sources for his writing. The problem is a complex one. The formal realism defined as being inherent in the novel begins the matter – as Valentine Cunningham expresses it, 'In a sense, "originals" are what the novel, especially the Victorian novel, is all about.'[1] Hardy himself is an acute example of this, since there is a particularly difficult relationship between fact and fiction in his writing. 'I find it a great advantage to be actually among the people described at the time of describing them', he wrote as early as 1874 (*Letters*, I, 27), and the reflection was a wise one. 'Hardy's best work', Michael Millgate authoritatively comments, 'tends to

* From 'I Look into My Glass'.

156

have strong and specific roots in his own background and experience. Their absence is generally a cause of failure.'[2]

None the less Hardy's attitude towards revealing the models for his work was dualistic, inconsistent – sometimes, it must be said, macro-economic with the truth. On the one hand, Hardy stimulated interest in the physical background to his books; on the other, he constantly tried to shut off interest in the personal. Topographical studies met with his blessing; biographical endeavour provoked his displeasure.

Hardy's notion of Wessex was gradual, not fixed. Only in the 1880s did Wessex as a region begin to become a coherent concept for him, and, for various reasons, it gained strength thereafter. Revisions of the novels reveal this process. The Osgood McIlvaine collected edition of 1895–7 is of particular significance, since it offered Hardy the chance to revise all his fiction from a common standpoint. It gave him the opportunity to see his work as a whole *oeuvre*, 'to place each work in the pattern of existence that Wessex had become for him', as Simon Gatrell, the expert on the topic, expresses it.[3] Thus the Heath of *The Return of the Native* had until this time been (not altogether inappropriately) in its own geographical limbo, without point of topographical reference to other Hardy novels or locations, barring only Eustacia's Budmouth aspirations. In the 1895 edition, however, the original adjoining town of Southerton has altogether disappeared, and the references to it are altered miscellaneously to Casterbridge, Anglebury and Weatherbury, locations familiar to the reader of other novels. 'What was once of mysterious extent and of shifting definition is now a limited tract of land any tourist can tramp over', Gatrell comments.[4]

Such indeed is partly the point. The 1895–7 collected edition contained at the front of each volume a map of 'Wessex'. In the same decade tourists began to take up Hardy's work as guidebooks to the region, a process which Hardy teasingly encouraged. 'In respect of places described under fictitious or ancient names – for reasons that seemed good at the time of writing –', the 1895 Preface to *Tess* explains, 'discerning persons have affirmed in print that they clearly recognize the originals.... I shall not be the one to contradict them.' Then, with an eye to sales, Hardy began in the early years of this century actively to co-operate with those who wished to provide topographical handbooks. The greatest assistance was given to Hermann Lea, with his *Handbook to the Wessex Country of Mr Thomas Hardy's Novels and Poems* (1905) and *Thomas Hardy's Wessex* (1913), both of them brought up to date in Denys Kay Robinson's *Hardy's Wessex Reappraised* (1971). Such publications are fun, especially for the tourist, but their critical value is debatable. Doubtless many Hardy readers enjoy the sensation of entering a discrete fictional world – or picking up a toy train. But one exercise may not be critically all that more informative than the other. As the judicious Richard H. Taylor succinctly expresses it: 'The real Hardy country is off the map and in the mind.'[5]

The relationship between Hardy's biography and his writing is a more complex and exacting topic. 'The human mind is a sort of palimpsest I suppose; and it is hard to say what records may not lurk in it', Hardy told William Archer for his *Real Conversations* (1904).[6] Missions to find the source of Hardy's writings in his experience have been various. *The Life of Thomas Hardy*, 'by Florence Emily Hardy', is simultaneously where the interested reader has to start and where he should not: it has the *imprimatur* one most looks for yet much mistrusts. With it, Hardy attempted to deter biographers by rendering their task superfluous; ironically, he probably succeeded only in making their sniff for a skeleton more keen.

The interested reader cannot be without this book; the intelligent reader should not neglect a detached perspective on many of its pronouncements. 'To your enquiry if *Jude the Obscure* is autobiographical I have to answer that there is not a scrap of personal detail in it, it having the least to do with his own life of all his books', the *Life* dutifully quotes (p. 425). The efforts of biographers have shown that there is as much to mislead here as there is in Hardy's presentation in the *Life* of other novels and events. Both in overall story and in supporting detail much of *Jude* was incontrovertibly suggested by elements of Hardy's own family history. His uncle John Antell, a Puddletown shoemaker, driven to drink and an early grave as a result of lack of access to a proper education, certainly lies behind the hero; whilst Sue's supporting names, Florence Mary, probably acknowledge the influence Florence Henniker and Mary Hardy had on the evolution of her personality. The detail of the writing shows the same underlying debts: when Jude quotes his favourite passages from the *Iliad*, these are Hardy's own, as can still be found by any student who cares to turn to them in the back of Hardy's copy, preserved in the Dorset County Museum.

The additional acknowledgement of the *Life*, that 'speaking generally, there is more autobiography in a hundred lines of Mr Hardy's poetry than in all the novels' (p. 425), says in this altered perspective far more than Hardy might have wished as to what the poems may themselves contain. At face value, the poems about Emma's death do of course provide an informative commentary on Hardy's reaction to one of the most important events of his life; studied more deeply they also reveal how little his poems should be relied upon to provide a factual record. 'Best Times' speaks sentimentally in printed editions of Hardy's relationship with Emma, even in its final phase. 'And that calm eve when you walked up the stair, / After a gaiety prolonged and rare' is a distorted version of Emma's last night alive. Heavily deleted from the manuscript is the more laborious 'climbed' instead of 'walked up', revealing Emma's acute physical pain; and instead of the 'gaiety prolonged and rare' the altogether more mundane 'After a languid rising from your chair'. Other examples would be easy to furnish. But using the poetry as no more than a biographical source book is a method sterile and unproductive, reducing to detective work what is, as we shall see, far more demanding as a problem of literary appreciation.

A large number of eyewitnesses left accounts of Hardy's personality or of visits to Max Gate. The most substantial collection is *Illustrated Monographs on the Life, Times and Works of Thomas Hardy* (1962–71) gathered together by J. Stevens Cox, and containing accounts some personal, some insightful, some wrong-headed, some detailed, yet never, to the real enthusiast, irrelevant, from contributors as diverse as parlour-maids, barbers, gardeners, favourite drivers, doctors and producer's daughters, Henry Moule, Gertrude Bugler and Lady Cynthia Asquith. More polished fare, but as yet unpublished as a collection, are the accounts left by distinguished writers. Particularly good examples in differing genres are Virginia Woolf in *A Writer's Diary* (1959, entry for 25 July 1926, beginning 'At first I thought it was Hardy and it was the parlour-maid, wearing a proper cap'); T. E. Lawrence in a letter of 8

September 1923 to Robert Graves; Graves's own account in the autobiographical *Good-bye to All That* (1929); and Siegfried Sassoon's poem 'At Max Gate':

> Old Mr Hardy, upright in his chair,
> Courteous to visiting acquaintance chatted
> With unalert aloofness while he patted
> The sheep dog whose society he preferred.
> He wore an air of never having heard
> That there was much that needed putting right.
> Hardy, the Wessex wizard, wasn't there.
> Good care was taken to keep him out of sight.
>
> Head propped on hand, he sat with me alone,
> Silent, the log fire flickering on his face.
> Here was the seer whose words the world had known.
> Someone had taken Mr Hardy's place.

The proposed publication of an edited selection of such reminiscences by James Gibson in the Macmillan *Interviews and Recollections* series will release a particularly welcome and useful volume.

Full-scale biographies have been mixed in their achievement. Early biographers frequently suffered from a lack of supporting scholarly endeavour, though the studies by Edmund Blunden (1942) and W. R. Rutland (1938) more than compensate for this by their other virtues. In modern times, the principal three biographies have been those by Robert Gittings, in *Young Thomas Hardy* (1975) and *The Older Hardy* (1978); Michael Millgate's *Thomas Hardy: A Biography* (1982); and Martin Seymour-Smith's *Hardy* (1994). Gittings writes with a professional author's speed, a literary enthusiast's freshness, a historian's sense of period, and a canny energy for demythologising. Many of the same virtues can be found in Seymour-Smith's exceedingly long, sometimes randomly melodramatic and conjectural, but always redeemingly enthusiastic and crusading study. One would not wish to be without either book for its provoking viewpoint; at the same time, both might be misleading if allowed to become the only source of information.

Millgate's biography represented a new approach and a new fidelity of achievement. From the late 1970s onward, scholarly materials useful for the biographer as for the critic at last came to be published in numbers. Millgate himself co-edited with R. L. Purdy Hardy's *Collected Letters* in seven volumes (1978–88), scrupulously edited, and followed by *Thomas Hardy: Selected Letters* (1990) for those without the interest and fortitude to face all the details of the sorting of domestic arrangements and the acknowledgement of presentation copies of books. Lennart Björk completed the identification and publication of Hardy's *Literary Notebooks* (1985), an indispensable if also copiously detailed guide to Hardy's reading; and Samuel Hynes added critical (1982–5) and James Gibson variorum (1979) editions of the poems to the growing number of reliable editions of the texts of the novels. Thus for the reader anxious to be allowed to reach his own conclusions about Hardy, the materials at last came conveniently to exist. Not, however, that anyone need fear a distorting bias in Millgate. *Thomas Hardy: a Biography* seems unlikely soon to be surpassed for accuracy and fair-mindedness, not to mention balance and elegance of style: for any one requiring a biography, this is undoubtedly the first recommendation, just as Millgate's edition of the *Life* now represents the authoritative source for that text. 'Hardy's writing, no less than his life, possesses a kind of innerness and privateness into which criticism can only blunder', John Bayley had warned in the 1970s.[7] Millgate's comprehensive attention to Hardy at last provided a sensitive and sympathetic guide to the inner man and the outer achievement.

An alternative biographical-cum-critical approach has been to look at the literary products in aggregate, and to deduce from this the major concerns present in Hardy's life and mind, following his own admission that 'the characters, however they may differ, express mainly the author'.[8] A surprising critical starting point is Proust: in *A la recherche du temps perdu* Marcel explains to Albertine that '*les grands littérateurs n'ont jamais fait qu'une seule oeuvre* [great writers have only ever written a single work]'. The conversation looks for examples to Hardy, and the similarities between *Jude, The Well-Beloved* and *A Pair of Blue Eyes*.[9] The topic is one that has naturally lent itself to discussion in journal articles. In what is probably the most famous of these, J. O. Bailey identified a series of 'Mephistophelian Visitants' in figures such as Venn,

Farfrae, and Dare (of *A Laodicean*), who have diabolical over-tones and invade otherwise secluded regions in such a way as to disrupt their stability.[10]

Richard J. Beckman's 'Character Typology for Hardy's Novels' argues that 'the main characters in any one novel form a logically complete set of archetypal human natures' and suggests that such characters display four main kinds of response to the world, which may be related to the four seasons.[11] Thus in *The Mayor* (from which Beckman's thesis is principally illustrated), Henchard's hot summer cannot last, Lucetta languishes in an exotic autumnalism, Farfrae shows vernal opportunism, and Elizabeth-Jane, who is closest to winter, proves the best survivor of vicissitudes. Those who wish further to study the ramifications of Hardy's confession to William Archer that 'In character drawing several similar individuals will merge into one type',[12] can find stimulating alternative schemes discussed by Lascelles Abercrombie, D. H. Lawrence, Lord David Cecil, Peter J. Casagrande and Albert J. Guerard.[13]

Hardy's publishing history has perhaps been even slower than biographical study to reach any kind of maturity. The easiest area of focus is on the bowdlerisations required by editors in serial publication of Hardy's fiction. Studies of these, prompted by complaints in the *Life*, go as far back as those by J. W. Beach (1921) and Mary Ellen Chase (1927).[14] In common with other Victorian novelists, Hardy wrote in the first instance for serial publication: we no longer read his fiction in the format for which it was initially intended. The results of serial demand are twofold: superfluity of incident and superfluity of purity. The view of the *Life* on *The Mayor* is clear:

> It was a story which Hardy fancied he had damaged more recklessly as an artistic whole, in the interest of the news-paper in which it appeared serially, than perhaps any other of his novels, his aiming to get an incident into almost every week's part causing him in his own judgement to add events to the narrative somewhat too freely.   (p. 185)

Purity caused more widespread problems. The Reverend Donald Macleod, editor of *Good Words*, the magazine in which *The Trumpet-Major* first appeared, gave Hardy a representative account of what the serial writer should supply:

> We are anxious that all our stories should be in harmony with the spirit of the Magazine – free at once from *Goody-goodyism* – and from anything – direct or indirect – which a healthy *Parson* like myself would not care to read to his bairns at the fireside. Let us have as much humour (oh that we had more!) and character – as much manly bracing fresh air – as much honest love-making and stirring incidents as you like – avoiding everything likely to offend the susceptibilities of honestly religious and domestic souls.
>
> Do forgive this homily! But we have had such bothers in the past in consequence of a want of clear understanding beforehand on matters like this that I think it best to be frank.[15]

Problems with Macleod, however, and with Hardy's other editors – even Leslie Stephen – there almost invariably were. In the end it is difficult to avoid the conclusion that, if only subconsciously, Hardy sought out dispute with them; for it is unlikely that his *naïveté* could have extended to thinking that some of his story matter would pass their scrutiny. In the last analysis such disputes must have been amongst the reasons for Hardy ceasing to write fiction. *Tess* was rejected by three publishers, the first of them having already set some of it in type, and much altered at various stages at the behest of a fourth, Arthur Locker of the *Graphic*. Hardy published two passages in a separate form (the description of the baptism of Sorrow as 'The Midnight Baptism' and the Trantridge Dance episode as 'Saturday Night in Arcady'), and yet still found himself with further alterations required. Angel carrying the milkmaids across the flooded road in his arms was deemed too suggestive, and so in the serial he adopts the agency of a conveniently positioned wheelbarrow. Textual changes to the novel (though Hardy was less anxious to draw attention to this point) were also prolonged by other considerations. The Chaseborough Dance episode first appeared in printed versions of the novel as late as 1912, the reason being not Mrs

Grundy, but rather Hardy's desire to achieve 'a good commercial stroke' by an advertising stunt, as a letter to
Macmillan makes plain.[16]

Detailed studies of Hardy's textual history are beginning to
make possible better-informed judgements of the cruxes in
the novels. Does Eustacia meet with an accident or choose
suicide at Ten Hatches Weir? What did happen between
Henchard and Lucetta in Jersey? How sexually knowing is
Grace? Is Tess raped, seduced or willing? On all these issues it
is clear that Hardy, like his readers, expended much thought,
and the study of the changes he made in the course of the
novels' development and reprints at last allows critics to
reach more informed judgements.

The characterization of Farfrae provides a useful example.
The first-time reader of *The Mayor* may end up confused: is
Farfrae Henchard's unwitting or willing destroyer? How
much should one's sympathies be engaged by him? The
development of the text shows that Hardy intended the
reader to be bothered by this uncertainty, and that he increasingly wished Farfrae to be judged in an unsympathetic light.
Changes in the one-volume edition of 1886 are small but
telling, and draw attention to the implications of the Scottish
nationality of Farfrae, much stressed in the subsequently
written Preface, which Hardy progressively filled out from
1895–1912. Farfrae understandably has an interest in the
Casterbridge corn and hay trade. In all previous versions of
the text, we are told that 'with his native sagacity he saw
honest opportunity for a share' of it. But in 1887, and all subsequent editions, the word 'honest' was omitted, a change
small enough to have escaped the editor of the novel's most
authoritative edition, but with a large enough consequence
for what the informed Hardy reader will make of Farfrae's
method and motivation. Likewise, when, at the end of the
novel, Elizabeth-Jane and her husband are searching for the
dying Henchard on Egdon, an observation from Farfrae
added to the 1887 one-volume edition clinches the argument:
overnight accommodation 'will make a hole in a sovereign' –
the fact that this is exactly the amount that Newson paid
towards the skimmity ride increases the ironic reference of
the remark, suggesting almost a callousness about destruction
in Farfrae.

In the first Collected edition published by Osgood McIlvaine in 1895, further ironic perspective on Farfrae's sentimentality is provided. Previously Farfrae had sung at the festivities after his marriage to Elizabeth-Jane merely 'a song of his native country' (xliv). But in 1895 this became 'a song of his dear native country, that he loved so well as never to have revisited it'. As full critical editions of the novels, and studies of them, become available, Hardy's readers stand to be far more fully enlightened as to the patterns of his mind and the nature of his authorial intentions. R. L. Purdy's *Thomas Hardy: A Bibliographical Study* (1954) remains the standard reference work. Particularly informative detailed studies of individual texts are John Paterson's *The Making of 'The Return of the Native'* (1960), and J. T. Laird's *The Shaping of 'Tess of the d'Urbervilles'* (1975). Simon Gatrell has been involved with the issuing of scholarly texts for both the Clarendon and World Classics editions of Hardy, and hopes that in due course a collected critical edition of the fiction may appear – though exactly what version of the novel such an edition would in each case use as a copy text makes the project fraught with fundamental uncertainty. In the meantime Gatrell's *Hardy the Creator* (1988) makes use of the editing experience to provide what he calls a 'textual biography', and this informative book currently forms the best introduction to the novels' textual aspects.

'Why!' Robert Graves claimed Hardy had said to him, 'I have never in my life taken more than three, or perhaps four, drafts for a poem. I am afraid of it losing its freshness.'[17] If scholarly endeavour has shown the statement to be somewhat ingenuous, Hardy's secrecy with his manuscripts has ensured that the textual truth about some poems will never be known. Hardy's doubts about whether certain poems (for example the controversial 'Panthera') should be published are documented in his published correspondence, but the scale of the negotiations never reached that common with serial versions of the novels. What the variorum editions of Hynes and Gibson do, however, allow the reader to glimpse is the skilful professionalism characteristic of Hardy's poetic craft. According to Gibson, three of Hardy's most famous poems, 'Beeny Cliff', 'Afterwards' and 'During Wind and Rain', are particularly good for watching Hardy the textual reviser at work. The publication of Emma Hardy's *Some Recollections* had already enabled identification of the origins of many of the experiences to which the last of these poems refers. But a comparison of the manuscript and succeeding printed versions allows a far more profitable glimpse of the meticulousness with which Hardy revised his work:

During Wind and Rain

They sing their dearest songs –
He, she, all of them – yea,
Treble and tenor and bass,
    And one to play;
With the candles mooning each face ...
    Ah, no; the years O!
How the sick leaves reel down in throngs!

They clear the creeping moss –
Elders and juniors – aye,
Making the pathways neat
    And the garden gay;
And they build a shady seat ...
    Ah, no; the years, the years;
See the white storm-birds wing across!

They are blithely breakfasting all–
Men and maidens – yea,
Under the summer tree,
    With a glimpse of the bay,
While pet fowl come to the knee ...
    Ah, no; the years O!
And the rotten rose is ript from the wall.

They change to a high new house,
He, she, all of them – aye,
Clocks and carpets and chairs
    On the lawn all day,
And brightest things that are theirs ...
    Ah, no; the years, the years;
Down their carved names the rain-drop ploughs.

An examination of the last line of each stanza reveals how carefully Hardy worked to achieve a concluding effect. 'How the sick leaves reel down in throngs' replaced 'How the sickened leaves drop down in throngs'; 'See, the white storm-birds wing across' was simplified from 'See, the webbed white storm-birds wing across'; 'And the rotten rose is ript from the wall' substantially improved on 'And the wind-whipt creeper lets go the wall'; and 'Down their carved names the rain-drop ploughs' added considerable resonances to the original 'On their chiselled names the lichen grows'.

Hardy's theme, or his grand theme, is the next aspect of controversy to be considered. 'The invasion of the realm of metaphysics', Herbert Grimsditch wrote in 1925, 'is the most outstanding characteristic of Thomas Hardy's art, whether in prose or verse.'[18] E. M. Forster, in his seminal *Aspects of the Novel* (1927), seized on this as the particular of Hardy he could most interestingly dwell on. For Forster, what was 'eminent and memorable in the Wessex novels' was 'the fate above us, not the fate working through us'. This was, indeed, not just an overriding theme but an all pervasive flaw: Hardy, Forster suggested, had 'emphasized causality more strongly than his medium permits'.[19]

Analysis of this perhaps excessively pessimistic sense of what can most conveniently be called fate, with much attention to its background in various philosophies and in Classical aesthetics, has consistently been a part of Hardy criticism, especially in its earlier years. Lascelles Abercrombie, in his *Thomas Hardy: A Critical Study* (1912), related Hardy's achievement to his love of Sophocles, comparing his work to classical tragedy. The American scholar W. L. Phelps in his *Essays on Modern Novelists* (1910) remarked that 'The pessimism of Mr Hardy ... makes the world as darkly superb and as terribly interesting as a Greek drama.' Phelps additionally noted the possibility of a debt to Schopenhauer, which was enlarged on in works by Helen Garwood (1911) and Ernest Brennecke (1924)[20] which particularly drew Hardy's displeasure. W. R. Rutland's *Thomas Hardy: A Study of his Writings and their Background* (1938) and Harvey C. Webster's *On a Darkling Plain: The Art and Thought of Thomas Hardy* (1947) are wider-ranging and hence avoid that pitfall so frequent in approaches to Hardy, of grasping out for some consistent underlying philosophical scheme, rather than recognising Hardy's writing as dramatised searchings for one. Ironically, just such a scheme can famously be found in a work dedicated to a wider theme, John Holloway's *The Victorian Sage* (1953), which perhaps deserves to be seen as the finest product of this largely deterministic critical school.

Holloway sees Hardy as a man with a 'sense of the unalterable sequence of things'.[21] Essentially he puts to one side Hardy's overt pronouncements on religion and philosophy, preferring to examine the texture of what he writes. He particularly focuses on Hardy's view of Nature, which he claims presents 'a system of rigid and undeviating law'.[22] Society as presented by Hardy is but a microcosm of nature. Hardy's work thus contains a widely pervasive and highly distinctive 'sense of what the world is like and how it functions', a strong feel of 'a determined system of things which ultimately controls human affairs without regard for human wishes'.[23] Much of the argument is conducted via an intelligent and sensitive study of Hardy's imagery. In *Tess*, for example, Holloway seizes on what he calls '*proleptic* images; they hint at the whole determined sequence of things'.[24] Examples are the novel's sequence of images of wounded or caged birds, or dairyman Crick's fork, 'planted erect on the table like the beginning of a gallows' (xviii). By such means Hardy does not have to reason out an argument, but more effectively creates an impression of man's insignificant and ineffectual position in the general scheme of things.

Though it would be unfair to deny the force of Holloway's argument, and impossible to doubt its analytic skill, it is now undoubtedly far less possible than before to entertain exclusively an approach to Hardy of the deterministic kind once so popular. No study has done more to bring this about than Roy Morrell's *Thomas Hardy: The Will and the Way* (1965), a book of refreshing originality and vigour. Still less widely known than it should be, the book has retained well its challenging tone. Morrell stresses the extent to which Hardy's characters do have free will and are presented with choice: their decisions are of course a reflection of their character, but no reader should under-estimate the extent to which their character determines their fate. Again *Tess* is scrutinised. Chapter 3, 'A Note on "The President of the Immortals"', analyses this most famous phrase from the last chapter, a last-minute addition to the manuscript. 'Through this slight blunder', Morrell argues, 'Hardy's reputation has suffered out of all proportion to its seriousness.' Morrell's distinctive contribution is to view the phrase as ironic, and to argue that the 'irony ... is aimed, at least partly, against the reader':[25]

> 'Some people, God help them, may still suppose,' Hardy is saying, 'like Aeschylus long ago, or like Joan Durbeyfield, shifting the blame from her own shoulders, that fate can be blamed for Tess's disaster. The reader may wish to believe this too: but surely I have shown where the real blame lies.'[26]

This blame, Morrell argues, is with Alec and Angel, with Tess's family, with Victorian morality and society and, let it not be forgotten, with the faults of personality present in Tess herself. The same trend of thought is seen also in other novels. Eustacia blames 'some indistinct colossal Prince of the world' (*Return of the Native*, IV, viii) rather than herself. Henchard, gambling on his luck, puts himself into Fate's hands, and then blames Fate instead of himself. In the same novel Hardy, quoting George Eliot's *Mill on the Floss* (in which Eliot in turn was quoting Novalis), remarks that 'Character is Fate' (*Mayor of Casterbridge*, xvii). Since Morrell's book, no self-respecting critic of Hardy has been able to neglect the prominence of the idea. On the one hand, it is still possible to share Lord David Cecil's view that always Hardy 'conceives man in relation to ultimate human destiny'.[27] But on the other, since Morrell, the kind of critic who could write 'The philosophy Hardy worked out was a tragic one with Fate ruling a superstitious group of people who believed in witchcraft and sorcery and were for ever seeking the aid of witches and conjurors if fortune served them ill' has seemed haplessly flat-footed and outmoded.[28]

'All we can do is to write on the old themes in the old styles, but try to do a little better than those who went before us', Robert Graves also claimed that Hardy had told him,[29] and the remark is sufficiently consonant with other pronouncements by Hardy to ring true: 'There is no new poetry; but the new poet ... comes with a new note', the *Life* remarks (p. 322). Both in his life and in his work Hardy was acutely conscious of tradition, of the tread of each generation on its predecessor. How he relates to the styles of writing that he inherited, and – more particularly – how he was assessed by the writers who came after him is central to any appreciation of his status.

That not all writers should have found Hardy to their taste is hardly surprising. But that so many distinguished writers should have seen Hardy's status as so paltry is unusual, and demands some exploration. The critic F. R. Leavis assumes a special importance here. Less a Cambridge don than a luminous cultural missionary whose dicta could not by his substantial apostolic body be challenged, Leavis was to important sections of succeeding generations an influential arbiter of taste. Leavis was not afraid – indeed he relished it as part of his role – to place some writers on pedestals above others. 'The great English novelists are Jane Austen, George Eliot, Henry James and Joseph Conrad',[30] *The Great Tradition* (1955) announces in its opening sentence. Dickens this book discounts as merely 'a great entertainer' (Leavis later recanted), whilst Hardy is summarily dismissed with a quotation from Henry James: 'The good little Thomas Hardy has scored a great success with *Tess of the d'Urbervilles*, which is chock-full of faults and falsity, and yet has a singular charm.'[31] Likewise Leavis's survey *New Bearings in English Poetry* (1932) sidelines Hardy as 'a naive poet of simple attitudes and outlook',[32] granting major status to Eliot, Pound and Gerard Manley Hopkins. Leavis's judgements perhaps represent the acme of the difficulties felt by Modernists with Hardy's work. Eliot (as we have seen) scorned Hardy; Forster belittled him; and for many it was Leavis who managed finally to cast Hardy out. Leavis's rejection of Hardy thus represents not merely the personal judgement of one critic but also a whole set of values and traditions in English creative and critical writing. Modernism was suspicious of just that communication with the masses in which Hardy managed to excel – for John Carey in his study of Modernism, *The Intellectual and the Masses* (1992), this is what links Leavis with the creative writers of the period.

Many critics would now see Hardy rather than Conrad or James as the pivotal novelist between Eliot and Lawrence. Virginia Woolf, indeed, twinned the two authors excluded by

Leavis – Dickens and Hardy – as 'unconscious writers', who 'seem suddenly and without their own consent to be lifted up and swept onwards', in a way quite different from the Continental, more distinctively crafted and self-conscious methods of James or Flaubert.[33] Failure to link Hardy to Lawrence involves negligence of Lawrence's extraordinary 'Study of Thomas Hardy', written in 1914, but not published in its entirety until the posthumous *Phoenix* (1936). 'It will be about anything but Thomas Hardy', Lawrence promised,[34] but the disclaimer is only partly true, for with sprawling energy and utter conviction of insight Lawrence is, by Chapter 3, prepared for his analysis of Hardy's art:

> This is the tragedy of Hardy, always the same…. This is the theme of novel after novel: remain quite within the convention, and you are good, safe, and happy in the long run, though you never have the vivid pang of sympathy on your side: or, on the other hand, be passionate, individual, wilful, you will find the security of the convention a walled prison, you will escape, and you will die, either of your own lack of strength to bear the isolation and the exposure, or by direct revenge from the community, or from both. This is the tragedy, and only this … .[35]

If the essay is uneven in its focus it is even more inconsistent in its judgement. At one moment Lawrence is fulminating 'let it be said again that Hardy is a bad artist',[36] at another he will be reverently picking out some subliminal quality which he argues Hardy shares only with Shakespeare, Sophocles and Tolstoy. But the inconsistency is not one that should be criticised. The 'Study' is Lawrence's attempt to cope not only with the disbelieving anger engendered in him by the First World War, but also by the attempt to separate *The Rainbow* from *Women in Love*. It is a challenging, at times exasperating, but ultimately unique example of all that the critical exploration of one writer can do for the creative achievement of another. The Hardy student is unlikely to find any more attractive *bonne bouche*.

Thomas Hardy and British Poetry (1973), an influential book by the poet and critic Donald Davie, represents another interesting point of cross-reference to Leavis's critical tradition, and another example of a creative artist working out his own methods via the examination of those of Hardy. Davie argues that 'in British poetry of the last fifty years (as not in American) the most far-reaching influence, for good and ill, has been not Yeats, still less Eliot or Pound, not Lawrence, but *Hardy*'.[37] The italic is an expression of Davie's surprise and concern. Yeats represents for Davie an approach to creativity and content irreconcilably at odds with that of Hardy, and Davie's masterful analysis of Hardy's style, along with his examination of poems by Lawrence, Auden, Larkin, Tomlinson and Fisher, leads him to regret Hardy's influence as being greater than that of Yeats, for 'in most of the senses of "great" as we apply it to poets, Hardy is not a great poet at all'.[38] Davie puts forward several reasons for this. A chief limiting factor is Hardy's modesty. This is the modesty of 'the expert technician, imperious within his expertise, diffident or indifferent outside it'. Hardy is a kind of engineer with words rather than a poet, a 'triumphant technician' or 'honest journeyman' rather than a craftsman or major intellectual. It limits his subject matter, preventing him from tackling 'Major issues of national policy'.[39]

The poem which Davie fastens on for analysis is 'Overlooking the River Stour', one of Hardy's reflections on the Sturminster 'idyll', in which the poet realises how even at this time he neglected to cultivate a proper relationship with his wife:

> The swallows flew in the curves of an eight
> >   Above the river-gleam
> >   In the wet June's last beam:
> Like little crossbows animate
> The swallows flew in the curves of an eight
> >   Above the river-gleam.
>
> Planning up shavings of crystal spray
> >   A moor-hen darted out
> >   From the bank thereabout,
> And through the stream-shine ripped his way;
> Planing up shavings of crystal spray
> >   A moor-hen darted out.

Closed were the kingcups; and the mead
　　Dripped in monotonous green,
　　Though the day's morning sheen
Had shown it golden and honeybee'd;
Closed were the kingcups; and the mead
　　Dripped in monotonous green.

And never I turned my head, alack,
　　While these things met my gaze
　　Through the pane's drop-drenched glaze,
To see the more behind my back … .
O never I turned, but let, alack,
　　These less things hold my gaze!

Davie sees the poem as a first-rate example of Hardy's
'cunning irregularity':

> The symmetries, stanza by stanza, are all but exact to begin
> with; once we know that the occasional inexactitude is no
> less engineered, 'engineered' seems more than ever the
> only word to use. Once again there is an analogy with
> Victorian civil engineering, which topped off an iron
> bridge or a granite waterworks with Gothic finials, just as
> Hardy tops off his Victorian diction with an archaism like
> 'sheen' or 'alack'. Within its historically appropriate idiom,
> the poem is 'a precision job'; that is to say, its virtuosity is
> of a kind impossible before conditions of advanced
> technology.[40]

The poem is then used to develop Davie's argument that
there is in Hardy a major deficiency in 'the quality of his
attention to experience and the poetic rendering of it',
making the poetry and the poet a 'sort of cop-out, a modest
(though proudly expert) workman in a corporate enterprise
which from time to time publishes a balance sheet called *The
Golden Treasury* or *The Oxford Book of English Verse*'.[41] Parts of
the argument will already be familiar to the reader from the
discussion in Chapter 2 of 'The Last Signal', Hardy's tribute
to his friend William Barnes, who is presented there as a
neighbour, to be described using techniques dear to him, not
elevated into some kind of vatic seer. Davie, so expert here as

elsewhere – especially in his masterful essay 'Hardy's Virgilian Purples' (1973)[42] – in his analysis of Hardy's poetic technique, has to conclude damningly that Hardy's achievement represents 'a crucial selling short of the poetic vocation, for him and for his successors'.[43]

Other writers and poets have taken the reverse of Davie's view. As Davie himself explains in his poem 'Hawkshead and Dachau in a Christmas Glass', 'At Dachau, Yeats and Rilke died'; so that, in the Hardy allusion of another poem, ('Remembering the Consequence'), 'A neutral tone is nowadays preferred.'[44] Not all postwar tastes in tradition have been those of Davie. This perhaps particularly applies in the case of one of Hardy's most influential postwar champions, the poet Philip Larkin. In 'Wanted: Good Hardy Critic' in the *Critical Quarterly* (Vol. 8., 1966) Larkin did not claim to be responding to his own advertisement. There was indeed no need, for here as elsewhere he showed himself Hardy's unashamed champion, even including 'The Sunshade' in his *Oxford Book of Twentieth Century English Verse*, where Hardy was accorded more poems than any other author. 'May I trumpet the assurance that one reader at least would not wish Hardy's Collected Poems a single page shorter', Larkin wrote (in defiance of the statement of Leavis that only twelve poems stood out from Hardy's output), 'and regards it as many times over the best body of poetic work this century so far has to show.'[45] As early as his second volume of verse Larkin chose to replace Yeats by Hardy as his poetic mentor; and his biographer, the poet Andrew Motion, states that this dilemma 'represents, in miniature, that struggle between two literary traditions which has dominated English poetry for the last sixty odd years'.[46] Writing in the *Listener* to mark the fiftieth anniversary of Hardy's death, Larkin explained the reason for his choice:

> What I like about him primarily is his temperament and the way he sees life. He's not a transcendental writer, he's not a Yeats, he's not an Eliot; his subjects are men, the life of men, time and the passing of time, love and the fading of love.[47]

In other words, just that unassuming ordinariness which Leavis and Davie objected to was for Larkin (as for others) a source of attraction, and acknowledged by them as a tradition to which they wished to attach themselves.

The sources of such a tradition are studied by the poet and critic John Powell Ward in *The English Line* (1991). This 'Line' Powell Ward takes to be predominantly Wordsworth, Clare, Hardy and Frost, though he also analyses Tennyson, Arnold, Coleridge's conversation poems, Owen, Edward Thomas, Housman, MacNiece, and the Movement poets, especially Larkin. The canons of Leavis and Eliot are spurned, Powell Ward for example pointing out that the poets examined in *New Bearings in English* [sic] *Poetry* are two Americans and an English Catholic. Taking his cue from Motion and the American Hardy critic Samuel Hynes, Powell Ward claims that the Englishness of the line he sees 'lies in the verbal reserve and the pragmatic and laconic suspicion of the visionary or the extravagant, for which the English were commonly renowned'. From Wordsworth through to Larkin, poets of Powell Ward's English line have insisted on the ordinariness of their language, and have tended also towards ordinariness in their subject matter, displaying what Powell Ward calls a characteristic 'vocational pessimism' whilst striving to create, in a phrase taken from J. S. Mill's appreciation of Wordsworth, 'poetry of the unpoetic'.[48]

The roots of the tradition go deep – as deep as the mediaeval English lyric in Hynes's view, or *Piers Plowman* and such Old English elegies as 'The Wanderer' and 'The Seafarer' in the view of Powell Ward. For Hynes, quoted as one of Powell Ward's epigraphs, this is 'the principal tradition in English verse'. Even for the less partisan, it is a powerful reminder that there are more ways of looking at Hardy than that of Leavis.

In a highly simplistic but none the less useful way, two traditions of looking at Hardy can be identified in the last sixty years, as the above opposition makes plain. On the one hand, devaluers of Hardy can be centred around Leavis, with his topographical-cum-intellectual sphere of influence centred on Cambridge, and his tastes centred on a tradition more likely to appeal to those with Modernist and cosmopolitan sympathies. On the other, there is a group of poets and critics associated with the more conservative traditions of English promulgated at Oxford, with its historical approach and compulsory reference back to Anglo-Saxon literature and culture. Major influences here have been the critics Lord David Cecil, with his highly readable *Hardy the Novelist* (1943), and John Bayley, in the less approachable but if anything more influential *Essay on Hardy* (1978); and a series of poets all educated at Oxford and championing Hardy: Edmund Blunden with his urbane and balanced critical biography *Thomas Hardy* (1942); the poet laureate Cecil Day Lewis, whose marks of respect range from his excellent introductory lecture to 'The Lyrical Poetry of Thomas Hardy' (1951) to the request that he too should be buried in Stinsford churchyard; the brief critical essays by Larkin; and the unusual *Thomas Hardy: The Poetry of Perception* by Tom Paulin (1975), which relates Hardy backwards to the empirical philosophers Hume and Locke, forwards to poets such as Larkin and Grigson, and in doing so provides a kind of halfway point in the Larkin–Davie disagreement.

Despite Hardy's enthusiasm for the University Boat Race, traditions of Hardy criticism are too multifarious to be presented simplistically and blinkeredly as some kind of clash of light- and dark-blue blades. In the United States, for example, Hardy's reputation has been far more broadly based than in this country: as one commentator has expressed it 'not only Ransom and Tate, but also Robert Penn Warren, James Merrill, Harold Bloom, John Hollander and J. Hillis Miller have published work on Hardy that shares little beyond the distinction of its authors'.[49]

Many excellent works clearly owe nothing to any camp – not least because what distinguishes all camps is how difficult they find it to embrace all of Hardy's variety. Thus J. Hillis Miller in his seminal *Thomas Hardy: Distance and Desire* (1970) concludes that it is impossible to talk of any idea of Hardy himself, only of the voices that he assumes. Sharing several ideas with Miller is Jean R. Brooks's *Thomas Hardy: The Poetic Structure* (1971), one of the most thought-provoking books the Hardy student can read. It aligns Hardy not backwards with Wordsworth or Shelley or Browning, as this study has tended to do, but forwards to the French existentialists, Sartre and Camus, and to Beckett:

Often in Hardy's world, as in Samuel Beckett's, nothing happens, nobody comes, nobody goes, as a glance at some of his titles may indicate – 'A Commonplace Day', 'A Broken Appointment', 'Nobody Comes', 'You were the sort that men forget'. Yet, like Beckett, Hardy extracts significance from the insignificant.[50]

Brooks's book has been influential on a new strain of criticism that is just emerging and claiming that it will force Hardy scholarship into a radical reappraisal of itself. The key force here is Peter Widdowson, author of *Hardy in History: A Study in Literary Sociology* (1989) and editor of the *Tess* volume (1993) in the Macmillan New Casebook series, which is designed to illuminate 'the rich interchange between critical theory and critical practice that characterises so much current writing about literature'[51] – that is, to reflect the change brought about in literary thinking by structuralism and subsequent ideological developments. Highly intelligent and fluently articulate in a language which commands study, Widdowson is certainly a breath – perhaps even a rush – of fresh critical air. He is particularly judicious in the prominence he gives to feminist approaches, which, in studies such as Penny Boumelha's *Thomas Hardy and Women* (1982) and Rosemarie Morgan's *Women and Sexuality in the Novels of Thomas Hardy* (1988), have suggested an especially vigorous area of study for future years.

Like Brooks, Widdowson stresses that 'Hardy was indeed a contemporary of the Modernists', 'an *anti*-realist, challenging and demystifying the limits and conventions of realism and humanist essentialism'.[52] He is highly dismissive of previous Hardy criticism, especially in its failure to achieve this perspective. Whereas previous attempts to fit Hardy into traditions have generally failed, Widdowson feels that he is now able to offer the concept of a 'disruptive postmodern Hardy' which is 'nearer the mark'. Post-structuralist criticism, most obviously in deconstruction, he explains, 'has re-emphasised textuality as the primary concern of criticism', and it sees the text as 'a fissured, riven, deranged, unstable linguistic terrain'.[53] Hardy's texts are, he argues, particularly suitable for this kind of analysis. Feminist and post-structuralist initiatives have at last enabled readers to appreciate 'the dynamically unstable textuality of Hardy's fictional writing: its plural discourses and competing styles, its irony, mannerisms and self-deconstructing artificiality, its self-conscious vocabulary and modes of address, its language of tension'.[54] Accordingly Widdowson concludes by offering us a new 'faithful presentation' of *Tess*:

> Hardy's novel, then, well ahead of its time, seems to be dismantling the bourgeois-humanist (patriarchal and realist) notion of the unified and unitary human subject, and to be doing so by way of a discourse so self-reflexive and defamiliarising about representation, so unstable and dialogical, that it deconstructs itself even as it creates. Which is why, I believe, we can justly discover a contemporary post-modern text in *Tess of the d'Urbervilles*.[55]

Firmly rooted in the novel, and quoting persuasively from it as well as from Hardy's writings about his methods, Widdowson's essay represents a fascinating and utterly convincing version of the text. It is harder, however, to see that it says anything radically new, however obvious it may be to observe that it prides itself on having found a rather complicatedly new way of saying it. A précis of the paragraph above might suggest that *Tess* is a novel conscious that it represents a series of impressions, not an argument. Here there is nothing new, though much that is fundamental. And the same pertains throughout Widdowson's discourse. Re-reading Virginia Woolf's essay 'The Novels of Thomas Hardy' (1928), it is striking how many of Widdowson's supposedly novel ideas are lucidly anticipated. 'Certainly it is true to say of him that, at his greatest, he gives us impressions; at his weakest, arguments', Woolf writes of Hardy.[56] She acknowledges that he will not conveniently fall into any tradition of great novelists, that he is highly unorthodox in his treatment of probability and in terms of his style. She even focuses on the same phrase as Widdowson, 'moments of vision', in her attempt to define Hardy's technique. But the difference is of course in style. Woolf's essay was to be collected in *The Common Reader*, and here is a concept of audience Woolf bears constantly in mind. Widdowson writes, rather, with regard to a university readership. Writing in a volume that bears Widdowson's influence, the 1993 issue of *Critical Survey* devoted to Hardy, the editor Roger Ebbatson argues that 'Only through a fundamental unsettling of the canon, by recovering some of the allegedly "minor" works and by re-viewing some of the "major" texts, can we begin to produce those multiple Hardys necessary to a fuller understanding both of textuality and of our rural history.'[57] Two assumptions are important here. First, the critical cart is now before the creative horse. Hardy is there to service theory. As John Lucas writes in the last essay in the volume, 'contemporary writing has cancelled the privilege that was formerly attached to works called "literary works". Now there is only writing and most of that writing is criticism.'[58] Secondly, any idea that some of Hardy's novels are superior to others is frowned upon. Here, there is a thrust that might bring about a revolution in the way Hardy is looked at. Ironically, however, such a change is probably to be determined by that general reader on whom recent criticism, for all its political protestations, is, at any rate in its terminology, generally happy to turn its back.

Hardy and genre is the penultimate point of controversy. Is he a poet? Is he a novelist? Is he both? Is he neither? The responses to Hardy of the early reviewers are well documented in *Thomas Hardy: The Critical Heritage* (1970), edited by R. G. Cox, and *Thomas Hardy and his Readers* (1968), edited by Laurence Lerner and John Holmstrom. Early reviewers were disadvantaged through having known Hardy the poet first as Hardy the novelist, and frequently blundered accordingly. Thus the *Saturday Review* for 7 January 1899 approached Hardy 'predisposed to respect' on account of the novels, but greeted his first volume of verse harshly:

> as we read this curious and wearisome volume, these many slovenly, slipshod, uncouth verses, stilted in sentiment, poorly conceived and worse wrought, our respect lessens to vanishing point, and we lay it down with the feeling strong upon us that Mr Hardy has, by his own deliberate act, discredited that judgement and presentation of life on which his reputation rested.[59]

Unmelodiousness, the lack of what the *Saturday Review* termed a 'singing voice', frequently wrong-footed reviewers until gradually Hardy's distinctive style came to be better understood. Hardy's friend Edmund Gosse, recording a tribute to Hardy in March 1928 (transcription published 1968), explained that:

> To early readers of his poems, before the full meaning of them became evident, Hardy's voice sounded inharmonious, because it did not fit with the sophisticated melodies of the later Victorian age. But he did not attempt to modify his utterance in the least; and now we can all perceive that what seemed to himself harsh in his poetry was his peculiar and personal mode of interpreting his thoughts.[60]

Thus it has eventually become possible to see Hardy not as novelist in one compartment and poet in another separate one (as too many university exam papers encourage) but as the distinctive and all-but-unique poet-novelist which enlightened observers, sometimes perhaps more from good manners than intuitive judgement, have observed all along. William Stebbing, as *The Times* leader writer ever accustomed to the middle thought, expressed just this idea when writing to thank Hardy for his birthday greetings:

> Lover – all my life – as I am of poetry, I do not wonder at your preference for writing it; but let me say, that always, before I knew (as I well know now) of you as thus writing, I had read the Poet in the charm of your prose.[61]

Recognition of Hardy's special status as some kind of generic hybrid is now a central tenet of Hardy criticism. Leslie Stephen, recalling 'the poetry which was diffused through the prose' in *Far from the Madding Crowd*, and recognising 'the same note' in his autographed copy of *Wessex Poems*, perhaps passed the idea on to his daughter Virginia Woolf, who, as already mentioned, saw in the novels the moments of vision which gave their title to one of the collections of poems.[62] The result of such a critical thrust has been to dispose of ideas of Hardy as, on the one hand, a novelist *manqué*, a George Eliot who could not quite manage her formal realism, and on the other, as a poet debilitatingly hungover with a certain prosaicness acquired from his previous career.

A crucial volume here was the summer 1940 edition of the *Southern Review*, a celebration of the hundredth anniversary of Hardy's birth. The championing of Hardy's poetry by W. H. Auden helped force on a widespread critical revaluation. 'I cannot write objectively about Thomas Hardy because I was once in love with him', Auden admitted, with a characteristic mixture of outrageousness and whimsy in his metaphor. 'Hardy comforted me as an adolescent, and educated my vision as a human being, but I owe him another and, for me personally, an even more important debt, of technical instruction.'[63] Less rhetorically but still more influentially, perhaps, in an essay entitled 'Hardy in Defence of his Art: the Aesthetic of Incongruity', M. D. Zabel analysed a common principle underlying both novels and poems. In this essay, helpfully reprinted in the excellent *Twentieth Century Views* volume on Hardy (ed. Albert J. Guerard, 1963), Zabel identified Hardy as 'a realist developing toward allegory ... an imaginative artist who brought the nineteenth-century novel out of its slavery to fact'. Hardy is thus seen as a conscious anti-realist, 'the contemporary, in other words, of Baudelaire, Flaubert, and Turgenev, of James, Moore, Yeats, Proust, Pound, Valéry, and Eliot, but a colleague of none of them' – a writer never afraid to heighten reality symbolically, even if the effect can appear overwrought and grotesque to conventional tastes, always a poet by nature, if often a prose writer by medium.[64]

This theme the student can find continued, as already mentioned, in the fine study by Jean Brooks, as well as in A. J. Guerard's *Thomas Hardy: The Novels and Stories* (1949, revised 1964) and Richard Carpenter's *Thomas Hardy* (1964). Hardy, modest to some eyes, paranoically self-protective to others, at different times feigned indifference to his achievement in either genre. 'I never cared very much about writing novels', he remarked in the course of his discussions with Vere H. Collins for the latter's *Talks with Thomas Hardy at Max Gate, 1920–22* (1928).[65] 'Well: the poems were lying about, and I did not quite know what to do with them', he remarked to Gosse after the publication of *Wessex Poems* (*Letters*, II, 208). In fact,

Hardy must now be seen as an author who remarkably trans-fused two genres. Ezra Pound's famous statement may lack arithmetical skill and chronological knowledge, but its insight, of course, still holds: 'Now *there* is clarity. There *is* the harvest of having written twenty novels first.'[66]

'Hardy's double achievement is stupendous', an amplified Lord David Cecil agreed, telling his totally full and largely nodding audience at a Thomas Hardy Society summer school that 'He is one of the very great English writers.'[67] Hardy's reputation may indeed end up as such, but all it is fair to be certain about will be that it has aroused an unusually wide spectrum of disagreement. 'In the past fifty years Hardy has spanned the entire range of readers as no other writer', Charles Lock remarks in his general survey.[68] Certainly the Public Lending Right Office reports Hardy at the head of its list of the top thirty classic authors borrowed from public libraries (followed by Tolkien, Dickens, A. A. Milne, Jane Austen, D. H. Lawrence and Trollope). But such statistics should not of course have any conclusive weight against critical convictions, deeply and persuasively held, like those of R. S. Thomas:

> Hardy, for many a major
> Poet, is for me just an old stager,
> Shuffling about a bogus heath
> Cob-webbed with his Victorian breath.[69]

The discrepancy is no nearer resolution because of contin-ued disagreement as to what should be regarded as Hardy's best work. As already stated, there is a wide gap between those who see Hardy's poetic output as hugely uneven and those (like Larkin) who would not be without a single poem – a difficulty expressed and perhaps exacerbated by the fact that no single anthology has yet been agreed on as pre-eminent. The picture is little clearer with the fiction. On the one hand, most critics (like Hardy's once-exclusive pub-lisher Macmillan) have been happy to place novels into a premier league and distinct also-rans. Until the publication of the New Wessex edition of 1975–8, indeed, purchasing a new copy of *Desperate Remedies*, *A Pair of Blue Eyes*, *The Hand of Ethelberta*, *A Laodicean*, *Two on a Tower* or *The Well-Beloved* was all but impossible. Only with the loss of copyright did copies become widely available and paperback editions of that minor fiction now so refreshingly recommended for reconsideration by post-structuralists come on to the market.

In addition, within the more commonly accepted texts, critical opinion remains divided on relative merits. In what is probably the best single book on Hardy's fiction, Michael Millgate's *Thomas Hardy: His Career as a Novelist* (1971), *Tess*, which Henry James had found so 'chock-full of faults and falsity' is identified as 'unmistakably' Hardy's finest novel.[70] Other critics, thinking the later novels overwrought, argue that in fact Hardy developed little if at all for the better after his early work. Thus Charles Lock can conclude that *Far from the Madding Crowd* is considered 'by a number of both early and recent critics' to be the best of the novels, whilst in the first issue of the *Critical Quarterly* (1959) John F. Danby remarked of *Under the Greenwood Tree* that 'already in 1872 it says as much as Hardy will ever be able to say, and maybe in a form more satisfactory than any he later devised'.[71]

Views of Hardy's style are seldom far removed from the polarities of critical assessments of his status. Driffield, the author figure in Maugham's *Cakes and Ale* (1930), for a long time thought to be based on Hardy, may indeed share one of his features:

> He was for long thought to write very bad English, and indeed he gave you the impression of writing with the stub of a blunt pencil.[72]

James found Hardy's style 'ingeniously verbose and redundant', and Blunden referred to its 'inartistic knottiness'. Day Lewis, criticising Leavis for condemning Hardy's 'gaucherie, compounded of the literary, the colloquial, the baldly prosaic, the conventionally poetical, the pedantic and the rustic', himself in the next breath had to admit that 'Often Hardy seems to lose all touch with his medium, and will dress up his subjects in the shoddiest, reach-me-down verse.'[73] A kind of totem of this stylistic controversy has been Hardy's use of allusion. Edmund Blunden's blunt impatience does not seem unforbearing:

He often adorns his page with a brief allusion to classical learning. Does it help? No. The reader cannot be expected to hunt up these references in order to do what his author should have done if he set out to enrich and illustrate a plain tale at all.[74]

On the other hand, the most complete modern survey of the topic, Marlene Springer's not always convincing *Hardy's Use of Allusion* (1983) argues that Hardy 'out-alluded virtually every allusionist, – not only in substance but in skill as well'.[75] Frequently, the honest critic has to confess that he does not know where he or the author stands. Can it really so casually be the case, as Robert Gittings seems pretty persuasively to suggest, that when in later editions of *The Return of the Native* Hardy wished to alter an allusion to the mediocrity of mind of Bishop Sumner (an attribute of which he had learnt in the *Saturday Review*), he simply substituted the name of the previous Bishop of Winchester, Tomline, rather than search for a prelate of comparably indifferent intellectual capacities?[76] Eustacia as some 'Queen of Night' has likewise often seemed to critics arbitrary or, more harmfully, overblown. Yet in his new critical study, *Thomas Hardy and the Proper Study of Mankind* (1993), no less careful a critic than Simon Gatrell argues persuasively for its integral relevance.[77]

The discrepancies of opinion over what Hardy was trying to achieve – over his technical proficiency, as indeed of his status as a whole – are in the end all the more difficult to resolve because there has always been fundamental disagreement over his personality, and yet at the same time discussion of that personality has been the frequent recourse of many a critic seeking to analyse Hardy's greatness. The circle is a full and vicious one. 'Any critic can, and often does, see all that is wrong with Hardy's poetry, but whatever it was that makes for his strange greatness is much harder to describe', wrote Irving Howe in his highly capable general survey *Thomas Hardy* (1967). Like so many critics, especially early ones of the poetry, Howe is driven back on suggesting that the power of the personality and the merits of the *oeuvre* are inextricably mixed. 'Can there ever have been a critic of Hardy', he asks despairingly, 'who, before poems like "The Going" and "During Wind and Rain", did not feel the grating inadequacy of verbal analysis, and the need to resort to such treacherous terms as "honesty", "sincerity", and even "wisdom"?'[78]

The same dilemma affected Day Lewis. 'Personalities as a rule should be kept out of the criticism of poetry', he accepted. 'But it is extraordinarily difficult, and possibly undesirable, to dissociate Hardy's poetry from his character.' Thus Lewis's final judgement of Hardy the author was in essence a judgement of Hardy the person. The poems are praised because they 'offer us images of virtue ... breathe out the truth and goodness that were in him, inclining our own hearts towards what is lovable in humanity', thus in a way confirming Hardy's assessment, quoted by Day Lewis, that 'The ultimate aim of the poet should be to touch our hearts by showing his own' (*Life*, p. 131).[79] Woolf's judgement of the novels was in many ways the same: they are 'a vision of the world and of a man's lot as they revealed themselves to a powerful imagination, a profound and poetic genius, a gentle and humane soul'.[80]

Such assertions are awkward. Not for nothing do the *Literary Notebooks* contain a lengthy *Times Literary Supplement* review of Bridges' *Demeter: A Mask*, a clear demonstration of Hardy's interest in how the author could conceal his own personality in the way Sassoon had noted at Max Gate. Perhaps it was modest to place self-effacing poems such as 'He Resolves to Say No More' at the end of volumes of verse. But there is something about the regularity of the gesture – whatever the delectability of the resultant anthology pieces – that fails to ring true; indeed grates. What is the tone of the penultimate poem of *Late Lyrics and Earlier*, 'After Reading Psalms XXXIX, XL, etc.'? The quotations from the psalms seem on the one hand skittish, on the other as though Hardy is quite happy to draw his reader's attention to all that he has accomplished, to mark himself out as one of the literarily chosen. Robert Gittings's biography, in a more practical fashion, exposed (too strongly for some tastes) the more ungenerous side of Hardy's personality, the diary-destroyings and manuscript burnings, and the poems less as literary units than as items of biographical shame, generated by 'profound remorse' since 'His full guilt was too horrible to face.'[81] 'This was the rather tremendous truth about Hardy; that he had humility', Chesterton remarked in his *Autobiography* (1936), but he followed it with a repetition of the allegation that had given Hardy so much offence, that he possessed the 'sincerity and simplicity of the village atheist'. 'He was the most touching old dear I have ever seen', another visitor to Max Gate, Frances Cornford, reported; but he added the highly perceptive rider, 'I never saw anyone so modest, or so needing appreciation.'[82]

In the last analysis, the problem with Hardy is one of comprehension in a double sense: a difficulty in *understanding* Hardy which results from the extreme difficulty of *encompassing* the number of influences on him. Hardy bemuses his critics. 'Will the real Mr Hardy stand up?', asked the editor of a critical edition of *Far from the Madding Crowd*, commenting on the difficulty of detecting a coherent pattern in Hardy's development of the text of the novel.[83] He is notoriously craggy and uneven, yet undeniably possessed of certain consistent features: 'The worst chapter of *The Hand of Ethelberta* is recognizable, in a moment, as written by the author of the best chapter in *The Return of the Native*', Gosse perceptively remarked.[84] As Richard Taylor concludes in his splendid survey of Hardy's critics:

> the poet-novelist resists the conventional moulds and the geometrical rule of easy definition... . At the beginning and in the end, there is only one experience of remarkable reward: with the imperative urgency of Pound's exhortation for Eliot – READ HIM.[85]

Yes, Hardy bemuses his critics – but few have explicitly done what perhaps they ought, and thanked Hardy for it. More than anything else, perhaps, Hardy's challenge, what John Bayley has called his 'baffling status as a great writer',[86] is the source of his appeal. He refuses to fit easily into one period, to one reputation, to one tradition, to one personality, to one assessment of his merit – and so the problem for this chapter is how finally to fit him into it. The answer must be that it can't. In matter, as in manner, Hardy is protean. He is too multiform ever satisfactorily to be tidily placed. The critical task is, in that sense, impossible. Lance St John Butler, in a recent review, puts the problem clearly:

Changing Hardy changes on in the ineluctable counter-points of cultural history. When we need a universal mind, Hardy is there contemplating the universe; when we need the local, there is Hardy too, the local historian; when we need a quintessentially English voice (because, for example, we are at war again) Hardy is standing by to provide it.... We are presented with more and more Hardys: the feminist Hardy, the post-structuralist Hardy of course but also the Hardy who dropped out of sight during the 'critical waste-land between 1940 and 1963', the marginal Hardy, the crypto-socialist Hardy. In all cases we are forced to ask why the various short periods that have succeeded each other since, say, the 1890s have produced or made for themselves such very different versions of the work of the Sphinx.[87]

But Sphinx, in matter as in manner, Hardy has always been. Since this chapter has taken Hardy way out of his time, the best critical strategy may be to return Hardy to it, and to end with the earliest critical comment of all, with John Morley's assessment for Macmillan of that Hardy novel we no longer have, *The Poor Man and the Lady*. Hardy moved on from it, but criticism can profitably move back to it, and see, in the Hardy it has been deprived of, much of the Hardy it has since been bafflingly familiar with:

> A very curious and original performance: ... much of the writing is strong and fresh. But there crops up in parts a certain rawness of absurdity that is very displeasing, and makes it read like some clever lad's dream: the thing hangs too loosely together. There is real feeling in the writing, though now and then it is commonplace ... .[88]

Biographically, Hardy's beginning was almost Hardy's end; critically, Hardy's end may conversely not be so very differ-ent from Hardy's beginning. 'An Ancient to Ancients', by the several Thomas Hardys, writers in their times, gives good advice:

> And ye, red-lipped and smooth-browed; list,
> Gentlemen;
> Much is there waits you we have missed;

Much lore we leave you worth the knowing,
Much, much has lain outside our ken:
Nay, rush not: time serves: we are going,
    Gentlemen.

Chronological Table

1840   Born at Higher Bockhampton.
1846   Corn Laws repealed.
1847   Opening of railway from Dorchester to London.
1848   Enters school at Lower Bockhampton. Chartism finally collapses.
1850   Transfers to Isaac Last's school in Dorchester. Death of Wordsworth.
1851   Great Exhibition.
1854   Outbreak of Crimean War.
1856   Articled to the Dorchester architect John Hicks.
1857   Joseph Conrad born.
1859   Publication of Darwin's *On the Origin of Species*.
1860   Publication of *Essays and Reviews*.
1862   Departs for London, working there for Arthur Blomfield, and immersing himself in a programme of self-study as well as the life of the capital.
1863   Death of Thackeray.
1865   'How I Built Myself a House' published in *Chambers's Journal*. Bicycle invented.
1866   J. S. Mill presents first Women's Suffrage Petition to parliament.
1867   Returns to Dorchester to work for Hicks. Second Reform Act increases suffrage.
1868   *The Poor Man and the Lady* submitted unsuccessfully for publication.
1870   Meets Emma Lavinia Gifford whilst undertaking an architectural commission in Cornwall. Death of Dickens. Education Act extends provision of elementary education.
1871   *Desperate Remedies* published.
1872   *Under the Greenwood Tree* published.
1873   *A Pair of Blue Eyes* published. Suicide of Hardy's friend Horace Moule.

1874   Publication of *Far from the Madding Crowd* allows
        Hardy the financial stability to marry Emma Lavinia
        Gifford.
1876   Publication of *The Hand of Ethelberta*. Acquire for the
        first time a house to themselves, at Sturminster
        Newton. *The Return of the Native* written here, and the
        marriage enters its happiest period. Invention of tele-
        phone and phonograph.
1878   Publication of *The Return of the Native*. Moves to
        London, making the acquaintance of literary society,
        but also becoming dangerously ill.
1880   Death of George Eliot. Publication of *The Trumpet-Major*.
1881   Publication of *A Laodicean*.
1882   First petrol engine constructed. *Two on a Tower*
        published.
1884   Third Reform Act extends suffrage to virtually all
        adult males.
1885   Moves into Max Gate, a house on the outskirts of
        Dorchester designed by himself.
1886   Publication of *The Mayor of Casterbridge*.
1887   Publication of *The Woodlanders*.
1888   First book of short stories, *Wessex Tales*, published.
1891   Publication of *A Group of Nobles Dames*; and of *Tess of
        the d'Urbervilles*, after problems of censorship.
1892   Death of Hardy's father.
1894   *Life's Little Ironies* published.
1895   *Jude the Obscure* published, to some public outcry. The
        novel's treatment of the marriage theme does little to
        improve Hardy's increasingly troubled relations with
        Emma.
1897   *The Well-Beloved* published, the last of Hardy's novels
        to appear in book form.
1898   *Wessex Poems* published, to general critical puzzle-
        ment.
1899   Outbreak of Boer War.
1900   Labour Party founded.
1901   Death of Queen Victoria.
1902   *Poems of the Past and the Present* published.
1904   Death of Hardy's mother. *The Dynasts* begins publica-
        tion (third and last volume published 1908).
        Britain begins considerable expansion of its fleet.

1905 Einstein's *Special Theory of Relativity* published.

1909 *Time's Laughingstocks* published. Death of Meredith leaves Hardy in a clear position of eminence amongst English authors.

1910 Receives the Order of Merit.

1912 The Wessex edition of the novels begins publication. Death of Emma Hardy gives rise to a lengthy period of mourning, revisiting of old haunts, and composition of expiatory poems.

1913 Publication of last volume of short stories, *A Changed Man and Other Tales*.

1914 Marries his former secretary, Florence Dugdale. Publication of *Satires of Circumstance*, including the 'Poems of 1912–13', commemorating Emma. Outbreak of First World War. Hardy agrees to write for the allied cause.

1915 Death of Hardy's sister Mary.

1917 *Moments of Vision*, including 'Poems of War and Patriotism', published.

1918 Limited female franchise granted in Britain.

1919 Rutherford achieves a transmutation of atomic elements.

1922 Publication of *Late Lyrics and Earlier*, for which Hardy had prepared an introductory 'Apology'.

1923 Publication of *The Famous Tragedy of the Queen of Cornwall*.

1925 Publication of *Human Shows*.

1928 Dies at Max Gate. Ashes buried in Westminster Abbey; heart interred in Emma's grave at Stinsford. *Winter Words* published posthumously.

Notes

INTRODUCTION
1. *Literary Notebooks*, ed. Lennart A. Björk (London, 1985) vol. I, p. 194.

CHAPTER 1   THE LIVES OF THOMAS HARDY
1. Lord Macaulay, 'Sir James Mackintosh', *Critical Historical and Miscellaneous Essays* (Boston, Mass., 1878) vol. III, p. 279.
2. A. P. Stanley, *The Life and Correspondence of Thomas Arnold*, 12th edn (London, 1881) vol. II, p. 110.
3. Michael Millgate, *Thomas Hardy: A Biography* (Oxford, 1982) p. 37.
4. Lascelles Abercrombie, *Thomas Hardy: A Critical Study* (London, 1912) p. 63.
5. Millgate, *Biography*, p. 301.
6. Ibid., p. 356.
7. Charles Lock, *Critism in Focus: Thomas Hardy* (London, 1992) p. 18.
8. Millgate, *Biography*, p. 389.
9. Ibid., p. 452.
10. Ibid., p. 470.
11. Ibid., p. 499.
12. Viola Meynell, *Friends of a Lifetime* (London, 1940) p. 296.
13. Edmund Gosse, *Thomas Hardy* (Bulphan, Upminster, 1968) p. [7]; Virginia Woolf, *Collected Essays*, I (London, 1966) p. 256.

CHAPTER 2   HARDY AND THE ROMANTICS
1. Quotations from Michael Millgate, *Thomas Hardy: A Biography* (Oxford, 1982) pp. 564, 442. See also the latter reference for Hardy's view of the past.
2. R. B. Martin, *Tennyson: The Unquiet Heart* (Oxford, 1980) p. 231.
3. *Shelley's Poetry and Prose*, ed. Donald H. Reiman and Sharon B. Powers (New York, 1977) p. 508.
4. Roy Gridley, *Browning* (London, 1972) p. 64.
5. Martin, *Tennyson*, p. 147.
6. Charles Kingsley, *Alton Locke*, Everyman edition (London, n.d.) p. 168.
7. Letters to Clough, early Feb. 1849, and Dec. 1847 or early 1848. *The Essential Matthew Arnold*, ed. Lionel Trilling (London, 1949) pp. 622, 615.
8. *Letters*, V, 253.
9. *Literary Notebooks*, I, 129.

10. Ibid., I, 153.
11. Emma Hardy, *Diaries*, ed. Richard H. Taylor (Ashington, Northumberland, 1985) p. 145.
12. 'The Seafarer', in *Sweet's Anglo-Saxon Reader*, ed. Dorothy Whitelock, 15th edn, 2nd corrected impression (Oxford, 1975) ll. 72–3.

CHAPTER 3   HARDY AND CONTEMPORARY SOCIETY

1. See, for example, Christopher Gillie, *Longman Companion to English Literature* (London, 1972) p. 206ff.
2. *The George Eliot Letters*, ed. Gordon S. Haight, vol. IV (London, 1956) p. 97; R. H. Hutton, review in *Thomas Hardy and his Readers*, ed. Laurence Lerner and John Holmstrom (London, 1968) p. 23; and Michael Millgate, *Thomas Hardy: A Biography* (Oxford, 1982) p. 168.
3. *Novelists on the Novel*, ed. Miriam Allott (London, 1959) p. 303.
4. Ibid., p. 94.
5. Charles Kingsley, *Yeast* (London, 1888) p. 95.
6. Benjamin Disraeli, *Sybil*, ed. Stephen Gill (Harmondsworth, 1970) p. 45; ed. Sheila M. Smith (Oxford, 1981) p. 65.
7. Charles Dickens, *Hard Times*, ed. David Craig (Harmondsworth, 1985) pp. 238, 312.
8. Thomas Hardy, *Literary Notebooks*, ed. Lennart A. Björk (London, 1985) vol. I, p. 136.
9. George Eliot, *Middlemarch*, ed. W. J. Harvey (Harmondsworth, 1965) p. 392.
10. Millgate, *Biography*, p. 110
11. Sir Arthur Conan Doyle, *The Memoirs of Sherlock Holmes* (Harmondsworth, 1950) p. 215.
12. F. M. L. Thompson, *The Rise of Respectable Society* (London, 1988) p. 151.
13. Phillip Collins, in Norman Page (ed.), *Thomas Hardy: The Writer and his Background* (London, 1980) p. 49; Michael Millgate, *Thomas Hardy: His Career as a Novelist* (London, 1971) p. 38.
14. *Tess of the d'Urbervilles*, vi, and J. T. Laird, *The Shaping of 'Tess of the d'Urbervilles'* (Oxford, 1975) p. 119.
15. R. G. Cox (ed.), *Thomas Hardy: The Critical Heritage* (London, 1970) p. 281.
16. Page (ed.), *Thomas Hardy: The Writer and his Background*, p. 70.
17. J. F. C. Harrison, *Late Victorian Britain* (London, 1990) p. 174.
18. Alfred Lord Tennyson, *The Princess*, V, 437–8.
19. Coventry Patmore, 'The Angel in the House', Book I, canto iii.
20. W. M. Thackeray, *Pendennis*, Introd. Anne Ritchie (London, 1903) p. 13.
21. David Rubinstein, *Before the Suffragettes* (Brighton, 1986) p. 5.
22. Charlotte Brontë, *Jane Eyre*, ed. Q. D. Leavis (Harmondsworth, 1966) p. 141.
23. Millgate, *Biography*, p. 356.

24. Rubinstein, *Before the Suffragettes*, pp. 72–3.
25. Millgate, *Biography*, p. 356; *Collected Essays* (London, 1966) vol. I, p. 260.
26. Robert Gittings, *The Older Hardy* (London, 1978) p. 95.
27. P. B. Shelley, *Notes on Queen Mab* (1813) Note to V, 189.
28. See W. E. Houghton, *The Victorian Frame of Mind, 1830–70* (New Haven, Conn., 1957) p. 354, for a good example of mid-Victorian emphasis on sexual restraint.
29. *Letters of Henry James*, ed. Percy Lubbock (London, 1920) vol. I, p. 205.
30. 'Mr Thomas Hardy's New Novel', *Pall Mall Gazette*, 31 December 1891, p. 3; Cox (ed.), *Thomas Hardy: The Critical Heritage*, p. 189.
31. Houghton, *Victorian Frame of Mind*, p. 352.
32. Cox, *Thomas Hardy: The Critical Heritage*, p. 204.
33. Benjamin Disraeli, *Lothair*, ed. Vernon Bogdanor (London, 1975) p. 78.
34. T. H. Huxley, *Methods and Results: Essays* (London, 1893) p. 42.
35. Richard Jefferies, *Hodge and his Masters*, Introd. Raymond Williams (London, 1966) vol. II, p. 37.
36. Kenneth Bourne, *The Foreign Policy of Victorian England 1830–1902* (Oxford, 1970) p. 302.
37. Charles Dickens, *Our Mutual Friend*, ed. Stephen Gill (Harmondsworth, 1971) p. 174.
38. Houghton, *Victorian Frame of Mind*, pp. 206, 203.
39. Harvey Brooks, *The Religious Aspect of the Volunteer Movement* (n.p., 1861) p. 10.
40. Rudyard Kipling, 'The White Man's Burden', in *A Choice of Kipling's Verse*, ed. T. S. Eliot (London, 1963) p. 136.
41. Denis Richards and Anthony Quick, *Britain, 1851–1945* (London, 1967) p. 154.
42. Robert Gittings, *The Older Hardy* (London, 1978) p. 100.
43. Millgate, *Biography*, p. 403.
44. Gittings, *The Older Hardy*, p. 170.
45. Millgate, *Biography*, p. 498.
46. Virginia Woolf, 'Mr Bennett and Mrs Brown', in *Collected Essays* (London, 1966) vol. I, p. 320.
47. Ibid., p. 321.
48. Gittings, *The Older Hardy*, p. 170.

CHAPTER 4   HARDY AND THE IDEAS OF HIS TIME

1. Benjamin Disraeli, *Lothair*, ed. Vernon Bogdanor (London, 1975) p. 47.
2. R. S. Smith, *Impressions on Revisiting the Churches of Belgium and Rhenish Prussia* (London, [1875]) p. xi.
3. David L. Edwards, *Leaders of the Church of England, 1828–1944* (London, 1971) p. 160.
4. Walter Pater, 'Robert Elsmere. By Mrs Humphrey Ward', *Manchester Guardian*, 28 March 1888, p. 469.
5. Legh Richmond, *The Dairyman's Daughter* (Otley, 1817 [1816?]) p. 29.

6. Beatrice Webb, *My Apprenticeship*, 2nd edn (London, n.d.) p. 123.
7. Charles Darwin, *The Origin of Species*, ed. J. W. Burrow (Harmondsworth, 1968) p. 293.
8. Cited by Darwin, ibid., p. 116.
9. Ibid., p. 116.
10. Arthur Symons, *A Study of Thomas Hardy* (London, 1927) p. 58.
11. Gideon Algernon Mantell, *Wonders of Geology* (London, 1838) p. 679.
12. Edward Clodd, *Pioneers of Evolution* (London, 1902) p. 93.
13. Thomas Hardy, *Literary Notebooks*, ed. Lennart A. Björk (London, 1985) vol. I, p. 106.
14. T. H. Huxley, *Science and Christian Tradition* (London, 1894) pp. 245–6.
15. Leslie Stephen, *Essays on Free Thinking and Plain Speaking* (London, 1873) p. 32.
16. Ibid., p. 362.
17. *Oxford Companion to English Literature*, 4th edn (Oxford: 1967, reprinted with corrections 1975) p. 774.
18. Michael Millgate, *Thomas Hardy: A Biography* (Oxford, 1982) p. 246.
19. Mary Augusta Ward, *Robert Elsmere* (1888; London, [1907]) p. 575.
20. David Hume, *Inquiry Concerning Human Understanding*, ed. Antony Flew (London, 1962) p. 132.
21. William Archer, *Real Conversations* (London, 1904) p. 37; Viola Meynell, *Friends of a Lifetime* (London, 1940) p. 305.
22. Leslie Stephen, *An Agnostic's Apology* (London, 1893) p. 343.
23. J. S. Mill, *On Liberty*. Taken from Hardy's copy, People's Edition (London, 1867) p. 36.
24. Letter to Hardy, 17 Feb. 1874, Hardy Memorial Collection, Dorset County Museum.
25. Millgate, *Biography*, p. 199.
26. Quoted by R. Gittings, *Young Thomas Hardy* (London, 1975) p. 146.
27. Letter to Clodd, 12 February 1906, Hardy Memorial Collection, Dorset County Museum.
28. Meynell, *Friends of a Lifetime*, p. 307.
29. Ibid., pp. 309–10.
30. W. K. Clifford, *Lectures and Essays* (London, 1879) vol. II, p. 247.
31. *Literary Notebooks*, vol. I, p. 146.
32. *The Letters of T. E. Lawrence*, ed. David Garnett (London, 1964) p. 429.
33. Cited by Webb in *My Apprenticeship*, p. 115.
34. Ibid., p. 114.
35. Auguste Comte, *A General View of Positivism*, trans J. H. Bridges (London, n.d.) p. 241.
36. Letter to Hardy, 29 Dec. 1891, Hardy Memorial Collection, Dorset County Museum.
37. Comte, *A General View*, p. 252.
38. Ibid., p. 209.
39. William Ralph Inge, *Outspoken Essays*, second series (London, 1922) p. 179.
40. Augustus John, *Chiaroscuro: Fragments of Autobiography* (London, 1952) p. 134.

CHAPTER 5   HARDY AND THE OTHER ARTS

1. Vera J. Mardon, 'Thomas Hardy as a Musician', Monographs on the Life of Thomas Hardy, no. 15 (Beaminster, 1964) p. 11.
2. Michael Millgate, *Thomas Hardy: A Biography* (Oxford, 1982) p. 285.
3. Ibid., p. 286.
4. Joan Grundy, *Hardy and the Sister Arts* (London, 1979) pp. 59–64.
5. Evelyn Hardy, 'Thomas Hardy and Turner', *London Magazine*, June–July 1975, p. 25.
6. Millgate, *Biography*, p. 362.
7. Nikolaus Pevsner, in *Victorian Architecture*, ed. Peter Ferriday (London, 1963) pp. 29, 244.
8. *Thomas Hardy's Personal Writings*, ed. Harold Orel (London, 1967) p. 208.
9. Thomas Rickman, *Attempt to Discriminate the Styles in English Architecture*, 4th edn (London, 1835) p. 6.
10. A. W. N. Pugin, *Contrasts* (1836), introd. H. R. Hitchcock (Leicester, 1973) p. 1.
11. John Ruskin, *Unto This Last, and Other Writings* (1860), ed. Clive Wilmer (Harmondsworth, 1985) p. 79.
12. J. Mordaunt Crook, *The Dilemma of Style* (London, 1989) p. 160.
13. *Personal Writings*, p. 203.
14. Millgate, *Biography*, p. 146.
15. Extracts from the obituary are given in Hardy's *Architectural Notebook*, ed. C. J. P. Beatty (Philadelphia, 1966) p. 37.
16. Ruskin, *Unto This Last*, p. 104.
17. Roger Dixon and Stefan Muthesius, *Victorian Architecture*, 2nd edn (London, 1985) p. 22.
18. Ruskin, *Unto this Last*, p. 82.
19. Brandon, Joshua Arthur and John Raphael, *An Analysis of Gothick Architecture* (London, 1847) vol. I, p. 5.
20. Patrick Yarker, 'Meredith, Hardy and Gissing', *Sphere History of Literature in the English Language*, vol. 6, ed. Arthur Pollard (London, 1970) p. 245.
21. *Personal Writings*, pp. 207, 215.
22. H. H. Statham, 'Modern English Architecture', *Fortnightly Review*, vol. XX (1876) pp. 481, 490.
23. Millgate, *Biography*, p. 259.
24. Ruskin, *Unto This Last*, p. 98.
25. Millgate, *Biography*, pp. 259–60.
26. Ruskin, *Unto This Last*, pp. 85–6, 91, 92.
27. *Personal Writings*, p. 214.
28. Ruskin, *Unto This Last*, p. 108.
29. Lawrence Lerner and John Holmstrom (eds), *Thomas Hardy and his Readers* (London, 1968) p. 13.
30. Crook, *Dilemma of Style*, p. 189.
31. Ibid., p. 138.
32. Ibid., pp. 134, 137.
33. Ibid., p. 137.
34. Robert Gittings, *Young Thomas Hardy* (London, 1975) pp. 74–5.

35. Millgate, *Biography*, p. 259.
36. T. S. Eliot, *After Strange Gods* (London, 1934), pp. 54–5.

CHAPTER 6   THE CRITICS OF THOMAS HARDY

1. Valentine Cunningham, *Everywhere Spoken Against* (Oxford, 1975) p. 5.
2. Michael Millgate, *Thomas Hardy: A Biography* (Oxford, 1982) p. 200.
3. Simon Gatrell, *Hardy the Creator* (Oxford 1988) p. 118.
4. Ibid., p. 129.
5. Richard H. Taylor, in Norman Page (ed.), *Hardy: The Writer and his Background* (London, 1980) p. 223.
6. William Archer, *Real Conversations* (London, 1904) p. 52.
7. John Bayley, Introduction to the hardback New Wessex edition of *Far from the Madding Crowd* (London, 1975) p. 19.
8. *Personal Writings*, p. 124.
9. Marcel Proust, *A la recherche du temps perdu*, ed. Clarac and Ferré (Paris, 1954) vol. III p. 375.
10. J. O. Bailey, 'Hardy's "Mephistophelian Visitants"', *PMLA*, vol. 61 (1946) pp. 1146–84.
11. Richard J. Beckman, 'Character Typology for Hardy's Novels', *Journal of English Literary History*, vol. 30 (1963) p. 70.
12. William Archer, *Real Conversations* (London, 1904) p. 30.
13. Lascelles Abercrombie, *Hardy: A Critical Study* (London, 1912) pp. 108–112; D. H. Lawrence, 'Study of Thomas Hardy', in J. V. Davies (ed.), *Lawrence on Hardy and Painting* (London, 1973), *passim*; Lord David Cecil, *Hardy the Novelist* (London, 1943) pp. 83–4; Peter J. Casagrande, *Unity in Hardy's Novels* (London, 1982) p. 233; Albert J. Guerard, *Thomas Hardy: The Novels and Stories* (London, 1949) pp. 100–59. See also Timothy Hands, *Thomas Hardy: Distracted Preacher?* (London, 1989) pp. 55–79.
14. J. W. Beach, 'Bowdlerised Versions of Hardy', *PMLA*, vol. 36 (1921) pp. 632–43; Mary Ellen Chase, *Thomas Hardy: From Serial to Novel* (Minneapolis, 1927).
15. Quoted in Gatrell, *Hardy the Creator*, p. 53.
16. J. T. Laird, *The Shaping of 'Tess of the d'Urbervilles'* (Oxford, 1975) pp. 19–20.
17. Robert Graves, *Good-bye to All That*, 3rd edn (London, 1961) p. 270.
18. Herbert Grimsditch, *Character and Environment in the Novels of Thomas Hardy* (London, 1925) p. 11.
19. E. M. Forster, *Aspects of the Novel* (1927), pocket edn (London, 1958) p. 90.
20. Quoted by Taylor in *Hardy: The Writer and his Background*, p. 241; see also H. Garwood, *An Illustration of the Philosophy of Schopenhauer* (Philadelphia, 1911); E. J. Brennecke, *Thomas Hardy's Universe* (London, 1924).
21. John Holloway, *The Victorian Sage* (1953; Hamden, 1962) p. 270.
22. Ibid., p. 252.
23. Ibid., pp. 264, 280–1.

24. Ibid., p. 270.
25. Roy Morrell, *Thomas Hardy: The Will and the Way* (Kuala Lumpur, 1965) p. 39.
26. Ibid., p. 40.
27. Cecil, *Hardy the Novelist*, p. 84.
28. E. W. Martin, 'Thomas Hardy and the Rural Tradition', *Blackfriars*, vol. 30 (1949) pp. 253–4.
29. Graves, *Good-bye to All That*, p. 271.
30. F. R. Leavis, *The Great Tradition* (London, 1948) p. 1.
31. Ibid., pp. 19, 22.
32. F. R. Leavis, *New Bearings in English Poetry* (1932; Harmondsworth 1963) p. 52.
33. Virginia Woolf, *Collected Essays*, vol. I (London, 1966) p. 258. See also Henry James in *The Art of Fiction* (London, 1888) on the English novel's lack of theory (p. 44).
34. Quoted by J. V. Davies in *Lawrence on Hardy and Painting*, p. 3.
35. Ibid., p. 23.
36. Ibid., p. 100.
37. Donald Davie, *Thomas Hardy and British Poetry* (London, 1973) p. 3.
38. Ibid., p. 39.
39. Ibid., p. 39.
40. Ibid., p. 23.
41. Ibid., p. 40.
42. To be found in the special Hardy edition, edited by Donald Davie, of *Agenda*, vol. 10 (1972).
43. Davie, *Thomas Hardy and British Poetry*, p. 40.
44. For further discussion, and these references, see David Timms, *Philip Larkin* (Edinburgh, 1973) p. 16.
45. The article is reprinted in Philip Larkin, *Required Writing* (London, 1983), quotation taken from p. 254.
46. Timms, *Philip Larkin*, p. 15.
47. Quotation from Larkin, *Required Writing*, p. 175.
48. John Powell Ward, *The English Line* (London, 1991) pp. 7, 12, 11.
49. Charles Lock, *Criticism in Focus*, p. 100.
50. Jean R. Brooks, *Thomas Hardy: The Poetic Structure* (London, 1971) p. 55.
51. Peter Widdowson (ed.), *Tess of the d'Urbervilles: New Casebook* (London, 1993).
52. Ibid., pp. 11, 5.
53. Ibid., p. 11
54. Ibid., p. 6.
55. Ibid., p. 20.
56. Woolf, *Collected Essays*, vol. I, p. 263.
57. Roger Ebbatson, in *Critical Survey*, vol. V (1993) p. 113 (issue devoted to Hardy).
58. Ibid., p. 192.
59. Reprinted in *Thomas Hardy Poems: A Casebook*, ed. James Gibson and Trevor Johnson (London, 1979) p. 41.
60. Edmund Gosse, 'Thomas Hardy' (Bulphan, Upminster, 1968) p. 12.

61. Letter of 17 May 1913, Hardy Memorial Collection, Dorset County Museum.
62. Letter of 3 January 1899, Hardy Memorial Collection, Dorset County Museum; Woolf, *Collected Essays*, vol. I, p. 258.
63. Reprinted in *Hardy: A Collection of Critical Essays*, ed. Albert J. Guerard (Englewood Cliffs, N.J., 1963) pp. 135, 140–1.
64. Ibid., pp. 43, 26.
65. Vere H. Collins, *Talks with Thomas Hardy at Max Gate* (London, 1928) p. 42.
66. Taylor in *Hardy: The Writer and his Background*, p. 254.
67. In *Hardy and the Modern World*, ed. F. B. Pinion (Dorchester, 1974) p. 106.
68. Lock, *Criticism in Focus*, p. 3.
69. R. S. Thomas, 'Taste', *Poetry Review*, 1970.
70. Henry James, letter to Stevenson, 19 March 1892, reproduced in Edmund Blunden, *Thomas Hardy* (London, 1942) p. 75; Michael Millgate, *Thomas Hardy: His Career as a Novelist* (London, 1971) p. 263.
71. Lock, *Criticism in Focus*, p. 22; John F. Danby, in *Critical Quarterly*, vol. 1 (1959) p. 5.
72. Quoted by Douglas Brown, *Thomas Hardy* (London, 1954) p. 101.
73. Henry James, review of *Far from the Madding Crowd*, quoted in Lawrence Lerner and John Holmstrom (eds), *Thomas Hardy and his Readers* (London, 1968) p. 30; Blunden, *Thomas Hardy*, p. 190; Day Lewis, reprinted in *Thomas Hardy Poems: A Casebook* (ed. Gibson and Johnson) p. 149.
74. Blunden, *Thomas Hardy*, p. 193.
75. Marlene Springer, *Hardy's Use of Allusion* (London, 1983) p. 1.
76. Robert Gittings, *The Older Hardy* (London, 1978) p. 5.
77. Simon Gatrell, *Thomas Hardy and the Proper Study of Mankind* (London, 1993) p. 48.
78. Irving Howe, *Thomas Hardy* (London, 1967) p. 164.
79. *Thomas Hardy Poems: A Casebook* (ed. Gibson and Johnson), pp. 147, 159.
80. Woolf, *Collected Essays*, vol. I, p. 266.
81. Gittings, *The Older Hardy*, p. 153.
82. Frances Cornford, *Autobiography* (London, 1936) p. 278; Timothy O'Sullivan, *Thomas Hardy: An Illustrated Biography* (London, 1975) p. 168.
83. Robert C. Schweik, Lecture to the Thomas Hardy Society Summer School, Dorchester, 3 August 1982.
84. Edmund Gosse, in *Thomas Hardy: The Critical Heritage*, ed. R. G. Cox (London, 1970) pp. 237–8.
85. Taylor, *Hardy: The Writer and his Background*, p. 258.
86. Bayley, Introduction to hardback New Wessex edition of *Far from the Madding Crowd*, p. 30.
87. Lance St John Butler, Review of Charles Lock, *Criticism in Focus: Thomas Hardy*, *Thomas Hardy Journal*, 1992, p. 77
88. Robert Gittings, *Young Thomas Hardy* (London, 1975) p. 105.

Select Bibliography

WORKS BY HARDY

Novels (with date of book publication)

References in the text cite both part numbers, where appropriate, and chapter numbers.

Desperate Remedies (1871)
Under the Greenwood Tree (1872)
A Pair of Blue Eyes (1873)
Far from the Madding Crowd (1874)
The Hand of Ethelberta (1876)
The Return of the Native (1878)
The Trumpet-Major (1880)
A Laodicean (1881)
Two on a Tower (1882)
The Mayor of Casterbridge (1886)
The Woodlanders (1887)
Tess of the d'Urbervilles (1891)
Jude the Obscure (1895)
The Well-Beloved (1897)

Short stories

Wessex Tales (1888)
A Group of Noble Dames (1891)
Life's Little Ironies (1894)
A Changed Man and Other Tales (1913)

Poems

Wessex Poems (1898)
Poems of the Past and the Present (1902)
Time's Laughingstocks (1909)
Satires of Circumstance (1914)
Moments of Vision (1917)
Late Lyrics and Earlier (1922)
Human Shows (1925)
Winter Words (1928)
The Complete Poems, ed. James Gibson, are available in one volume (London, 1976). There are also critical editions in one volume by Gibson (London, 1979) and in three volumes by Samuel Hynes (Oxford, 1982–5).

Dramatic works

The Dynasts (1903–8)
The Famous Tragedy of the Queen of Cornwall (1923)

Other writing

Architectural Notebook, ed. C. J. P. Beatty (Philadelphia, 1966).
Collected Letters, ed. R. L. Purdy and M. Millgate, 7 vols (Oxford, 1978–88); referred to in text as *Letters*, citing volume and page number.
The Life of Thomas Hardy, ed. Michael Millgate (London, 1984); referred to in text as *Life*, citing page number.
Literary Notebooks, ed. Lennart A. Björk, 2 vols (London, 1985).
Personal Writings, ed. Harold Orel (London, 1967).

WORKS ABOUT HARDY

Bayley, John, *An Essay on Hardy* (Cambridge, 1978).
Blunden, Edmund, *Thomas Hardy* (London, 1942).
Boumelha, Penny, *Thomas Hardy and Women* (Brighton, 1982).
Brooks, Jean R., *Thomas Hardy: The Poetic Structure* (London, 1971).
Brown, Douglas, *Thomas Hardy* (London, 1954).
Cecil, Lord David, *Hardy the Novelist* (London, 1943).
Collins, Vere H., *Talks with Thomas Hardy at Max Gate* (London, 1928)
Cox, J. Stevens (ed.), *Monographs on the Life, Times and Works of Thomas Hardy* (St Peter Port, 1962–71).
Cox, R. G. (ed.), *Thomas Hardy: The Critical Heritage* (London, 1970).
Davie, Donald, *Thomas Hardy and British Poetry* (London, 1973).
Gatrell, Simon, *Hardy the Creator* (Oxford, 1988).
Gittings, Robert, *The Older Hardy* (London, 1978).
——, *Young Thomas Hardy* (London, 1975).
Gosse, Edmund, *Thomas Hardy* (Bulphan, Upminster, 1968).
Grundy, Joan, *Hardy and the Sister Arts* (London, 1979).
Guerard, Albert J. (ed.), *Hardy: A Collection of Critical Essays* (Englewood Cliffs, N.J., 1963).
——, *Thomas Hardy: The Novels and Stories* (London, 1949).
Hands, Timothy, *Thomas Hardy: Distracted Preacher?* (London, 1989).
Hardy, Emma Lavinia, *Some Recollections*, ed. Evelyn Hardy and Robert Gittings (London, 1961).
Holloway, John, *The Victorian Sage* (Hamden, 1962).
Laird, J. T., *The Shaping of 'Tess of the d'Urbervilles'* (Oxford, 1975)
Lawrence, D. H., 'Study of Thomas Hardy', ed. J. V. Davies (London, 1973).
Lerner, Laurence, and Holmstrom, John (eds), *Thomas Hardy and his Readers* (London, 1968).
Lock, Charles, *Criticism in Focus: Thomas Hardy* (London, 1992).
Miller, J. Hillis, *Thomas Hardy: Distance and Desire* (Cambridge, Mass., 1970).
Millgate, Michael, *Thomas Hardy: A Biography* (Oxford, 1982).

——, *Thomas Hardy: His Career as a Novelist* (London, 1971).

Morrell, Roy, *Thomas Hardy: The Will and the Way* (Kuala Lumpur, 1965).

Page, Norman (ed.), *Hardy: The Writer and his Background* (London, 1980).

Paterson, John, *The Making of 'The Return of the Native'* (Berkeley, Cal., 1960).

Paulin, Tom, *Thomas Hardy: The Poetry of Perception* (London, 1975).

Pinion, F. B., *A Hardy Companion* (London, 1974).

——, *Thomas Hardy: Art and Thought* (London, 1974).

Purdy, Richard Little, *Thomas Hardy: A Bibliographical Study* (London, 1954).

Robinson, Denis Kay, *Hardy's Wessex Reappraised* (Newton Abbot, 1971).

Springer, Marlene, *Hardy's Use of Allusion* (London, 1983).

Ward, John Powell, *The English Line* (London, 1991).

Widdowson, Peter, *Hardy in History* (London, 1989).

Williams, Merryn, *Thomas Hardy and Rural England* (London, 1972).

Woolf, Virginia, 'Thomas Hardy', in *Collected Essays*, vol. I (London, 1966).

Index